"Here is an infectiously good tale about the art of the con. In David Howard's capable hands, a lost world of sharks in tailored suits and their bodacious scams comes to crackling life on the page. I could feel the trickles of sweat from the high-stakes lies, could hear the muffled voices over primitive FBI surveillance gear. And as I read along, I kept checking my back pocket to make sure my wallet was still there."

—Hampton Sides, author of *Hellhound on His Trail*

"I can't recall the last time I had so much fun with a true-crime book. The plot bobs and weaves, the '70s underworld jet-set scene is rendered with groovy precision, the main characters are big, vibrant, and complex, and the supporting cast seems snatched from a John D. MacDonald caper. *Chasing Phil* is superb reportage mixed with edge-of-your-seat storytelling."

—Jonathan Miles, author of *Dear American Airlines* and *Anatomy of a Miracle*

"You'd never have wanted to invest with Phil Kitzer—con man extraordinaire, the criminal who initiated the FBI's age of undercover operations—but boy would it have been great to hang out with him. What a life! David Howard's suspenseful, propulsive, 1970s-infused book is the closest any of us will ever come to a boozy, airplane-hopping evening with Phil. *Chasing Phil* is an outstanding, heart-thumping read."

—Michael Finkel, author of *The Stranger in the Woods* and *True Story*

"David Howard takes you so deep inside the FBI's high-stakes, high-testosterone pursuit of one of the '70s great con artists, you can practically taste the Camels and the Cutty Sark. A terrific true-crime tale, masterfully told."

—Mark Adams, author of *Turn Right at Machu Picchu*

"*Chasing Phil* snared me with a tale as spellbinding as *Catch Me If You Can* and *American Hustle*: a world-class swindler, two FBI agents on his tail, and all the high drama and bad hair the late '70s had to offer. David Howard's story of the FBI's first body-wire undercover mission crackles with sharp dialogue and hairpin plot turns. Strap in. This is a true-crime thrill ride."

—Bruce Barcott, author of *The Last Flight of the Scarlet Macaw* and *Weed the People*

CHASING PHIL

The Adventures of
Two Undercover Agents
with the World's Most
Charming Con Man

DAVID HOWARD

B \ D \ W \ Y
Broadway Books
New York

Library of Congress Cataloging-in-Publication Data
Names: Howard, David, 1967– author.
Title: Chasing Phil : the adventures of two undercover agents
    with the world's most charming con man / David Howard.
Description: New York : Crown, 2017.
Identifiers: LCCN 2017008813 | ISBN 9781101907429 (hardback)
Subjects: LCSH: Kitzer, Phillip. | Swindlers and swindling—
    United States—Biography. | Espionage—United States. |
    Criminal investigation—United States. | United States.
    Federal Bureau of Investigation. | Swindlers and swindling—
    United States—Biography. | BISAC: TRUE CRIME /
    Espionage. | HISTORY / United States / 20th Century.
Classification: LCC HV6692.K48 H69 2017 | DDC 364.16/3092
    [B]—dc23
LC record available at https://lccn.loc.gov/2017008813

ISBN 978-1-101-90743-6
Ebook ISBN 978-1-101-90744-3

Printed in the United States of America

Cover design by Matthew Garrett, Pan Macmillan art department
Cover photography: Chayantorn/Tongmorn/Shutterstock
Title page photograph courtesy of James J. Wedick Jr.
Map illustration by David Lindroth, Inc.

10 9 8 7 6 5 4 3 2 1

First Paperback Edition

For Vaughn, who loves a story

Trust everybody, but cut the cards.

—FINLEY PETER DUNNE

Contents

Part III: Fear City

Part IV: The Reckoning

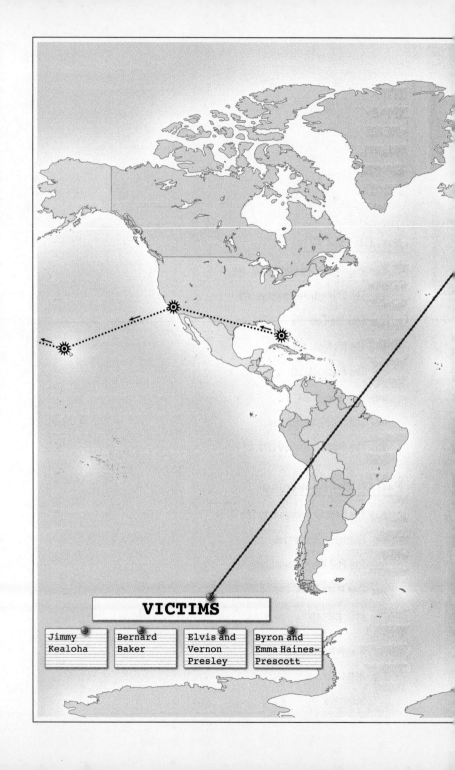

VICTIMS

Jimmy
Kealoha

Bernard
Baker

Elvis and
Vernon
Presley

Byron and
Emma Haines-
Prescott

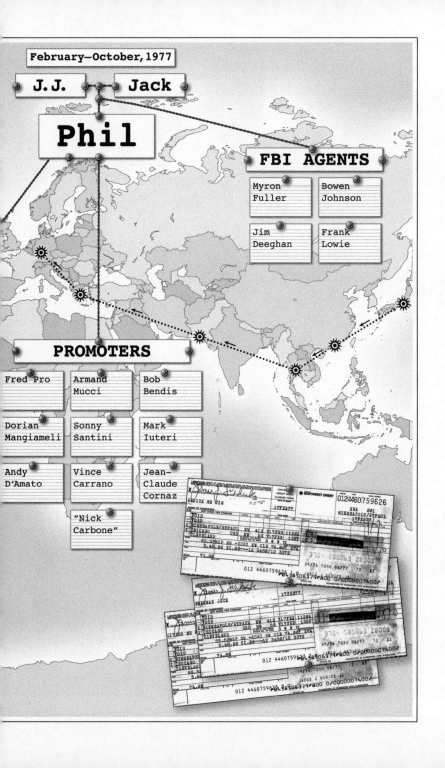

Prologue

Jim Wedick yanked at his collar as he walked across the parking lot toward the Thunderbird Motel, a sprawling Native American–themed lodge in suburban Minneapolis. It was early evening and the sun had long ago plummeted below the tabletop horizon, leaving the temperature hovering just above zero. Still, Wedick was overheating in his blue pin-striped three-piece suit. His heart banged out a punk-rock cadence as he strode alongside Jack Brennan, both of them working hard to look nonchalant. They eyed a massive totem pole, erected for maximum visibility from Interstate 494, then entered the Thunderbird's spacious lobby, packed with bearskin rugs, peace pipes, tepee-shaped light fixtures.

Once the warmth of the lobby hit them, the agents shrugged off their overcoats and scanned the room. Wedick was vaguely aware of the sweat soaking the armpits of his Brooks Brothers dress shirt, but his suit coat was staying on. He needed as many layers as possible to conceal the Nagra SNST audio recorder lashed to the small of his back. The device was diminutive for the era—five and a half inches long, just under four inches wide, and one inch thick—but was still larger than a pack of cigarettes, and right now it felt like a cinder block. He'd snipped a hole in his pants pocket to accommodate a remote-control unit. This allowed him to inconspicuously flip the recorder on and off, but he'd noticed outside that the setup also allowed cold air into his nether regions.

Wedick, an FBI agent who had just turned twenty-seven, was about to begin his first undercover assignment. Brennan was four years older, but he was also a first-timer in this kind of role. They both understood the stakes: They had traveled from their post in Gary, Indiana, to meet Phillip Kitzer. A high school dropout from Chicago, Kitzer had over the past fifteen years swindled banks, real estate developers, entrepreneurs, and everyday investors out of countless millions of dollars. The agents had come to see if they might crack open a window into his activities.

The odds looked steep. Their informant had told them that Kitzer possessed a preternatural ability to read people. Wedick and Brennan had already learned firsthand how slippery he could be, but they were young and ambitious and maybe a little naïve, and had lobbied hard for permission to fly to Minneapolis to take a shot. Their bosses had agreed reluctantly. Neither Brennan nor Wedick had received any training in undercover work—the FBI had only recently begun to offer such instruction. And they were using their real names. Nonetheless, they had on their own concocted an elaborate cover story about being young con men in training. Wedick had gone as far as creating a phony shell corporation.

After circling the lobby, they spotted a sign that read, "Cocktail fantasies in the intimate atmosphere of our exclusive Pow-Wow Cocktail Lounge." That was the meeting place. They took a few tentative steps inside the Pow-Wow Lounge and scanned the room. It was mostly empty—no surprise for a Tuesday night. One couple lingered over drinks at a corner table. And there was a gentleman in a suit and tie, sitting alone at a long wooden bar that swooped gently into the shape of a question mark. Kitzer was perched atop one of the barstools, which were designed to look like tom-tom drums on tepee legs. He sat with his back to the bar, facing the door. He was obviously waiting for them. He puffed on a Pall Mall through a white plastic filter as they approached.

The FBI agents crossed the carpeted room. Wedick sucked in a breath and produced an enthusiastic grin, willing himself to feel as if it were the most natural thing in the world for him to be there. He stuck out his hand. "Hi, I'm Jim."

Kitzer's expression was cast iron as he appraised them, first one, then the other. "Christ," he said. "You guys look like a couple of feds."

Part I

THE CHASE

The indian was standing with the rifle across his shoulders, his hands hanging over it. You come out you walk towards the moon, he said.

What if it aint up yet?

The indian spat. You think I'd tell you to walk towards a moon that wasnt there?

—**Cormac McCarthy**, *The Crossing*

1

How to Steal a Bank

JULY 1976

Heading out to dinner on a summer Saturday night, Byron and Emma Haines-Prescott (not their real names) couldn't have expected much. Byron, a British banker, was meeting two Americans who had arrived at his door two days earlier to discuss acquiring his small twelve-year-old bank, Seven Oak Finance, Ltd.

Haines-Prescott had put his bank (which was more of a depository, really) up for sale more than a year before, attracting a parade of big shots who had rolled into London ready to cut a sweetheart deal. But he wasn't about to give it away. Haines-Prescott was only thirty-six, so maybe the sharks expected to take advantage of his youth, or perhaps word had gotten out that he was flailing financially. Regardless, his latest suitor, Phillip Kitzer, could easily have been just one more in the parade of empty suits with hollow offers.

But Kitzer's arrival at Seven Oak had made an impression. At forty-three, he was wiry but dashing in his tailored suit, light blazing behind the eyes, brown hair parted on the left and swept back. Although his head looked slightly too large for his body, he had a narrow, creased face, a smile that revealed deep dimples, and the prominent chin of an early Hollywood star; he emanated a kind of effortless charisma unique to successful people. He'd arrived with a business partner, Paul Chovanec, who looked a decade younger. Chovanec had dark hair and black horn-rimmed glasses and was taller and heavier, but he was clearly second-in-command. Kitzer had talked up his background, then invited Byron and Emma for a follow-up meal at a swank London restaurant.

As they settled in at their table, Kitzer was funny and charming with Emma. He described a stratospherically successful career. He had already owned an assortment of banks and insurance companies, and had traveled the world brokering loans for the United Nations. He had global contacts across the uppermost strata of finance. All of that endeared him to the couple—but what happened after dessert made even more of an impression. Chovanec pulled Haines-Prescott aside and handed him an envelope.

"Here, this is for your time," Chovanec said. "We want to talk. We're serious."

Haines-Prescott opened it. Inside was $5,000 in cash.

The negotiations for Seven Oak began the following week. Kitzer and Chovanec showed up at the bank daily, riding the Tube thirty-five minutes to the suburbs from London's Brittanica Hotel. Sitting in the office with Byron and Emma, they pored over financial statements and lists of depositors.

As he grew more comfortable with the Americans, Haines-Prescott revealed the details of his situation. The rumors of his struggles were true: The bank was a smoking crater. Just a couple of months earlier, Seven Oak had promised readers of the *Illustrated London News* a return of 14 percent on deposits. "If you have a minimum of £500 that you wish to invest safely and profitably, then send off the coupon below." But Haines-Prescott had siphoned out £175,000—about $300,000—in deposits to fund a business called Cidco. He'd used his accounting background to conceal this shortfall by preparing a false first-quarter report. He'd then sent the document to an accountant whom he'd paid to certify the fabricated figures before he submitted them to the U.K.'s Board of Trade. Exactly how long Haines-Prescott could shield this financial sand castle from the oncoming tides of government oversight was unclear. Beyond the £175,000, Seven Oak was £7,000 in the red to two banks with which it had relationships.

Haines-Prescott was relieved to find that Kitzer wasn't put off by this. Kitzer assured him that none of that was any problem—in fact, he could help the Brit put his house back in order.

As the summer wound down, they reached the crux of the negotiation: how much Kitzer and Chovanec would pay. Haines-Prescott wanted, at the bare minimum, £175,000—so he could erase his debt, file a truthful statement with the Board of Trade, and walk away clear. But Kitzer took a tough stance.

"If you think that anybody is going to buy this bank and put a hundred and seventy-five thousand pounds into it [in] cash, you are badly mistaken," he said. "That will never, never happen. That's one of the reasons you haven't sold the bank. You'd better come up with a better idea."

"Phil, we can work it out," Haines-Prescott replied. "It doesn't have to be cash. We can come up with something." By then he'd invested about six weeks in the Americans, and he felt pressured to file his late second-quarter paperwork with the government.

Kitzer then furnished a better idea. He and Chovanec would provide a letter indicating that Sterling and Company, Chovanec's Milwaukee-based corporation, would transfer about £175,000 to cover the bank's debts—Haines-Prescott would never touch the money, but he would walk away assured he was in the clear. As a bonus, the Americans would pay him £50,000 in cash.

Haines-Prescott agreed to that offer. When he wrote up a preliminary agreement on September 14, he asked whom to put down as the purchaser.

"Make it 219 Dearborn Corp.," Kitzer said.

Chovanec looked over and lifted his eyebrows inquisitively: *Who?* Kitzer smiled and said he would explain later.

Naturally, Haines-Prescott wanted assurances that Kitzer and Chovanec would honor the deal, and in the next few days he spelled out his demands. First, he wanted a notarized letter from Sterling and Company confirming that it was holding $300,000 on behalf of Seven Oak. Haines-Prescott also required further references—banks that could assure him that Sterling had sufficient assets or that would back the company up with their own funds. And he wanted a notarized letter providing assurance that Chovanec could authorize such transactions for Sterling.

Haines-Prescott wrote out what he wanted, then stood there while Kitzer dictated it to Chovanec, who had flown back to Milwaukee.

> Dear Sirs,
>
> We hereby confirm that we are holding the sum of U.S. $300,000 on behalf of Seven Oak Finance, Ltd. of Priory Buildings, Churchill, Orpington, Kent, England. The authorized signatory being Phillip K. Kitzer.
>
> Yours faithfully, for and on behalf of Sterling and Company, N/A,
>
> P. Chovanec, President

Kitzer had suggested using his name because he'd stayed in England and could therefore sign in person. The letter came back bearing a stamp: "Signature guaranteed by Midland National Bank, Milwaukee, Wisconsin."

Chovanec provided a list of references on Sterling letterhead. A letter from William Kelly at North Ridge Bank highlighted his bank's solid relationship with Sterling and explained that Sterling had maintained $300,000 in deposits at various times during the previous year. A second bank reported that Sterling had authorized six-figure transactions in recent months.

Just before five in the afternoon London time, Haines-Prescott dialed one of Chovanec's references. Roger Lewis, the executive vice president of St. Francis Savings and Loan Association, in Wisconsin, confirmed that he knew Chovanec and that Sterling maintained an account holding hundreds of thousands of dollars.

Haines-Prescott jotted, "Yes, six figures. We have had a good relationship with them." Then he hung up.

"Okay, now the second one," Kitzer said.

"No, that's it," Haines-Prescott said. "I don't have to go any further. I got it from one, I imagine I will get it from them all."

Kitzer pressed, but Haines-Prescott waved him off.

"Phil, this is fine, this is exactly what I need," he said. "Let's close the deal."

On September 30, Haines-Prescott made out a deposit slip for £175,000, and Kitzer handed him two bills of exchange—the British version of a personal check—to cover the bonus. They were postdated because, Kitzer had explained, he needed to spread out the payments.

Kitzer signed various pages of paperwork, and Haines-Prescott assigned him and Chovanec his stock in Seven Oak—all one hundred thousand shares. They shook hands, and having spent a productive couple of months in England, Kitzer headed home.

Haines-Prescott hoped to move quickly to clean up his accounting mess. There was one problem: The transfer of the £175,000 didn't happen. A few days passed, then a week, and the Americans assured Haines-Prescott that the transaction was imminent.

But after ten days, the Brit received notice that the bank responsible for wiring the funds had declined payment for insufficient funds. Squelching his rising panic, Haines-Prescott tried to call Kitzer and couldn't reach him. But he contacted Chovanec, who said that the declined payment was a mix-up that he would soon straighten out.

When he still hadn't received the money by October 17—two and a half weeks after the deal closed—Haines-Prescott must have suspected that he'd been scammed. He figured he'd strike back while he still had some leverage: He wired Kitzer a message saying he planned to notify Seven Oak depositors that their money was in jeopardy. He would trigger a run on the bank.

But Haines-Prescott had initiated a chess match, and his first move was a stumble: October 17 was a Sunday. The bank was closed. This gave Kitzer time to send notice back to England that he had fired Haines-Prescott; his wife, Emma; and the entire board of directors, effective immediately—thereby eliminating their ability to communicate with the bank's customers. Seven Oak's four employees would receive this directive when they arrived at work on Monday.

Haines-Prescott studied the deal he'd signed, turning to the guarantee he had received from Midland National Bank. He would soon find that the stamp didn't match Midland's corporate seal—that, in fact, it was a counterfeit created by a stamp maker Chovanec had hired.

Then there was the document's wording: "Signature guaranteed by Midland National Bank, Milwaukee, Wisconsin." A careful reading revealed a hidden catch. The letter didn't mean that Midland guaranteed the $300,000. All it said was that the bank guaranteed *Kitzer's signature*.

Haines-Prescott might have taken comfort from the $50,000 Kitzer had given him. The bills of exchange were each for $25,000 and were postdated for three and six months after the sale date—but in light of events, Haines-Prescott decided to try cashing them. Kitzer had built in a trapdoor there, too. After acquiring Seven Oak, Kitzer had sent a telex instructing the staff to place a stop payment on any checks or bills of exchange from any past bank officers or directors "until a determination can be made if in fact they were issued for the personal benefit of past officers and directors."

Haines-Prescott realized, to his horror, that he had even inadvertently helped Kitzer cover his tracks. *He* had written the terms of the deal. If he dragged Kitzer and Chovanec into court, they could simply show Haines-Prescott's notes: *See? We gave him exactly what he asked for.* Except, of course, for the money—and in that setting, Kitzer could simply draw attention to Haines-Prescott's accounting improprieties.

Haines-Prescott ultimately figured that was worth the risk, because on October 18 he played his final move. He met with Kenneth Guilbert, a detective inspector in the fraud department of Scotland Yard, handed over the sale documents, and explained how two Americans had stolen his bank.

2

The Informant

OCTOBER 18, 1976

It was midafternoon on a typically chilly autumn day in Chicago when the phone rang in Norman Howard's pizza shop. Howard, in his early fifties, was a sturdy, soft-spoken black man with a fringe of gray hair. When he lifted the receiver, he was surprised to hear his old friend Phil Kitzer's voice. During the 1960s and early '70s, they had engineered many financial frauds together, but they hadn't spoken for more than a year.

As a young man in 1954, Howard had joined the police force in his native Chicago. He began selling insurance policies while walking his beat and discovered that it perfectly suited his disarming eloquence. He was struck by how easy it was to convince people to pull out their checkbooks. Howard resigned in 1960, after finding that enforcing the law didn't provide the same thrills—or income—as breaking it. He quickly advanced from writing bad policies to running high-risk auto insurance companies in order to systematically fleece them of cash. He later graduated to sophisticated schemes involving phony financial guarantees, performance bonds, and other kinds of securities, sometimes working with organized crime. Several arrests barely slowed him down, prompting the Illinois Department of Insurance to warn the industry that Howard's "history of fraud and flimflam is uncontested."

Which was exactly why Kitzer was calling. He said he'd just returned from acquiring a bank in England called Seven Oak and wanted to talk deals. "This is the perfect vehicle," he said. "I can do anything I want with this vehicle."

Howard said he would come by for a visit and hung up. In the past, he would have reflexively risen to this shiny lure, knowing that working with Kitzer meant easy money. But at that moment, he saw a different kind of opportunity. He picked up the receiver again and dialed Jack Brennan, an FBI agent in nearby Gary, Indiana.

Brennan and Howard also had a productive business relationship, though theirs was of a far different kind. Brennan had collared Howard the previous year for writing illegal bail bonds, and because of his extensive criminal history, Howard faced as many as forty-five years in prison. Desperate for lenience, Howard eagerly offered Brennan his services as a tour guide through the underworld. After cutting a deal with the government, the informant shared tales of corruptible Swiss banks, Mexican presidential candidates unwittingly investing in bogus $100 million letters of credit, and huge labor unions run by mobsters. Some of the most riveting stories were about a group of high-finance con men— Howard called them "promoters"—who worked in tandem to pull off intricate capers, one of which had recently cost the City of Los Angeles almost $1 million. Brennan's background was in finance, so he was intrigued.

Brennan sent leads to other FBI offices around the country and flew with Howard to the West Coast, where the informant secretly recorded conversations with suspects. The FBI paid scant attention to white-collar crime, but Brennan realized that if Howard's stories were true, the bureau was missing out. The promoters were stealing far more than any bank robber ever could.

When Howard phoned on October 18, Brennan was entangled in a long and complicated trial and didn't have time to talk. But when the agent managed to call back, Howard sounded excited, and Brennan stopped what he was doing to focus on what Norman had to say.

You want to go after those promoters I was telling you about? Howard asked.

Brennan did.

Well, then, Howard breathed into the phone, I can give you the top guy.

At thirty years old, Brennan was already an established star in the FBI's Gary office, having recently quarterbacked several high-profile investigations. He stood out not just for his youth and size—six feet tall and burly enough to have played on the offensive line in junior college football—but also for his speaking style and comportment. Unlike the stereotypical agent, who employed bluster and threats, Brennan spoke gently and with a lilting southern inflection. He had sandy hair, striking pale blue eyes, and an enormous smile that came easily and stretched the length of his round face. For all his capabilities and intelligence, he would never be chosen to play the tough guy. When it came time to convince people to talk—and much of an agent's job was developing informants—Brennan attacked them with charm and empathy. "C'mon, let's just chat," he would say. Then he would sit quietly, laughing easily or levering his expressive eyebrows downward into looks of avuncular concern. For Brennan, listening came effortlessly.

His retiring demeanor was particularly striking considering the way the bureau was intertwined with his DNA. In 1908, his great-grandfather Edward Brennan was one of the first eight men hired to what was then the Bureau of Investigation. Edward ran some of the FBI's biggest and busiest offices, in New York, Chicago, and St. Louis, and pioneered the agency's system of linking suspects to crime scenes by matching fingerprints. In 1921, he organized a training program for new agents, and one of the greenhorns was his son John, who went by Jack and who had joined the FBI at the age of nineteen, over his father's protestations. Jack became one of the bureau's first firearms instructors and had a knack for turning up wherever the action was. When J. Edgar Hoover and Clyde Tolson descended on Chicago to take down the Roger Touhy gang, Jack killed two gangsters in a shootout. He also helped capture Pretty Boy Floyd and participated in some of the most sensational kidnapping cases of the era.

He retired in 1950 just as his son, Edward, joined the bureau—maintaining the family tradition of ignoring his father's admonitions to seek a safer, stabler life. The FBI moved Edward and his family from Philadelphia to Mobile, Alabama, during the fifties, launching him headlong into the carnage of the civil rights movement. His elder son, Jack, was in the fourth grade when the family relocated, so he heard about the lynchings, shootings, and bombings. "When a civil rights worker was killed," Jack said, "he would go for three or four months at a time."

Seeing a certain inevitability in the family's fealty to the bureau, Edward took the novel approach of not trying to preemptively discourage Jack and his younger son, Scott, from joining. It almost worked. Jack finished his secondary schooling at Murphy High School, where his stellar academic and athletic performance—he was a guard on Murphy's football team, which played for a state championship—earned him a nomination to the U.S. Naval Academy. But Jack possessed a sunny, freewheeling disposition, and the last thing he wanted was years of predawn bugle reveilles.

He enrolled at Auburn and gravitated toward mathematics and the computer lab, where researchers were doing trajectory work on the Apollo moon mission. He was the kind of kid who had begun purchasing inexpensive stocks in high school to try to make money, so at Auburn he and a fraternity brother pooled their funds and started trading commodities on a highly volatile mercantile exchange. They had enough success with cattle futures that, after graduation, his broker landed him a job at Lind-Waldock, a huge commodities-trading firm. He moved to Sandusky, Ohio, traded frozen pork bellies during the week with other people's money, and on weekends flew south to see his girlfriend, Becky Heldreth, at Auburn. In his early twenties, he was making four times more money than anyone back home. He woke early, worked like a demon, then retired to a golf course and bars. "My philosophy was that money was just a tool to do what you wanted to do," Brennan said.

But he was also aware, in the recesses of his limbic brain, that he was hurtling toward a spectacular early-life flameout. "It was high stress," he said. "Not healthy."

He and Becky married in 1970, and he bailed on commodities. They were in Atlanta and he was working in Texaco's tax and property division when, one day, his father called, and Jack's particular genetic mutation blinkered to life. His father explained that the bureau required each agent to recruit three people annually. And so the man who'd joined the FBI against his father's wishes induced his largely uninterested son to do the same. Jack wasn't committing to anything, so he was happy to help his father by applying. But a few months later, a letter arrived saying that J. Edgar Hoover wanted to offer him a job.

After talking it over with Becky, Jack decided to give it a try. He entered the FBI Academy and was soon helping senior agents work kidnappings and extortion cases and bank robberies. "I learned that there are whole worlds out there that we know nothing about," he said.

In 1972, the bureau assigned him to New Orleans, where, working alongside an agent who specialized in tracking fugitives, the former commodities trader learned how to talk to people on the street, to develop informants. He forged a rapport with a Chicago mafioso who explained to him about organized crime, which became useful when, after a year, the FBI transferred him to Gary.

His successes in his new post came in rapid succession. His mob contact helped him snuff out a home-invasion ring, as well as a band of thugs who were stealing truckloads of televisions from Chicago and selling them out of eighteen-wheelers in Gary. He was working on a case involving massive fraud against the federal government by the bishop of a large church when he met Norman Howard.

The name Phillip Kitzer sounded familiar, but it wasn't until the morning after he talked to Howard that Brennan connected the dots. By coincidence, the *Wall Street Journal* published a story that day under the headline "Uncollectible Drafts on West Indian Bank Flood U.S. and Total Millions of Dollars." The article focused on Mercantile Bank & Trust Co., an institution run out of a one-room office in Kingstown, St. Vincent, in the British West Indies. The bank had issued tens of millions of dollars' worth of uncollectible cashier's checks, certificates of deposit, and letters of credit. Bankers were honoring them partly out of confusion: Mercantile's name was virtually identical to that of Mercantile National Bank, a long-established Chicago-based financial institution. The story mentioned that Kitzer was an officer.

Brennan remembered where he'd heard Kitzer's name before. The FBI occasionally flew groups of agents from all over the country to Quantico for in-service classes. One instructor asked each person to outline an interesting case he was working on. Allen Ezell, from Charlotte, told of a young North Carolina couple, Bobby and Susanna Duckworth, who had sought a half-million-dollar loan to purchase a motel, the Summer Wind Motor Inn, in Myrtle Beach. Lacking any real collateral, they'd struggled to find funding.

Eventually the couple spotted an ad in a Charlotte newspaper: A broker named Arthur Norman Murley offered to help secure loans through Mercantile Bank. Murley explained that Mercantile itself wouldn't provide the money; instead, it would furnish collateral against which their local bank would lend the half million. All he required was a fully refundable $19,500 fee.

This sounded reasonable enough. The Duckworths signed a mound of paperwork, and on January 26, 1976, Mercantile notified Southern National Bank in Charlotte that it was holding a $500,000 letter of credit on the couple's behalf.

The letter of credit was to serve as a kind of safety net. In this case, if the Duckworths defaulted on their half-million-dollar loan, Mercantile would pay Southern back on the couple's behalf.

Still, everything had to check out. Southern's bankers requested further documentation—specifically, they wanted proof that there really was $500,000 set aside in Mercantile's coffers. These inquiries went nowhere, however, and Southern rejected the Duckworths' application. When the couple, in turn, asked for their $19,500 back, their calls went unreturned.

The Duckworths contacted the FBI, and Ezell pursued Mercantile, learning what later appeared in the *Wall Street Journal:* The bank seemed to have virtually no assets, much less half a million dollars, but had charged people around the world for certificates of deposit and letters of credit in deals just like the Duckworths'.

Grasping the intricacies of Mercantile's fraudulent operation was one thing. Arresting and convicting Kitzer and his crew was exponentially harder. Mercantile left no trail to follow, and Kitzer operated in a way that spanned various borders, so that any prosecution would require cooperation among law enforcement from different states and countries. Everyone suggested to Ezell that the phony bank was someone else's problem: the Securities and Exchange Commission's, the British Crown's, Interpol's. Even worse: St. Vincent had no bank regulations, and therefore Mercantile had to file virtually no reports on what it was doing.

Ezell eventually gathered enough evidence to haul Kitzer into Charlotte in August to testify before a grand jury. The agent approached Kitzer in the courthouse and said he was seeking an indictment for mail and securities fraud and interstate racketeering. Kitzer's lawyer, Frank Oliver, advised him to invoke his Fifth Amendment right against self-incrimination. With no one testifying to the workings of Kitzer's criminal operation, Ezell couldn't counter the argument that the bank was legitimately chartered and that the Duckworth situation involved a bank loan that simply hadn't worked out.

This was a problem. Ezell and the federal prosecutors had

to convince a jury that Kitzer had *intended* to defraud the Duckworths and Southern. It was easy to surmise but hard to prove. Without any informants, Ezell could do nothing but watch Kitzer walk away.

Thinking over the challenges Ezell had faced, Brennan saw that he would have to try a different strategy—and Howard's cooperation presented one. But Brennan was juggling two complicated trials. He needed help.

Brennan thought about his colleagues in Gary. Some of them wouldn't understand what Kitzer was up to, and even more of them wouldn't care. It didn't sound like a bureau case. Besides, a majority of the office's twenty-five agents were busy just trying to survive. Gary had been home to the nation's highest per capita murder rate for several years running, and the lakeshore had become the Chicago mob's preferred repository for dead bodies. Agents there were prone to burnout. And the FBI had recently rescinded a policy that allowed them to request their office of preference after five years in one city, so everyone was now marooned there, including a few agents who were only months away from a transfer. The sole ambition for some was to make it to five o'clock so they could go drink in peace. When Brennan arrived, young and hungry, and wanted to pursue promising but risky cases, veteran agents discouraged him.

To take on Kitzer, Brennan needed someone willing to swim upstream against the culture of resignation—not to mention the bureau's own resistance to these kinds of cases. He could think of only one guy, the agent everyone called J.J.

James J. Wedick Jr. was, by all appearances, the yang to Brennan's yin. He was pure kinetic energy, a vivacious, speed-talking New Yorker who seemed to enjoy the steady adrenaline jag Gary delivered. But like Brennan, he was smart and ambitious and a hard worker.

Brennan found him near the coffee machine. He explained the case—how exciting it could be, how Howard was a stick of dynamite but a guy who knew plenty about the underworld, how this would be something new and challenging and potentially big.

Wedick stirred five or six spoonfuls of sugar into a cup of coffee as he listened. When Brennan was finished, he shook his head. "Not interested," he said. "Really. Sorry, Jack, but no way."

3

You Owe Me Fifty Bucks

OCTOBER 19, 1976

Unlike almost everyone else in the Gary office, J.J. Wedick was doing exactly what he wanted. He was twenty-six, single, and working sixteen-hour days chasing fugitives and bank robbers. He was six foot two and thin as turpentine, and had dark brown hair parted on the side and a full mustache curling around his mouth. What Brennan was proposing—pursuing a guy in a suit slinging fraudulent securities on a case that could take years—did nothing for him. (In fact, it triggered memories of his days studying accounting at Fordham University—a chapter of his proximate past he was happy to have left behind.)

He'd grown up Irish Catholic in a middle-class neighborhood in the Bronx, the second of four kids. The entire family was wedged into a two-bedroom apartment—Jim packed into a room with his older sister and younger brother. His father, James Sr., was stern and intense—a fire department battalion chief who before he gave them up smoked three packs of Camels a day. "He didn't fool around," Wedick said. "He didn't want a lot of nonsense with kids not doing their schoolwork."

Young Jim was chatty and energetic, an extrovert who frequently hung around the neighborhood playground. He naturally absorbed the colorful patois of the streets, the accents, and with his enthusiasm and excitability, he made friends effortlessly. An indifferent student, he wanted to help people and craved thrills—even as his father pressed him to think about how he could get ahead in life. A typical father-son chat entailed the elder Wedick lecturing his offspring on how a good employee showed up on time and outworked everyone else. When Jim was old enough to get a job, his father said, he should always take a rag and wipe down surfaces when heading out on his breaks. "Don't just lallygag to lunch," Jim Sr. advised.

After ruling out the Secret Service (too much standing around), investigative journalism (too much writing), and the CIA (too much travel), young Jim settled on the FBI. At age fourteen, after his family had moved to a more spacious home in Staten Island, he wrote to the bureau asking about careers. One day he stood in the kitchen as his parents chastised him about his grades. The phone rang. "This guy says he's with the FBI and he wants to talk to you," his father said. "What's this about?"

Jim took the phone, and a recruiter explained that he'd received Wedick's letter and wanted him to come in for an interview. Jim eventually managed to interject that he had only just started high school.

Even without his father's admonitions, he naturally gravitated toward responsibility. He embraced the role of altar boy at St. Helena's Church, soaking up the Latin, relishing the precision and repetitions of the ceremony. When, at age sixteen, he was working as a counselor at Camp Notre Dame in New Hampshire, the head counselor suddenly departed in midsummer, and Jim was next in line. He happily blew a whistle in the mess hall and began making announcements about how he was going to run the place.

To help pay for his college classes, Wedick decided to become a New York City lifeguard; the competition for the position, a lucrative union job, was, however, quite intense. He'd never thought much about swimming and would be going up against teenagers who had competed on swim teams for years. Several times a week, he took a ferry and a subway to get to the East Fifty-fourth Street pool in Manhattan, where he swam laps until he nearly sank from exhaustion. He landed the job and learned a life lesson. "I had this work ethic," he later recalled. From that point on, he said, "I'm for doing everything to the maximum. I don't know halfway."

In 1969, after graduating from high school, he enrolled in an accounting program at Fordham because he'd heard that J. Edgar Hoover mostly hired lawyers and accountants, and he figured he'd start with the latter. Between classes one day, he spotted a flyer with an FBI logo on it: The bureau was seeking part-time office help. This was a possible entry point. *I could get in there,* he thought, *and then I'll be golden.*

For the next few years, he juggled a slate of classes and jobs as a lifeguard and an FBI clerk. He sometimes worked seven days a week, napping during two-hour subway rides between Manhattan, Coney Island, and Staten Island, often waking up three stations past his stop. But he was on his way. He eventually became a driver for John F. Malone, an assistant director of the FBI's New York office, and during their trips Malone regaled him with stories of bank robberies and plane hijackings.

The fantasy nearly fizzled. During Wedick's senior year at Fordham, the bureau offered him a full-time job as a special-agent accountant. He wasn't interested in forensic analyses of financial ledgers, but everyone leaned on him. One bureaucrat in a three-piece suit told him, "Jim, if you don't do this, you're not gonna be in the FBI." Even Malone pushed him to accept it.

He gambled and refused the job, and the FBI instead offered him a spot in its next class of trainees. He enrolled at Quantico in 1973 at twenty-three, the youngest member of his class. The other recruits nicknamed him Bronx. His counselor, Al Whitaker, was a lifer from Gary, Indiana, and he told the recruits riveting tales about the pursuit of Baby Face Nelson and John Dillinger. By the time they graduated, three months later, the whole class knew that Bronx wanted to go to Gary.

This was a source of hilarity among recruits who knew the city's reputation as a Rust Belt pothole. Anyway, the FBI didn't send anyone where he *wanted* to go. The joke was that the bureau handed a monkey a dart bearing a recruit's name and pointed at a map on the wall. But when his orders came in May 1973, Wedick's destination read Indianapolis. Gary was one of Indianapolis's resident offices. And fifteen months after Wedick arrived, Special Agent in Charge James Martin called him into his office. "Jimmy, I'm very sorry," he said, "but I'm sending you to Gary." The FBI normally assigned Gary to agents only after they'd accrued significant experience elsewhere, because it was so dangerous. But Martin had no one else to send.

Wedick thanked Martin and cleaned out his desk. When he arrived in Gary, he said, "downtown was all burned down." The office had bullet holes in it, and people were being murdered in the park across the street. One of his new colleagues advised Wedick that when he walked out to his car late at night, he shouldn't keep his gun in a holster. Instead, he should wear a raincoat and slip his snub-nosed .357 into a pocket where it would be easy to grab. Wedick thanked him.

This is perfect, he thought.

During his first week, he took a case involving a ring of thieves stealing tractor-trailer trucks loaded with steel. He cultivated a local thug named Tom as an informant. There was one problem: Tom feared that mobsters would sniff out that he was a snitch. To deflect suspicion, Wedick staged a scene at two in the morning in which he walked into an underworld bar and said he was looking for Tom. Of course, Tom was sitting right there, and Wedick left after staring right at him—making it clear that he had no idea who Tom was.

The next day, Tom drove Wedick along the shores of Lake Michigan, into a warren of warehouses and junkyards and eerie incinerator silos. It was like a set for a dystopian movie. Tom stopped at a massive chop shop—a place where stolen trucks were cut apart with acetylene torches and their pieces sold off. Five rigs carrying massive steel coils were parked there. The thieves had targeted those trucks so they could melt down the steel and resell it. Together, the trucks and steel were worth more than $2.5 million.

The find established Wedick as an ambitious upstart, someone who wasn't about to wait his turn to claim center stage. He was intense and cocky, talked like a New Yorker, and grew a lush mid-seventies mustache that made him look a few years older. A single guy who could function on little sleep, he hurled himself into his cases, hounding after every detail so obsessively that he would skip lunch, then dinner, then wonder why he felt light-headed at ten o'clock. He nicknamed his desk "the vortex."

His unbridled chutzpah sometimes led to trouble. He once went out looking for a fugitive alone—a rookie mistake—and, during an ensuing foot chase, fell through ice into a pond. He hoisted himself out by grabbing an overhanging tree branch. On another occasion, as Wedick walked to his car in the small hours of the morning, he watched a vehicle pass slowly. *They're coming back,* he thought. Sure enough, the car circled around and stopped in front of him, and the two occupants got out and demanded his wallet. Wedick had already pulled his gun. The would-be muggers lunged back into the vehicle and squealed away.

Some agents viewed his near-ecstatic fervor as an affront. "There was an element of 'Who do you think you are, kid? You're going to blow the pecking order out of the water,'" he recalled.

He notched so many arrests in bank robbery and fugitive cases that the bureau assigned him a new 1976 Ford Thunderbird that year, passing over older colleagues.

But for Wedick, the office was more than an outlet for his fanatical work habits. His family was almost eight hundred miles away, so he created a surrogate version by harnessing his natural ability to connect with people. A relentless extrovert, he bought an office coffeemaker to create a water-cooler type of gathering point. He organized the office Christmas party, collecting money and putting up decorations, even holding it in his apartment complex one year. He bantered with everyone, greeting and chatting up the office janitor and the concession-stand guy as if they were pals from back on the Bronx playgrounds.

Wedick cast a wide social net. He befriended federal prosecutors and clerks and cops in Hammond, one town over. He wasn't just young and therefore invincible; he was also an FBI agent and thus even *more* invincible. Wedick shared a three-bedroom apartment with Kim Jordan, who was also in his twenties and the federal court chief judge's law clerk, and the scene was like his family's overflowing Bronx apartment. A rotating cast of visitors and friends occupied the third room, including *Hammond Times* reporter Bob O'Hearn, who wrote extensively about the FBI in Gary—in particular, Wedick's arrests. Wedick dubbed this extended circle "the Federalies." Sometimes he rallied the troops for happy hour drinks, and other times Wedick, who liked to exercise, persuaded everyone to go to Omni 41, a local health club.

Wedick was, as he put it, "happy as dirt"—and right where he wanted to be.

All of this made Brennan's Kitzer pitch sound distinctly unappealing. The only reason Wedick paused to consider it was Brennan himself. During his first assignment, in Indianapolis, Wedick had pulled overnight shifts in which his job was to sort incoming teletypes. He'd noticed Brennan's name on many of the big cases coming out of Gary, and when he was assigned there in August 1974, he watched how Brennan operated.

Brennan clearly knew a promising case—which was part of what made Wedick leery. If this one was so great, why wouldn't Jack work it himself—or keep it in reserve for a slow stretch, as many agents did? Wedick thought he knew the answer: It sounded like a meat grinder. Whoever took the case would likely find themselves endlessly conducting and transcribing interviews, reviewing financial records, applying for subpoenas—typical white-collar-crime sausage-making tedium.

But Brennan had a way of working people. He hid a bullish persistence under a kind of southern-gentleman act that was so disarming, you somehow ended up agreeing to do whatever he wanted. He continued to hector Wedick. "It'll just be one case," he said. "Norman Howard is a great informant who knows a lot, and you'd love working with him."

He tried another tack: appealing to Wedick's ego. So J.J. could handle the toughest cases? This guy Kitzer will be far more challenging than any nitwit bank robbers.

Wedick said he would think it over.

As Wedick pondered Brennan's proposition that night, he began to look at the Kitzer case differently. Allen Ezell had already tried the conventional route to nail Kitzer, and so far it hadn't worked.

They needed a new strategy, and the most obvious one Wedick could think of was also one that held serious appeal for him: They might need to work undercover.

The FBI had long avoided such operations, but lately it had begun to take a few tentative steps in that direction. Back in Indianapolis, Wedick had chatted up Dean Naum, the first agent there to take the bureau's bare-bones training class for undercover work. Naum wore street clothes instead of a standard-issue suit and walked with a swagger. Wedick had sought him out. "Dean, I'd like to work undercover stuff," he'd said.

Naum had waved him off. "Not ever in your dreams, kid."

But after arriving in Gary, Wedick openly campaigned for undercover training. In May 1976, his boss, Orville Watts, wrote a memo to headquarters outlining Wedick's "intense desire to attend a school associated with bureau undercover work, including the schooling in driving a tractor-trailer rig. SA Wedick's interest in such a school, desire to work in an undercover capacity, ability to meet and converse with people even under the most unusual or trying circumstances, age and physical appearance would all be an asset." Wedick had requested the truck-driving school thinking he could use that to infiltrate organized-crime theft rings.

Indianapolis already had Naum and another agent in place for undercover jobs, and the FBI's program was still in its infancy. The training was in high demand, and Wedick, who was young, probably wasn't going to be chosen for at least another year.

Maybe, he thought, the Kitzer case was a chance to jump to the front of the line. Which made it far more appealing than it had sounded at first.

There was one problem: Wedick knew that if he took the case, Brennan was likely to want to join in as soon as he was free from his current trials. Brennan had a way of reaching into cases in which he was peripherally involved if he thought they weren't moving quickly enough, or when he was suddenly freed up from other commitments. There was a paradoxical impulsiveness to his easygoing personality. Back home, when Brennan's four-legged console television set broke, he didn't bother reading the manual. He just took it apart with Becky standing by asking if he knew what he was doing and making sure he'd at least remembered to unplug the thing. Somehow he always managed to make it work— but Wedick didn't subscribe to this kind of seat-of-the-pants, often impulsive way of doing things. He had no interest in taking the Kitzer case only to have Brennan later insert himself and start tinkering. Brennan would have an obvious motivation to do so: He had opened the case, and he stood to get credit for any result. But to Wedick, the thought of both of them grappling for the reins of the case was distinctly unappealing.

Driving to work, Wedick thought up a solution, and when he arrived at the office, he tracked Brennan down. "Look, I'll do this, Jack, but I want no interference from you," Wedick said. "If you stick your hands into this, I'll prepare the memo to close this case faster than you can blink your eyes."

Brennan agreed without hesitation. He knew Wedick would work it hard, and he didn't want the opportunity to disappear.

Within hours, Wedick was sitting with Norman Howard, going over the way Kitzer operated. They agreed that they should strike quickly, while Kitzer was reaching out, and they invented a story they could use to lure him in.

Howard called Kitzer afterward and explained that a buddy of his had a brother, Nick Carbone, who owned a restaurant in South Bend, Indiana. Carbone had made some poor decisions that had created financial trouble, and his bank, St. Joseph, had balked at his $50,000 loan application. The bankers had indicated that Carbone lacked adequate collateral. Howard told Kitzer that Carbone would make an excellent prospect for a $50,000 Seven Oak Finance letter of credit, which Carbone could use to improve his bottom line.

Howard, of course, knew that Seven Oak didn't have $50,000. Kitzer was in the business of taking money, not handing it out. He offered the *illusion* of assets—a kind of financial hall of mirrors in which a banker or victim might be flummoxed into turning over money. For a fee, Kitzer would send a businessman a phony bank statement showing a six-figure balance—again, to insinuate wealth where none existed.

Kitzer told Howard that this sounded fine. He could provide the letter of credit for 10 percent of face value, or $5,000.

On October 21, three days after Kitzer called his pizza shop, Howard walked up to a fashionable apartment building on Fullerton Avenue, on Chicago's North Side—the home of Kitzer's friend Debra Marshall. Howard was wearing a hidden wireless transmitter that allowed Wedick to listen from a van parked outside. He told Wedick that he could get Kitzer to talk about the fraudulent nature of Seven Oak.

"Hey, buddy," Howard said when Kitzer answered the door.

"Hey, Norman," Kitzer replied. He introduced Marshall to Howard and then asked, "How about a drink?"

"What you got?"

"Scotch."

"Yeah, I knew you didn't have anything but Scotch," Howard said, laughing.

Marshall interjected that, in fact, she had wine.

"Good, give me a little wine," Howard said. "One cube of ice."

Kitzer asked what Howard had been up to.

"Just kicking around," Norman answered. "I'm mad at you, though."

"Why's that?"

Howard reminded him that at one point Kitzer had planned to include him in Mercantile Bank & Trust—maybe even send him to the Caribbean to run it.

Kitzer didn't hesitate: "Do you have fifty bucks in your pocket?"

"Say what?"

"Because you owe it to me."

Howard sounded baffled. "For *what*?"

"This is just the day before yesterday," Kitzer said, pulling out a copy of the *Wall Street Journal* article. "Here's the Caribbean thing—in the *Journal*."

"Oh, okay," Howard said, laughing. "I owe you fifty bucks."

Kitzer laughed, too.

"What, did it blow apart, huh?" Howard said.

"Yeah, it blew apart," Kitzer said. "I'm in it."

"I guess my name would have been in there if you didn't cut me out," Howard said, realizing where Kitzer was going.

"Because you were cut out, it cost you fifty."

"Fifty. Okay. All right."

"Was it worth it to keep your name out of the *Journal*?"

"Yeah, I guess so," Howard conceded.

Inside the van, Wedick marveled at how effortlessly Kitzer had flipped the conversation to put Howard on the defensive.

Howard asked about Seven Oak. "Let me see that stuff you got," he said.

Kitzer showed Howard the paperwork from London: financial statements, stock certificates. He controlled one hundred thousand shares of Seven Oak stock. "I call all the shots," he said.

"In other words," Howard said, "on a letter of credit, this guy, all he's got to do is come to you and you make the phone call and we got it, right?"

"That's right."

Flipping through the pages, Howard came across the name 219 Dearborn Corp. Kitzer explained that that was the holding company he'd formed.

"How did you come up with that?"

"How do you think?" Kitzer said. "You know what 219 Dearborn is."

"No, I don't, really. Is it the stock exchange?"

Kitzer laughed. "It's the federal building."

"Well, I'll be damned," Howard said. "That's the Everett Dirksen Building." He was referring to the skyscraper at 219 South Dearborn Street in downtown Chicago.

"Right, right," Kitzer said. "The FBI, the whole shot . . . the United States courthouse. I was being very facetious that day."

Howard then tried to help Wedick out by probing into the bank's legitimacy. "You don't have to comply with the laws of this country, relative to issuing?" he asked, referring to the British bank.

"You have to comply with the federal law."

"Uh-huh."

"We comply," Kitzer added. "Not going to do anything wrong."

Wedick pondered this. He hoped Kitzer might give him something to show intent to commit fraud. Instead, he was doing the opposite. Kitzer seemed to be playing Howard, trying to convince the old con man he'd gone straight.

"Uh-huh," Howard said. "In other words, this is checkable. . . . See, here's the thing about it. I don't want to take this guy's money and he screams. You get his money, I want him to be satisfied."

Kitzer reassured him about everything. Before leaving, Howard said Carbone might pay by cashier's check. Kitzer shook his head: cash only.

"You told me he's Italian, right?" Kitzer said.

"Yeah."

"So why don't you tell him to get a crooked banker?"

Howard laughed.

Kitzer added, "Tell him we'll meet in a phone booth."

"Okay, all right," Howard said, chortling. "We'll get it done."

They agreed to close the deal soon after that. Howard would bring Carbone to a Holiday Inn just off the Chicago Skyway in Hammond, Indiana.

Wedick felt pleased that things were coming together so quickly—but now he had to make this happen. He only had a few days to find someone to play the part of Nick Carbone.

4

The Shell Game

Jim Wedick scanned the grim, shag-carpeted interior of room 130 at the Holiday Inn and, for the hundredth time, ran through the mental checklist he'd built over the preceding four days. Kitzer would arrive soon, and Wedick had game-planned every scenario. Norman Howard would wear a concealed tape recorder. Playing the part of Nick Carbone would be Dean Naum, the undercover specialist from Indianapolis. Wedick had requisitioned the $5,000 that "Carbone" would pay Kitzer. Running the undercover operation gave him the chance to learn its intricacies.

To round out the cast, Wedick—using one of Brennan's connections from a previous case—had recruited the help of St. Joseph Bank in South Bend. A senior vice president, Dan King, had manufactured Carbone's $50,000 loan application by changing some of the numbers in a dead file. A document showed Carbone's net worth at $56,600, most of it restaurant equipment.

King wrote in the loan-rejection letter, "Nick, in looking at your financial statement, a copy of which is attached, it is apparent that once you borrow the $50,000 your net worth will be reduced to approximately $6,600. Traditionally, restaurant equipment carries little collateral value and as a consequence, it will be necessary to request additional collateral."

Wedick had scrambled to get all of this lined up. Within the hour, he would know whether he'd done enough.

The weather was unseasonably cold for late October, winter creeping into the Upper Midwest, and Kitzer was late. When finally he arrived, wearing a suit and accompanied by Paul Chovanec, Kitzer said that they'd encountered the season's first snow on their two-hour drive from Milwaukee.

"Christ," said Carbone. "I couldn't believe the weather. It's gonna be a bad winter comin' up this year."

"Oh yeah, well, last one was too easy," Chovanec said.

After dispensing with the small talk, Carbone broached the topic of the letter of credit. He said he had a friendly banker named Dan King who would help smooth the way for the bank to accept it. "Did Norm tell ya I was talking with this banker up there?" he asked.

"He's your pal?" Kitzer asked.

"Our wives went to school together," Carbone said, "and I've known him for about ten years now, I guess. I've had a little bit of problems tryin' to get some financing and I've been talkin' to him up there . . . tryin' to work something out with him, and from everything he says, we can do something here today."

Kitzer made sure Carbone understood that acquiring the letter of credit was not the same as obtaining $50,000, and that if he was issued a loan, he would still have to repay it. "The reason I say that point-blank to you like that, Nick, is 'cause a lot of people that receive these, they think they don't have to pay."

Carbone assured him that he understood. "There's no problem about repaying or anything like that," he said. "I'm not gonna try and walk away from it."

Kitzer assured Carbone that he wouldn't have any problems. King, he said, "can confirm it for the bank, the whole shot, no problems. At that point he should give you the money. If he doesn't give you the money, then he never wanted to to begin with."

Chovanec opened his briefcase and began filling out paperwork for Carbone to sign. He produced a Seven Oak brochure and some paperwork, including a promissory note, with copies for the bank's records. Kitzer explained that Seven Oak required a postdated $50,000 check made payable to the bank, and that Carbone should write "In payment of letter of credit #1078" on it. He asked Carbone to date it October 20, 1978—the day Carbone's two-year loan from the bank would be due. This was to protect Seven Oak in case Carbone defaulted, Kitzer said—but Carbone shouldn't worry about any of that. If he paid back his loan, Seven Oak would tear up the check.

Howard knew this was bogus—one of Kitzer's defense mechanisms. If some FBI agent tried to claim the letter of credit was worthless, Kitzer would hold up the check: See? If it was fraudulent, why would someone give me $50,000 for it? Kitzer knew he could never cash the check; he sold his documents to people who *needed* money. If Carbone had $50,000 in his bank account, he wouldn't need the letter of credit in the first place.

"Oh, you know damn well the check ain't worth a shit, is it now?" Howard said.

Kitzer ignored him.

Carbone filled the silence by asking, "How you want that made out, now?"

"Made out to Seven Oak Finance," Chovanec said.

When they were finished, Carbone took out the $5,000 and asked Kitzer to count it. "Now, yeah, you can draw the drapes," Kitzer said, and everyone laughed. He flipped through the bills and nodded. Carbone said he would have more business for Seven Oak if this deal worked out.

With that, it was done. Kitzer and Chovanec said good-bye and asked Howard to step out with them. They went to the men's room in the hotel lobby, and Kitzer handed Howard his $2,500 commission. Then they were gone.

Wedick mostly felt relieved as the team reconvened and he took the $2,500 from Howard. The meeting had gone smoothly. He still had work to do, but Kitzer had stepped right into the trap.

Wedick's next task was to prove that Kitzer had defrauded Carbone and St. Joseph Bank. He asked Dan King to telex England to see if the $50,000 in the letter of credit actually existed. What followed was a series of telexes over a period of weeks that traveled between South Bend; Kitzer's home in tiny Ellendale, Minnesota; and National Westminster Bank, a third-party institution in London that Kitzer claimed held the money.

Predictably, King couldn't find any trace of the fifty grand. National Westminster claimed to know nothing of the Seven Oak document. In his correspondence, Kitzer omitted a key piece of information in one telex, then gave a wrong number in the next one. The idea was to frustrate St. Joseph until the bankers gave up—because Kitzer didn't care if Carbone got his loan. He already had the $5,000.

Naum, playing Carbone, called Kitzer on November 21 about the problem. Kitzer told him that King had made a mistake in his confirmation request.

"Okay," Carbone said. "There's no problem with the letter of credit, though, is there?"

"There is no problem."

"'Cause, you know, I'm very concerned about this."

"Norman explained this to me," Kitzer said, "and I explained to Norman, I said, 'Norman, they asked the wrong question on the telex.'"

"All right."

"And then that is the last I heard about it, Nick."

Kitzer promised to call King the next morning. "I'll have a talk with him and see what he has done, who he's been in touch with," he purred. "And I'll try to instruct him which way to go."

But when he spoke to King the next day, Kitzer said there had been a miscommunication overseas and promised again that the confirmation was imminent. For Wedick, each call or telex that crossed a state or international border was another piece of evidence. By mid-January 1977, King had exchanged ten telexes with Kitzer, each deepening the conspiracy.

By Wedick's tally, the government could now charge Kitzer with seven counts of fraud and conspiracy—but he was sure it wasn't enough. Even with Howard, who had insisted he could draw something incriminating out of his old friend, Kitzer had said nothing to indicate he was committing fraud. It was uncanny—as if he knew someone was listening.

Wedick was certain that if he charged Kitzer with fraud, Kitzer's lawyer would repeat what he'd said in Charlotte: *Where's the proof?* Just as with Mercantile, Kitzer was using a legitimately chartered bank located in another country, so Wedick couldn't get his hands on the records. A federal prosecutor in Hammond reviewed the case and confirmed Wedick's suspicions that he didn't have enough—a jury might be either confused or unconvinced.

But Wedick was locked in. Howard was whispering in his ear that the scams went much, much deeper—Kitzer had swindled people out of millions of dollars, and would take millions more if someone didn't trip him up.

Wedick sat at work late one night with Kitzer's telexes spread across his desk, his hands wrapped around the back of his head. One thing was obvious: Pursuing Kitzer in the traditional way—by conducting interviews and gathering a paper trail—made no sense. Kitzer already seemed to know what the FBI was after. If Kitzer wouldn't admit that he was doing something illegal, maybe Wedick could catch him doing something that was. Howard had said that Kitzer sometimes dealt in stolen bonds. What if Wedick could get Kitzer to sell him one?

That would mean another undercover buy. Wedick liked that idea. And this time, he was doing it himself.

———

Getting permission to go undercover with zero training was no layup. But Wedick's immediate boss, the gray-haired senior resident agent Orville Watts, was easy. A few months earlier, a citizen had expressed his displeasure with the U.S. government by hurling a spear at the federal building in Gary. The missile shattered Watts's first-floor window and lodged itself, quivering, in the drywall across from his desk. After that, Watts's primary concern was talking to headquarters about moving to an upper floor, so he rubber-stamped most anything else laid in front of him.

Wedick's proposal prominently featured the words "stolen bonds." He figured that this term would make it easier to secure approvals from the bosses. The idea wasn't to try to make another buy but, rather, to gather more intelligence on what Kitzer was doing. (It helped, too, that Wedick wasn't asking for more money.) Wedick didn't go into much detail about the financial intricacies of Kitzer's operation. Better not to confuse anyone.

When the bureau signed off, Wedick decided he wanted Brennan to come along, to increase his comfort level. Howard would introduce them as young promoters trying to get into the game.

Wedick set out to fill in the details of their lives as embryonic con men. He researched how to create a shell corporation similar to what Kitzer had used in acquiring Seven Oak. A business name occurred to him after a few days: Executive Enterprises. The firm sounded simultaneously substantial and like nothing at all. It was a Rorschach test, and they hoped Kitzer would see an opaque entity of uncertain means and motives. Wedick ordered business cards naming himself as chief executive.

He applied for a post office box in South Bend, using his apartment in Griffith, a Gary suburb, as a backup address, so that nothing in the paperwork linked him to the FBI. He also subscribed to an answering service in South Bend so that he could give Kitzer a phone number.

Howard told Wedick that a telex machine would also help

project a solid image of a shady corporation. Kitzer used telexes routinely to mirror the activities of a legitimate bank. A telex service was like e-mail before there was any such thing: You typed in a message and it went through instantly to the recipient's teletypewriter. Wedick called RCA, who told him the machines cost $1,500 down and $750 a month. This would be the perfect prop, he thought. What FBI agent would go to this kind of trouble?

Wedick couldn't believe it when the FBI also approved this expense. *Now we're getting somewhere,* he thought.

There was one step he couldn't take. The FBI had the capability of providing fictional identities—but only for agents who had completed the undercover training. Wedick knew he wasn't getting into that program anytime soon, but he thought maybe he could reverse-engineer the situation. If he did the Kitzer operation without the normal safeguards in place, they might push him to the top of the list for the training. He didn't think it would be an issue, anyway: He and Brennan would have one meeting with Kitzer, maybe two, get a stolen bond, and boom.

By January 26, 1977, Wedick had finished creating his fictional biography. Howard called Kitzer and said he'd met a couple of young guys, J.J. and Jack, who wanted to meet about acquiring paper. Jack's grandfather owned an insurance company in Alabama that had hit a rough patch and run short on cash. States require such companies to keep a certain amount of money on hand to cover a sudden surge of claims, so Jack needed to plump up the financial statement to forestall any trouble. They figured this story would sound appealing because Kitzer would see an opportunity to seize control of and bankrupt the business, the same way he had hijacked Seven Oak.

Howard hung up the phone and told Wedick: He's going to call you. Be ready.

Wedick flipped on the turn signal of his Thunderbird and exited the frosty pavement of eastbound Interstate 90 in Portage, Indiana. Moments later, he drove into the parking lot of the Holiday Inn, walked into the lobby, and asked for his phone messages. Wedick had checked into the hotel the previous day, even though he'd had no plans to stay overnight. He'd just needed a room from which to call Kitzer. The clerk nodded and handed Wedick a slip of paper indicating that Kitzer had called, with a Minnesota number Wedick recognized.

Wedick was pleased to have missed the call. He thanked the clerk and slid back into his car. He would not call Kitzer back—not yet. He'd wait two or three days, then check into another hotel, in Indianapolis or Michigan City or Valparaiso, and try again.

This hard-to-get routine was calculated. Wedick wanted to seem interested but telegraph that he was in no hurry to connect. He hoped to project a busyness, a sense that he had far more going on than whatever Kitzer had to offer. Wedick also hoped to discourage any suspicions that he and Brennan were in law enforcement. What FBI agent would wait three days to return a call? "Jim Wedick from Executive Enterprises calling back," he'd say next time. "Sorry to miss you. Call when you can."

Wedick found that there wasn't much of an adrenaline rush in driving around the Midwest, collecting phone messages. He pondered the irony in this—pursuing a criminal by avoiding him—as he sped back toward Gary. But the challenge of penetrating the defenses of a master criminal was compelling and, in its own way, more exciting than tracking bank robbers. In his idle moments, Wedick found his mind drifting to Kitzer, trying to think what he might be thinking.

The agent hoped they could set up a meeting soon. After three months of stalking Kitzer, Wedick would finally sit across from him. He looked forward to that. True, this was a steep task for his first undercover venture, and he would have preferred to have taken the FBI's training classes.

But it was just one meeting. Wedick figured they could handle that.

Then it happened. After two more weeks of driving to hotels and leaving messages, Wedick spoke to Kitzer on February 14. They briefly discussed Jack's grandfather's situation and Executive Enterprises—just enough for Wedick to pile on more bait. Slipping in a few Bronx mannerisms, Wedick indicated that he had numerous deals in play, some of which involved connections in Italy. Kitzer invited him to come to Minneapolis the next day, and to bring Brennan.

After months of set building, the agents suddenly had twenty-four hours to hustle onto center stage—and there were still hurdles. First he had to obtain clearance to fly to another FBI jurisdiction. Wedick called Jim Deeghan, his immediate supervisor for this case. Deeghan had to get approval from his boss, Special Agent in Charge Frank Lowie, who, in turn, needed permission from both headquarters and the Minneapolis FBI office; this sort of procedure was standard anytime agents traveled onto someone else's turf. The bureau under J. Edgar Hoover rarely countenanced travel in an undercover role, but the legendary director had died in 1972. A new wave of more progressive thinkers was entering the bureau—and Lowie, fortuitously, was among them. A bespectacled, slender man in his mid-forties, he was a steady, calm, and reasoned thinker. His old-school predecessor wouldn't have given Wedick and Brennan a chance.

As the FBI bureaucracy clanked to life, Wedick bought a bottle of Cutty Sark—Howard had told him that Kitzer loved Scotch. He tried on the Nagra microrecorder, a device introduced out of Switzerland in 1970. The machine, made from a light metal alloy with trademark Swiss precision, was the first commercially available miniature cassette recorder, and it had been an instant hit among the likes of CIA operatives and East Germany's Stasi. Hollywood directors strapped Nagras to stuntmen to capture sound effects.

The device fit into a pouch built into an Ace bandage–type fabric that looped around Wedick's midsection. Two wires connected to tiny microphones, each about the size of a pencil eraser, that ran from the machine, situated on his lower back, up under his arms and around his chest to his sternum, where they were secured using surgical tape. The higher the microphones were positioned, the better they captured voices. Some agents placed them by their belt buckle to minimize the odds of discovery, but the tape sounded muddy and distant. A sharp recording was worth the risk, Wedick believed—plus, he was posing as an executive type, so he'd be wearing a suit and tie. A third wire connected to a remote-control on-off device. Wedick cut a hole in his right suit-pants pocket to thread the remote in. Each cassette could hold three hours of recordings.

Then Wedick and Brennan were on a plane in the early afternoon of February 15. It was a little surreal. Brennan sat quietly with his thoughts while Wedick fidgeted. Somewhere over the northern prairielands, Wedick looked at Brennan in alarm. A thought suddenly hit him: He'd spent so much time scrambling to get ready, he wasn't sure they were adequately prepared for their conversation with Kitzer. They were supposedly connected with Brennan's grandfather's insurance company—but what did they really know about that field? Meanwhile, Kitzer was an expert in high finance. What if he tested them?

Brennan told him to relax. As someone who had bought and sold commodities, he could bluff his way through whatever Kitzer threw at them. He explained a few basic terms and concepts, like stock market puts and calls.

Wedick, unconvinced, didn't necessarily see how one field translated to the other. "World's number one white-collar criminal, and I don't know squat," Wedick grumbled. "This is just great."

Then they sat in silence. It was too late at that point; either it would work or it wouldn't. If the investigation had been launched a decade later, the FBI would have provided a psychological screening to determine their readiness, plus in-depth training, new identities, and housing to safeguard their families, among other provisions. Brennan and Wedick weren't just going out there cold, using their real names, without much of a grasp of the insurance industry—they were, by almost any standard, an oddball pairing.

They needed Kitzer to believe that Brennan, the quiet, easy-going southern introvert, and Wedick, the chatty, high-energy New Yorker, were good friends *and* business partners.

Was this plausible? They couldn't be fully certain until they tried it.

Just one meeting.

Part II

THE GAME

The devil appeared like Jesus through the steam in the street

Showin' me a hand I knew even the cops couldn't beat

—Bruce Springsteen, "It's Hard to Be a Saint in the City"

5

The Thunderbird

FEBRUARY 15, 1977

Wedick held his smile, hoping it didn't look nearly as belabored as it felt, while Kitzer watched his reaction.

You guys look like a couple of feds.

There was no time to analyze the statement, to try to discern whether Kitzer was accusing them of something or just being provocative. Wedick's mind pinwheeled: Should they have dressed differently? Should they have anticipated this and had an answer ready? Would they set a record for the shortest undercover operation in FBI history? At least he had a mustache; Hoover had banned them during his reign.

Brennan stood next to him, grinning forcefully. Howard had told him that Kitzer was whip-smart, uncommonly perceptive, and dexterous in conversation. *He reads people,* Howard had said. Maybe, then, they should have expected Kitzer to test them—but the agents had assumed they'd have at least a few minutes to settle in first. For a couple of seconds that seemed like eons, they willed every muscle in their faces to hold steady.

Then Kitzer laughed, and stood and shook their hands, and the agents also laughed, they hoped not too enthusiastically. Kitzer said he *might* have suspected that Wedick was in the FBI if they hadn't spent the past few weeks trading phone messages.

"Jim Wedick," Kitzer said, "you're all over the place! I could never get ahold of you!"

Wedick shrugged as if to say, *Yeah, sorry, you know how it is,* but he felt relieved. He'd made an impression. Kitzer invited the men to sit, asked them what they were drinking—each wanted a Jack Daniel's—and put in their order. "Of course, Mr. Kitzer," the bartender replied.

Brennan and Wedick settled on either side of him at the bar and began to breathe again. Kitzer was drinking Scotch. His highball glass sat on the bar next to a pack of cigarettes and a gold-plated lighter with the word DUNHILL engraved on the bottom.

Kitzer asked about Howard, and Wedick said he was doing well and that he was a good guy who had helped them out, sprinkling in details about his pizza shop. Having Howard vouch for them was crucial—he was as solid a reference as they could hope to find. To build on their underworld bona fides, Brennan mentioned some organized-crime contacts in New Orleans he knew from having worked with them as an FBI agent.

After a half hour of this, the threesome circled around to the evening's business: Brennan's grandfather's insurance agency. Brennan explained that they were looking for stolen bonds to pump up his portfolio.

Kitzer leaned back, exhaled a stream of smoke, and fixed the men with a steady gaze. Then he shook his head. "That's a good way to go to the penitentiary," he said.

There was no time for the agents to feel disappointed. Wedick, in fact, had almost expected that answer—Kitzer was that cagey.

"Can you suggest another option?" Brennan asked.

Kitzer appraised them. Wedick unconsciously fidgeted with the remote control in his pocket. After a pause, Kitzer suggested that they go to dinner and get to know each other better.

They already had two drinks in them when they climbed into their rental car. Kitzer offered to drive, this being his turf, and Brennan idly wondered what the bureau might say if the cops pulled Phil over and slapped him with a DUI.

Kitzer drove out to the main road from the motel complex, then abruptly made a sharp right. They were now on a street that stretched the length of a city block before ending in a cul-de-sac. There were no restaurants—or any kind of businesses—in sight, and as they cruised toward the dead end, Brennan felt his chest tighten: *What is this?*

Brennan was about to ask where they were going when Kitzer swung into a three-point turn and headed back the other way. By the time Kitzer had merged back onto the main road, Brennan knew what Kitzer was doing. If someone had been following them—say, a surveillance team—Kitzer would have gotten a good look at them after turning around. There was no other reason to have made that maneuver.

Kitzer looked over and said, "Oops, wrong turn." And smiled.

Brennan thought, *Thank God we told the local agents not to provide cover.*

After dinner they returned to the Thunderbird, where they'd taken rooms for the night. At Kitzer's behest, they headed back to the Pow-Wow Lounge for another round. He seemed relaxed but not tipsy, despite ordering a steady stream of cocktails. The agents nursed their drinks and tried to gulp water.

Kitzer finally circled back to Jack's grandfather. He said there was one possibility: He knew some guys in Cleveland who might have stolen municipal bonds. Maybe Brennan and Wedick wanted to go there tomorrow and find out? He lifted his palms upward in a universal gesture of invitation. The agents looked at each other, then at Kitzer.

That sounds good, Brennan said.

Wedick immediately thought: *Cleveland? There's no way the FBI will let us go to Cleveland.*

Brennan said they would need to call their fence in New Orleans—an organized-crime contact who handled paper for them. Hoping to buy a little time.

Anyway, it was well after midnight. The agents said they were going to turn in and would firm up their plans in the morning.

Wedick was relieved to temporarily get away from Kitzer. He'd navigated an evening with him unscathed, but the pressure of staying in character, of mentally analyzing everything before saying it, was exhausting. The alcohol and stress had left him with a jackhammer headache.

Still, their night wasn't over. As planned, Wedick and Brennan left their room, slipped out of the motel through a side door, and walked to a nearby disco, where they'd arranged to meet with a Minneapolis-based FBI agent. There, they handed over the tape from the Nagra so their colleague could mail it back to Gary. Wedick was glad to get rid of it. They toppled into their beds around two a.m. Pulling off his clothes, Wedick ran a finger through the hole he'd snipped in his pocket before tossing the pants aside.

The next morning, they found Kitzer in the motel's Bow and Arrow Coffee Shop, wearing a different suit and tie and sipping coffee. He had news: His Cleveland contact had confirmed having some $100,000 municipal bonds from Arizona. The agents nodded and said they were waiting to hear from New Orleans.

Back upstairs, they locked their door and phoned Jim Deeghan in Indianapolis. Both Deeghan and Lowie generally had Wedick's back. They had history going back to when Wedick first arrived in Indianapolis, straight out of the academy, and they invited him to their regular after-work beer at the Knights of Columbus hall directly behind the office. Deeghan, who was about a decade older than Wedick and also from the Northeast—he was born in Pennsylvania and attended Rutgers—immediately liked the kid. Wedick, in turn, ingratiated himself over the next couple of years by volunteering for crap work they needed done, including some tasks connected to the Patty Hearst kidnapping case. He also offered his spare room to one of Deeghan's bureau friends who had been sent to Indianapolis for several months.

Still, Lowie who was not thrilled to hear about this new development. He'd agreed to a single day in Minneapolis; he now also needed to obtain clearance from his counterpart in Cleveland— again at the last minute.

Deeghan and Lowie called back on speakerphone, and Brennan answered. Lowie was unequivocal: "Do *not* get on a flight to Cleveland," he said.

Then he told Brennan to put Wedick on. Wedick knew why: They were worried that Brennan would board a flight regardless. Brennan was known to plow forward on cases in ways that didn't fully adhere to bureau protocol.

"Hey, J.J., listen to me: You are *not* getting on that plane," Lowie barked. "And tell Jack: He ain't getting on that plane either, okay?"

But Lowie said he would see what he could do. Wedick hung up and looked at Brennan. "They're having a heart attack," he said. "What do you think?"

Brennan rolled his eyes. When you needed a quick answer for anything outside the playbook, the default posture was: *Don't make me make a decision.* "It sounded a little squishy to me," he said.

Wedick stared at him. He didn't see how they had any leverage. In San Francisco, a new, extensive undercover operation had started up that featured a phony corporation complete with office space and a secretary. Brennan and Wedick were just a couple of young upstarts, and the vibe was: *You guys have no chance.* "That bureaucracy is big and tall, Jack," he said. "I don't know that they can get this cleared."

He also wasn't sure whether the trip to Cleveland made sense strategically. Maybe Kitzer's contact there was worth it—but maybe it was better for Kitzer to think they weren't so eager. An FBI agent would jump on the plane in a second, so Wedick thought it might be a good idea to do the opposite. He also felt like they should regroup, think things over.

The phone clanged to life. Deeghan had a friend in the Cleveland office who had helped smooth the way for the last-minute trip.

Lowie told them to get back to Indiana right after that. Brennan nodded and snapped his suitcase shut. Wedick felt ambivalent, but now they were going.

The agents brought their luggage down and checked out, then returned to Kitzer's table. The threesome made plans for Cleveland while eating breakfast; then Kitzer turned to Wedick.

"Why don't you put your luggage in my room until we're ready to go?" he said. "Here's my key."

Wedick stood and looked at his bag, and two realizations crashed over him. The first was that his suitcase contained the recording equipment he'd used the previous night. And the second: If he left his and Brennan's stuff in Phil's room, Kitzer might find a reason to go up there to rifle through it. To see what he might learn about his new friends.

Wedick hesitated, but he couldn't think of any plausible reason to say no. This was precisely why he'd wanted to hit the pause button: There were so many different things that could happen, and they didn't really know what they were doing, and Jack just wanted to plow ahead. Wedick picked up the two satchels and headed to the elevator.

Upstairs, he opened Kitzer's door, looked around, and tried to think the situation through. He immediately ruled out asking the motel staff to hold the Nagra for him; Kitzer, a regular, undoubtedly knew many of them and tipped them well. Wedick walked around the room. The closet was empty, and too obvious, and Kitzer might check it for forgotten items. The bathroom contained no hiding places. Under the bed? That seemed ridiculous.

Wedick gazed at the bed. On it lay a brown leather suitcase. Kitzer's bag looked far nicer than Wedick's boxy, clunky model. Kitzer had clearly packed already—there was not a stray sock lying around. While Wedick stared at the bag, a thunderclap of inspiration hit him. If Kitzer was already packed, he wouldn't go back into the suitcase, right? At first Wedick dismissed the notion—too crazy, too risky. But then he thought: *Anyone got a better idea?*

Moving quickly, not wanting to be gone too long, Wedick unzipped Kitzer's bag, trying not to think about all the ways this could go bad. He retrieved his Samsonite from near the door and tossed it onto the bed, snapping it open as it jounced on the mattress. He scooped out the recorder and accessories and slid the gear into the bottom of Kitzer's bag, underneath the clothing, smoothing out the shirts on top. Then he closed both, repositioned Kitzer's case where it had been, and hurried out, switching off the light.

Back downstairs, Kitzer was talking about Armand Mucci and Bob Bendis, the Cleveland promoters looking to peddle the bonds. The three men sipped coffee, and Kitzer suggested they get a haircut before leaving the motel; the barber was excellent and Kitzer himself immaculately groomed. After about ten minutes, he excused himself to make a call from his room.

Holy shit, Wedick thought. *I knew it.*

After Kitzer left, Wedick told Brennan what he'd done. He suggested they give Kitzer ten minutes before going back up—enough time for Kitzer to search their bags and satisfy his curiosity. But they didn't want to allow him much more time than that. They needed to get the recording gear back soon in case Kitzer was the type to double- and triple-check his suitcase before checking out. The agents came up with a plan, and after an agonizingly long ten minutes, they headed upstairs.

When Kitzer answered their knock, Wedick asked to use the phone to check his messages. Brennan, meanwhile, said he needed to use the bathroom. (They figured they both needed an excuse to be up there.) Kitzer nodded but said he was just finishing up in there. When Kitzer returned to the bathroom and closed the door, Wedick lunged at Kitzer's bag, whispering to Brennan to distract Kitzer if he came out too soon. He unzipped the suitcase, removed the recording equipment, and was just closing it again when he heard Kitzer turn the doorknob. Kitzer was saying "Okay, Jack, it's all yours" as Wedick stuffed the Nagra inside his jacket.

Wedick made small talk until Brennan emerged from the bathroom, then suggested that they take the bags downstairs and arrange for a cab. Kitzer agreed to this, and just then, the phone rang, and he turned to answer it. Wedick pantomimed that they would see him downstairs. As they stepped inside the elevator, Brennan looked at Wedick and said, "That's some balls, Jimmy boy. Some balls."

Maybe that had been a close call, or maybe Wedick had just imagined that Kitzer wanted to check them out. It didn't matter now. All Wedick could think was that they just had to get in and out of Cleveland in good shape, and that would feel like a significant accomplishment on its own.

6

Hello, Cleveland

FEBRUARY 16, 1977

By the time he buckled his seat belt for the flight to Ohio, Kitzer was bantering with the people seated next to him. He chatted up the stewardesses when they passed and asked neighboring passengers where they were from and offered jokes or questions or stories in response. *You're from Miami? You know that deli, Wolfie's, the place that makes pastrami sandwiches the size of my head? One time . . .*

The threesome had been unable to get seats together; Kitzer sat a row in front of the others and a few seats over, next to the window. As the airplane arced eastward, he torqued himself around and chatted with Wedick over the people sitting between them. This was partly by design: Seated between them was an attractive woman in her twenties. Kitzer worked to loop her into the conversation, eventually eliciting the information that her name was Cheryl and she lived in Bozeman, Montana.

Although Wedick, too, was naturally outgoing, he squirmed as Kitzer flirted. Phil claimed they were businessmen negotiating a major transaction and seemed utterly unself-conscious about sharing all of this with everyone in earshot. His folksy humor and good looks—highlighted by his easy, dimpled smile and his hair, combed back into a wave that morning but now tousled by the airplane seat—seemed to disarm. By the time they exited the plane for a layover in Chicago, he'd persuaded Cheryl to join them for a beer. Wedick had by then eased into the conversation, joking with both of them while the quieter Brennan hovered on the fringes, listening and laughing.

After asking for Cheryl's phone number, Kitzer invited her to accompany them to Cleveland, offering to pay to change her ticket. The agents were astonished by his brashness and spontaneity— and relieved when she declined, saying she had to get home. As if their situation weren't complicated enough.

As Cheryl waved good-bye and headed off to catch her flight, Kitzer grinned at Wedick and issued a challenge. "I'm going to get a date with her first," he said, adding that when they reached Cleveland, he would send her flowers.

Now that they weren't in danger of dragging along an unwitting accomplice, Wedick warmed to this bluster, the sort of thing that had been a staple of his life in the Bronx. Seeing a chance to deepen his connection with Kitzer, he suggested that they ramp up the competition by sending her a bouquet immediately, making sure it reached her front door before she returned home. Kitzer loved the idea, and they jumped up and headed for a bank of pay phones. Wedick, relying on an operator using the Montana Yellow Pages in the days before the Internet, was connected to a florist in Billings. When Wedick asked about delivery options, Kitzer interrupted to tell him to arrange for a taxicab to take the flowers to Bozeman, if necessary.

Wedick had jumped into this figuring it was a low-stakes lark. But now the florist was asking for credit card information, and they were talking about a cab trip from one city to another. He briefly hesitated, but again, as with the suitcases, there was no way to back out. He was the head of Executive Enterprises, so he couldn't plausibly balk at the expense—though, in his mind, he was anxiously adding up the cost of a showy bouquet and cab fare from Billings to Bozeman. He was hazy on Montana geography but felt certain that the towns were fairly far apart. He could only imagine the FBI accountants analyzing the receipt.

Eventually they boarded the flight to Cleveland, and Kitzer turned to the topic of their forthcoming meeting with the two

Cleveland-based promoters, Armand Mucci and Bob Bendis. Kitzer had met them for the first time only the previous month—or so he'd thought. As Mucci had recounted his past exploits, he and Kitzer had realized that back in the 1960s, they'd been on opposite sides of a deal involving artificially inflated stock.

Mucci specialized in fleecing the hospitality industry. He'd recently asked for Kitzer's help targeting the Shaker House Motor Hotel in suburban Cleveland, a 160-room edifice designed by an architect from Italy, complete with an underwater cocktail lounge, marble floors, and tiled walls. The owner had just filed for Chapter 11 bankruptcy. Many people then thought of bankruptcy in Monopoly terms—you're broke and out of the game—but Mucci knew better.

The hotel was still open, so paying customers were still rolling in. Mucci claimed noble aspirations, trying to ensure that the Shaker House wouldn't forever be stuck in its historical moment. But he really wanted to acquire the establishment with phony paper—a $600,000 letter of credit from Seven Oak Finance—so he could "bust it out." He would siphon off the cash coming in, then liquidate the furniture, televisions, and other assets. Meanwhile, Seven Oak's payment would never arrive. After Kitzer stalled for months, the promoters would blame each other for the hotel's collapse. Mucci would proclaim mock outrage that Seven Oak had reneged on its letter of credit. And Kitzer would produce paperwork showing that the funding was contingent on the Shaker House being a viable business—now that it was closed, the bank was off the hook. Mucci would lock the doors and abandon it, or sell the hotel to another con man running a new scam.

When they'd talked, Mucci had agreed to pay Kitzer $6,000 for the Seven Oak paper, though the fee would rise to 10 percent—$60,000—if he successfully acquired the Shaker House. Mucci had then mentioned that he had some stolen municipal bonds from Arizona: Did Kitzer have an outlet for them? They were, Mucci had said, "a little warm."

"How warm?" Kitzer had asked.

"Hot."

"Burning," Bendis had said.

Kitzer had shaken his head. Too risky. But then he'd run into these two young men from Indiana looking for the very same thing.

At around three p.m., Wedick, Brennan, and Kitzer walked off the jetway into Cleveland Hopkins International Airport, and the agents quickly scoped the gate area. With no time to make plans, they were left to hope that things would break right for them. They had no clue what to expect of Mucci and Bendis, and they were unarmed. Traveling undercover meant not carrying weapons.

Still, they weren't totally exposed. Deeghan had asked his contact in Cleveland for help with surveillance, and Wedick and Brennan knew that other agents would be mixed into the knots of tourists and businessmen, taking photographs. Deeghan had also told them that an agent would pass them recording equipment—though Brennan and Wedick had no idea how that would go down. The Cleveland agents knew what they were wearing and what flight they'd be on. Wedick expected to bump into someone—maybe literally—near the gate.

Exiting the plane, Wedick trailed behind and scanned the passing faces, although he had no idea whom to look for. After a few minutes, a man veered toward him, looking into Wedick's eyes. As he brushed past, the stranger pressed an object into Wedick's hand, and Wedick, in turn, tucked it into his pocket, his eyes darting around to see if anyone had noticed.

He had just started to breathe again when Mucci and Bendis emerged from packs of suitcase-hefting travelers. Mucci, squat and pudgy with a prominent nose and deep-set eyes, appeared to be in his late forties. He wore a dark sport coat with an open-collared shirt. Bendis, decked out in a business suit, had a push-broom mustache and a helmet of dark hair. They all exchanged cursory introductions and walked to a lounge. As they settled in, Wedick headed to the restroom. Once locked inside a stall, he pulled out the device and examined it. It was a transmitter, slightly larger than a deck of cards, that broadcast a signal—like a miniature radio station. Wedick screwed on the antenna, a couple of inches long, topped by a diminutive bulb-shaped microphone, which automatically turned the device on. Then he tucked it into his breast pocket and headed back out. There was no way under these circumstances to test in advance whether it worked. As with just about everything else they were doing, it seemed, he would just have to hope.

He arrived to find Mucci ticking through his past accomplishments: companies he'd busted out, stock he'd artificially inflated easier than one might blow up a child's birthday balloon. To Wedick and Brennan, unaccustomed to their roles, this was surreal—a criminal laying out his entire rap sheet. Wedick wondered whether the surveillance team was listening in; in the space of fifteen minutes, Mucci had offered up about a dozen leads.

Brennan and Wedick were also surprised by the reception. Mucci already knew Kitzer, so his self-congratulatory bloviating was obviously for their benefit. Wedick and Brennan had expected to have to explain who they were and justify their presence— instead, Mucci seemed to want to impress *them*. The reason gradually dawned on them: They were traveling with Phil Kitzer.

If nothing else, the interlude gave the newcomers a few moments to ease into the meeting. When the conversation moved to present-tense business, Kitzer held up a hand. "Gentlemen," he said, "we are about to enter into a conspiracy. Anyone who doesn't want to partake, get up and leave."

Kitzer explained that this was his standard practice, to invoke the term *conspiracy* so no one could later claim to have misunderstood the situation. "It's a pretty shocking word," he later said. "And I find that when you point it out to people, it usually catches someone's attention."

There was a pause. Wedick and Brennan avoided looking in the direction of a guy snapping photographs across the bar. Everyone agreed to partake of the conspiracy, and Mucci handed Brennan a $100,000 bond issued in Pinal County, Arizona.

Again, it seemed easy to the point of bewildering. Brennan could imagine a jury passing around the bond, Mucci watching from a defendant's table. He made a show of examining the ornate print. Brennan nodded at Wedick and they said they needed to call their fence in New Orleans.

They walked to a bank of pay phones and Brennan dialed Deeghan, using an AT&T calling card whose sixteen-digit number they had committed to memory. Deeghan took down information about the bond and gave Brennan the name and number of Lynn Del Vecchio in New Orleans. Del Vecchio was an agent who could pose as their fence if Mucci wanted to check up on them. After hanging up, Brennan got an idea that his great-grandfather, the fingerprinting pioneer, seemed to beam directly into his brain. Brennan knew he didn't need an ink pad to create a fingerprint; he could make one using his skin's oils. He rubbed the pad of his thumb alongside his nose, then flipped the document over and pressed it into the paper. Later, if they recovered the stolen bond, Brennan could point out the print as proof that they'd met.

Brennan returned to the table and told Mucci that his contact was concerned that the document was too exotic and preferred to invest in something more recognizable. Mucci shrugged, tucked the bond back into his briefcase, and moved on to another topic.

The meeting broke up an hour later, and before leaving, Bendis handed Kitzer $4,000, the balance of their payment for the Seven Oak letter of credit. Kitzer, Brennan, and Wedick, all of whom planned to fly back to their respective cities the next morning, lingered, and Kitzer told them that they were wise not to acquire the bond without knowing more.

With any stolen security, he said, they should know whether it had "hit the sheet"—the listings of the National Crime Information Center (the FBI's clearinghouse of information about crimes). The agents knew about the NCIC, of course—they sometimes posted information from their own cases on it—but now they learned about its value from an entirely new perspective. A stolen bond that *hadn't* hit the sheet was worth more to the promoters—typically 10 percent of face value, Kitzer explained. Once it was listed, its value tumbled by half. Another factor to consider: *How* had the bond been stolen? Was it quietly snatched from a safe-deposit box and unlikely to be missed anytime soon? If armed robbers had taken the bond at gunpoint, its underworld value would be diminished because law enforcement would be looking for it.

Then there was the issue of denomination: Although it sounded counterintuitive, a stolen $50,000 bond was worth more to a con man than a $100,000 or $1 million note. The higher amounts triggered more scrutiny. A bank might wonder why a person with a $500,000 bond needed a loan. But a person with a $50,000 bond and a plausible story could walk into a bank and flash it as collateral to borrow $30,000. You would leave the bond with the bank, take the thirty, and vanish.

Kitzer's impromptu colloquium stretched deep into their second evening together. Wedick and Brennan listened raptly as Kitzer puffed a Pall Mall tucked into his plastic filter—he'd read you could get cancer from holding cigarettes on your lips. Then he described where he was going with all this.

He explained that he ran vehicles—insolvent "briefcase banks" from which he sold worthless certificates of deposit, letters of credit, and other "paper." He peddled these phony securities to desperate businessmen and guileless entrepreneurs through a network of brokers. He detailed several recent deals involving his current vehicle, Seven Oak, including a $50,000 letter of credit he'd sold to a "dumb Dago" from South Bend. Wedick felt the hair on the back of his neck levitate at the oblique mention of Nick Carbone.

Kitzer was concerned that the banking industry was becoming familiar with his name, especially because the *Wall Street Journal* had recently published its Mercantile Bank story. He had no interest in taking a pseudonym, so he wanted to recruit front men: young promoters who could front his banks, serve as officers. He'd traveled for a couple of years with a guy named Chovanec, but they'd recently had a falling-out. From what Kitzer could see, Brennan and Wedick were smart and ambitious young guys, and he'd enjoyed the past couple of days.

He had a proposition: If they accompanied him in his travels, he would teach them the game. They had to pay their own way, but if they helped with his cons, they would get a cut of the take.

Were they interested?

Brennan and Wedick looked at each other. The questions they would have to answer before replying—with the FBI and, for Brennan, with his wife—were too numerous to even guess at.

But were they *interested*? They were.

"All right," Kitzer said, smiling and raising a glass of Scotch. "Let's try it."

His idea was to start a new vehicle later that year, after Seven Oak flamed out, with Brennan and Wedick. In the meantime, they would have to learn the business and meet and get to know the players—the other promoters he worked with. From time to time, they will be calling and wanting certain things done, he explained. And it's necessary you know them. It has to be a personal relationship.

There was no way, at that point, for the agents to imagine what that meant—the far reaches of the darkest corners of the labyrinthine world into which he would lead them. They had no clue that this would cause them to furrow new fields for the FBI, or that their newfound access to this stratospherically successful confidence man could alter the trajectory of their careers. In the months to come, Brennan and Wedick would come to understand the implications of what they were doing. But for now, they were just trying to understand how this new development might play out. Kitzer told them to go home and read a book, published a few years earlier, called *The Fountain Pen Conspiracy*, by *Wall Street Journal* reporter Jonathan Kwitny.

They had just signed up for a graduate-level course in high-finance confidence games. That was their first assignment.

The agents spent the flight back trying to process what had just happened. Wedick's thinking flip-flopped between the evidence they'd gathered and the new opportunity in front of them. Brennan's mind reeled. For him, Kitzer's offer created an even more complex algorithm for how to manage this life. After they landed in South Bend, he called his wife, Becky.

She was wrestling with their younger son, Chris, then just shy of two, when the phone rang. She wasn't surprised Jack had been gone a day or two longer than expected. She was now well versed in the mercurial elements of FBI life, though nothing about her childhood in Eufaula, Alabama, had prepared her for it. Tall and slender, with light brown hair and a quick smile, she spoke energetically but with a sumptuously thick accent that tacked extra syllables onto words like *on* and *there*. She hadn't traveled north of Atlanta until adulthood—and might never have if not for Jack.

They met playing bridge with mutual friends when they were both dating other people and going to different schools—she attended Birmingham-Southern. When they ran into each other a second time, on spring break in Panama City, Florida, during Jack's senior year at Auburn, they were both single and played cards for hours while their mutual friends went carousing. "There was," Becky said, "a little something there."

After returning to classes, Jack asked Becky out. She transferred to Auburn, and the swelling romance crested with a marriage proposal during her senior year, when Jack was in Ohio. They relocated to the South, and their first few years of marriage were breezy. When the FBI offer came, she signed on willingly, wanting Jack to be happy in his work. "I thought it was kind of exciting," she said. "I just had no idea what it would be."

His first assignment, in New Orleans, was mostly effortless.

They were not far from where Becky had grown up, and they'd rented a comfortable apartment. She had a good laugh telling folks back home about Jack's first case, which involved a shipment of stolen bowling balls. They ate their way around the city, checking off page after page in their copy of *The New Orleans Underground Gourmet*. Becky's first taste of life as an FBI spouse came when an armed man took hostages in a hotel. She watched as the TV showed FBI agents and the abductors exchanging gunfire from rooftops. She didn't know if Jack was shooting, but he didn't call, and she lay in bed wondering, for the first of many times, exactly what she'd gotten herself into.

Then Jack came home one night in 1972 and announced that he'd been transferred to Indianapolis. She thought that city was near Idaho: He showed her on a map that it was more than 650 miles north of Eufaula, but a straight shot up Interstate 65. *That'll be okay*, she thought—not so far from home. Then, a few days later, the bureau revised his orders to Gary.

During their first trip there, in January 1973, the clerk at a downtown Holiday Inn told them, "You don't want to stay here." Too many murders and muggings. The Brennans ended up at the suburban Crown Point Hotel, a converted farmhouse. They rented a room that had two twin beds and a sheet mounted to a ceiling track, hospital-style—the only room with its own bathroom. Which was a good thing, because Becky was pregnant.

They eventually bought a house in Crown Point, and their first son, John, was born in July. Life had infinitely more complexities now. That Christmas, they loaded the baby, their luggage, and Bernie, their 190-pound Saint Bernard, onto an overnight train to Alabama. When they reached Montgomery, Becky's mother met them and said, "I hate to tell you this, Jack, but your office called." She drove him straight to the airport for a flight back to Indiana.

A second baby, Chris, arrived in 1975. They slogged through the winters, and Becky tried hard to fit in. "I worked on my accent a lot when we got there, trying to sound not so southern," she said. But the neighborhood kids rang their doorbell just to hear her talk.

Life in Indiana never quite took. Becky loved her boys, but she'd grown up as a tomboy and wasn't fulfilled by spending her days alone with a toddler and an infant, and she felt far removed from home. "The people were really nice, and we had good friends, but it just wasn't the same somehow," she said.

At the same time, Jack's immersion in increasingly complex cases pulled him away for long days. Becky grew isolated and alone. "It was," she recalled, "very overwhelming."

By the summer of 1976, they had arrived at a crossroads. One of Jack's childhood friends, an executive at Waffle House, had opened a new franchise in the Florida Panhandle and invited him to become a partner. It sounded ideal; the Brennans owned a cabin near Panama City. They decided to go for it, and Becky was euphoric through the going-away parties and the U-Haul odyssey home.

But the plan imploded almost instantly. Jack, required to learn the business from the ground level, hated flipping hash browns and dealing with truant waitresses. He was at home in the South, but his soul belonged to the FBI. After a week, he revealed to Becky that he'd only taken a leave of absence. And he was going back. Blindsided and furious, Becky replied that she was staying. "At that point," she said, "we weren't sure we loved each other anymore."

They began to assemble separate lives. Jack stayed with single bureau friends—mostly Wedick, who had a spare bedroom. Becky spent long intervals with her older sister, Diane, a deeply religious homesteader. Diane, whom Becky called "Sista," quoted the Bible and told of witnessing miracles, and Becky wondered, *Why didn't I ever hear about this growing up in church?*

Sista eventually convinced Becky to give her life to the Lord and return to Indiana to seek Jack's forgiveness, because Becky's place was with her husband. Becky saw this with startling clarity. In October, she loaded a truck with her family and their belongings and drove to Indiana, even though she didn't have a clue about whether Jack still wanted to see her.

Becky knew that Jack loved the boys and was averse to repeating his family history. After spending a year on a kidnapping case in Minnesota, his grandfather had returned home to an ultimatum: his wife or the FBI. He'd chosen the bureau. Jack's father traveled frequently and under significant duress. In Mississippi, Edward Brennan helped exhume the bodies of three murdered civil rights volunteers, then photographed the autopsies. The time away and the psychic toll shredded his marriage, which ended in a toxic divorce when Jack was in the eleventh grade—old enough to get into his car and drive away. "I kind of abandoned my brother to my mother," he said. "He was her only audience to explain how terrible my dad was."

His FBI work helped him better understand his forebears—how the pressures of the job had split their lives apart like cordwood. This was the Brennan legacy. The bureau contagion leaped from one generation to the next. This early-life chaos shaped Jack's personality in a couple of ways. One was that, having been part of the collateral damage, Jack wanted a different outcome for his kids.

He had signed up for the Kitzer operation figuring it would involve one meeting, maybe two. Now that the master con man planned to take him and Wedick out on the road, Brennan had no idea how long it was going to last.

No Mickey Mouse

Wedick was wearing riot gear when he spotted Brennan coming his way. Wedick was on a break from SWAT training at the FBI Academy in Quantico, Virginia, and the sight of his partner yanked him out of a reverie related to a sharpshooting drill. Brennan, who had traveled to the academy for a different set of training exercises, had the expectant, hungry look of someone with something urgent to say. Two weeks had passed since they'd parted ways with Kitzer. They'd spent much of that time puzzling through the next steps in their blossoming fraud investigation, and the training had provided a short but welcome respite.

"We need to go back to Cleveland," Brennan said. "Kitzer wants us to meet."

Wedick stared at him for a few beats before responding: *"What?"*

Brennan explained that Kitzer was working a new scam and wanted them there to watch over his shoulder. Wedick instantly realized what had happened: After they'd returned from Cleveland, he'd given Brennan the number for Executive Enterprise's answering service. He now realized that this had been a lapse of judgment—Brennan tended to barrel ahead heedlessly. Of *course* Brennan had retrieved the messages.

Still, Wedick was furious. It had taken Orville Watts a year to get him enrolled in the SWAT class, and he wanted to finish it. Brennan was less of a box checker—one of the many differences that were becoming more obvious the more time the agents spent together. Wedick was a product of 1950s and '60s Catholic schools and stern parents; his work space was fastidious, and he preferred to meticulously plot things out. He believed in hierarchies.

Brennan found no advantage in going slow. Where Wedick saw an organized grid that should be systematically hopscotched, Brennan saw an open field that was best sprinted across before anyone could stop them. If there had been an established protocol for this kind of case, he and Wedick never would have been assigned to it—the work would have gone to someone who'd attended undercover school. FBI headquarters didn't know what they were doing yet, which Brennan saw as a huge advantage. He had noticed that when he was working on something new, he had about six months before the bureaucracy figured out how to control him. This was one advantage to being in a backwater location like Gary: less oversight.

For the moment, at least, the bureau leadership was in limbo and distracted. After taking office six weeks earlier, President Jimmy Carter had indicated that he wanted to replace Clarence Kelley as director, but he hadn't yet done so. No one was certain how new leadership might reshape the FBI, which was another reason to go now.

In Kitzer's invitation, Brennan saw nothing more than a superb opportunity to take a front-row seat during a fraudulent deal. "I had learned that it's better to do something than to do nothing," he said. "Get forgiveness, not permission."

These dynamics were complicated by the way the Kitzer case had come together. Wedick was the case agent, but Brennan also felt some propriety over it, having learned of it from his informant.

Wedick pointed out that Brennan had promised not to interfere. He didn't know why Brennan was in such a hurry. They stared at each other. "First of all, it's my name on the paper," Wedick said. "*You* sought *me* out. Now, you may not like this, but I'm in charge on this freaking case. Let's figure our moves out."

It was too late. Brennan said he had already directed Norman

Howard to tell Kitzer they would meet him the next day. Kitzer would be expecting them.

The same day, a few hundred miles away in Cleveland, Kitzer sat across from Armand Mucci and Bob Bendis at a table in the Sheraton Beachwood's bar in suburban Cleveland. He was pursuing a promising new deal. A couple of months earlier, he explained, a fellow promoter named Jack Elliott, whom Kitzer called Captain Jack, had introduced him to Jimmy Kealoha, the former lieutenant governor of Hawaii.

Once labeled "the wonder boy of Hawaiian politics," Kealoha was elected to Hawaii's House of Representatives at the age of twenty-six. He held various offices for much of the next thirty years, often winning races by overwhelming margins. His party chose him to run for lieutenant governor in 1959 in the state's first gubernatorial election—Hawaii became the fiftieth state that year—and his ticket rolled to victory. He eventually morphed into an entrepreneur, and during the seventies he'd launched his capstone project: a thirty-five-story, 206-unit condominium complex called KeAloha at Waikiki. He'd acquired one of the few large-scale development sites left on Waikiki Beach, across from a Hyatt on the island's sugar-sand shores.

But Kealoha was unlucky. He sent in the bulldozers just as the nation entered a profound funk. After a thirty-year gallop toward prosperity, America had been staggered by Watergate, Vietnam, and energy shortages. Although newly elected President Carter promised a new era, the national mood was sour. Unemployment hovered around 13 percent. Personal bankruptcy was soaring. Kealoha had approached many banks about financing the $10 million construction, but they wanted him to presell the condos before they committed. And no one was buying. With the market sagging, Kealoha bore the extra burden of selling units that didn't yet exist.

Adding to his bind, the city of Honolulu had specified a window of time in which Kealoha needed to start the work. A building permit there was a valuable possession: The city had recently declared a moratorium on high-rises, and this one was grandfathered in—but if he hadn't started construction by the deadline, Kealoha would have to reduce his building's size by 70 percent. Meanwhile, with the project stalled, Fireside Thrift, which had loaned him money to clear the land, was threatening to foreclose. Kealoha had sold only 85 of the condos. Desperate, he and his attorney, Ronald Yee, began hunting for an investor willing to purchase the 121 unsold units for $6 million.

Yee was connected to Jack Elliott, who, in turn, introduced Kealoha to Phil Kitzer. They met at the LAX Marriott in late 1976. Kitzer offered to put up a thousand-dollar letter of credit from Seven Oak as a down payment on each unsold condo—for a fee of $60,000. Kealoha agreed, and flew Kitzer to Honolulu for a closing.

Kitzer told Elliott that he could easily wring more out of Kealoha, who was so anxious to see the project through that he had teared up describing it. Elliott laughed and asked Kitzer, "What are you gonna do, take his pants [and] his kids?"

A few months later, in February 1977, Elliott called to tell Kitzer that Kealoha was still looking for what's known as a takeout commitment. Imagine you're going to build an office tower. You need two things: a short-term loan, to buy the bricks and glass, and permanent financing. That second, long-term loan comes from a mortgage company that commits to repay, or "take out," the short-term lender when the construction is finished. Elliott suggested that Kitzer provide the takeout—for another fee, of course.

Kitzer was now reluctant. He'd already used Seven Oak to buy the unsold condos and didn't think it would be wise to issue more worthless paper from the bank to the same customer. Part of his talent was in knowing how far to push his scams. But he promised that if he heard of anything that might fit, he would call. Then Mucci and Bendis told him about an acquaintance named Andrew D'Amato, who was operating a scam involving a Liechtenstein-based trust. Mucci said the trust would "stand up," meaning that its phony securities could withstand scrutiny from a legitimate bank.

Kitzer thought this sounded promising—but time was tight. Kealoha had already delayed one Fireside Thrift foreclosure, but he wouldn't be able to hold out much longer.

Mucci stood and announced that he would get D'Amato to Cleveland as soon as possible.

After they returned to Indianapolis, the complexities of what Kitzer had proposed hit Wedick and Brennan flush. Problem number one: They were taking on a deeply embedded culture that resisted the type of work they would have to do.

For most of its history, the FBI had avoided undercover investigations. Much of this was due to J. Edgar Hoover, who as a young and fast-rising administrator in the late 1910s watched Congress and the judiciary rebuke the bureau for such practices. "We do not question the right of the Department of Justice to use its agents in the Bureau of Investigation to ascertain when the law is being violated," a panel of prominent jurists wrote in 1920. "But the American people have never tolerated the use of undercover provocative agents or 'agents provocateurs' such as have been familiar in old Russia or Spain."

By the time Hoover was appointed director, in 1924, he'd embraced a mandate to shield the FBI from political pressure. Despite being fervently anti-Communist, in 1932 he discouraged the attorney general from expanding the bureau's authority to investigate leftist activities, expressing concern that his charges would need to do undercover work "to secure a foothold in Communistic inner circles." He resisted efforts to merge the FBI with the Bureau of Prohibition, in order to avoid even a whiff of scandal, and foisted the responsibility for pursuing racketeers onto the states. Hoover nixed undercover work involving the Mafia out of fear that his employees would be bought off.

By zeroing in on bank robberies, interstate theft and kidnapping, extortion, and fugitives, Hoover adopted an agenda any elected official could love. The idea was to investigate crimes only *after* they'd been committed. Hoover avoided "turning agents into investigators, working undercover in situations that required one to emulate, if not adopt, the language, style, and values of the criminal world," James Q. Wilson wrote in *The Investigators,* an in-depth examination of the FBI's practices. "Not only would this expose agents to temptations involving money and valuable narcotics, it would also require them to engage in enforcement policies that, though legal, struck many citizens as unsavory."

Undercover work was also impractical. As Wilson noted, "the dress code of the agents would have made it ludicrous for most of them to even attempt to go undercover—there are not many hijackers or auto thieves who could easily be impersonated by short-haired, clean-shaven agents."

To avoid congressional oversight and keep funds flowing smoothly, the FBI measured its achievements through misleading statistics. Job performances were judged largely by caseloads, even if it meant taking on "shit cases with which to cover your ass by making stats," as one agent told Wilson. The FBI took credit for the value of a stolen car even when the local police found and returned the vehicle and an agent did nothing more than inquire as to whether the perpetrator had moved it across state lines.

In each of the FBI's fifty-nine field offices, the special agent in charge had to answer for each agent's stats. In this environment, an agent who asked to go undercover long-term—which meant shirking a full caseload to focus exclusively on one investigation—was not warmly received. The emphasis on numbers also discouraged complex white-collar and organized-crime investigations.

Hoover's obsessive efforts to protect the FBI's gilded image were unraveling by the time he died, in 1972. In the five years that followed, Americans would learn that once-mythical G-men had used illegal bugs, wiretaps, and breaking and entering—practices referred to as "black bag jobs"—on citizens deemed to be political dissidents or while investigating the likes of the Weather Underground. Hoover's eventual successor, Clarence Kelley, under intense scrutiny from Congress for the FBI's role in Watergate and other pernicious episodes, began a top-to-bottom overhaul, setting organized crime, foreign counterintelligence, and white-collar crime as the new priorities. And in 1975, Kelley adopted a "quality over quantity" policy, in which each SAC decided which cases to pursue. Meanwhile, the FBI teamed up with local police departments in undercover investigations funded by Law Enforcement Assistance Administration grants, providing useful but limited experience. But the bureau retained plenty of rusty hinges. A 1977 manual opined that undercover operations "are far less valuable in the white-collar crime area than in other areas of criminal investigation" and predicted that they would be useful only for "an occasional and unusual opportunity."

Still, 1977 was the first year the Department of Justice expressly requested funds for such activities. The $1 million that Congress appropriated for that year funded fifty-three operations—this in an organization with 516 resident offices. By opening their Kitzer investigation, Wedick and Brennan were among the first to tap into that pool of money.

And they were the first to propose open-ended travel with the subject of a white-collar crime investigation.

The ground-level realities of their operation were even more daunting. They had no clue how long Kitzer's trips lasted, whom they'd be meeting, and what levels of danger might await. They would have to persuade the bureau to underwrite their travel. And then what if Kitzer flew outside the country and they needed diplomatic clearance? What would they do when they were witnessing a crime? Where would they draw the line with drinking? What if someone lit up a joint or snorted cocaine? There were no guidelines in place.

On top of all that, Kitzer's techniques were entirely new to the bureau. Wedick and Brennan sketched out his criminal enterprise on a conference call with SAC Frank Lowie and several other officials. When they were finished, Lowie said, "Well, so what?"

This was a time-tested tactic used by bureau supervisors. Old managers tended to ask a thousand questions about something new and unfamiliar, figuring the upstarts would just go away or fail to get all the boxes checked and return to counting stolen cars. Getting anything different done required mulish persistence. The idea—instilled by Hoover's image-conscious mind-set—was to avoid doing anything that might bring embarrassment or criticism.

Typical of the new generation, Brennan and Wedick thought it was time to move on from Hoover. They tried Lowie again, emphasizing that they suspected, based on their conversations with Howard and from reading *The Fountain Pen Conspiracy,* that Kitzer was pruning millions of dollars off banks' and entrepreneurs' bottom lines. He didn't use a gun or a ski mask, but Kitzer was ripping off far more money than the guys who did.

People still thought of con men as lonesome grifters who roamed small towns, living out of cardboard suitcases. *The Fountain Pen Conspiracy* limned the evolution of a whole new class of criminals during an era of unprecedented American prosperity, when millions of people who had scraped through the Depression suddenly had sizable nest eggs. Businesses were borrowing money and growing fast. Banks were booming. The government wasn't yet outfitted to regulate this deluge of financial activity.

The new confidence men wore three-piece suits, moved between high-end hotels, and targeted banks, high-rolling investors, and CEOs rather than barstool pigeons and old ladies on Social Security. They recognized that the powerful and rich weren't necessarily smarter but were often greedier—and thus more likely to give away money now on a promise to double it later. "When the cash value of promises goes up," *Fountain Pen* author Jonathan Kwitny wrote, "when tomorrows are being sold early, swindlers are among the first to profit."

Kwitny documented a loosely connected ring of about fifty "superswindlers" who invented rip-offs in entirely different strata: speculation scams involving mineral rights, stock schemes, bogus mutual funds, insurance fraud, offshore banks. They set up on islands off England's coast and in the Caribbean—places with no laws applying to foreign businesses and run by public officials who could be readily bribed. The superswindlers collectively stole hundreds of millions of dollars, Kwitny wrote. And Kitzer had told Brennan and Wedick that the book was outdated—he'd adopted more sophisticated methods, working with his own loosely organized global network of co-conspirators.

Lowie was unmoved. He didn't mind them meeting Kitzer in Minneapolis. But long-term? Maybe the Securities and Exchange Commission should take the case.

Wedick boiled. The bureau's other early undercover efforts were going nowhere at that point; he and Brennan had a shot at a mastermind fraudster.

With his anger rising, Wedick suggested that Lowie tell First National City Bank that he didn't care what Kitzer was doing. Kitzer had recently sold phony paper by using a virtually identical name—tacking on the words "of Grenada" in fine print.

"What do you think their opinion is gonna be about that?" Wedick said. "And tell them that as an SAC, you don't really give a shit."

Yes, Lowie replied, his voice rising. Of course that was a problem. It just wasn't *his* problem.

Wedick slammed the table. "Who the fuck am I talking to, you idiot?" he blurted. The words hung through a moment of stunned silence.

Lowie growled, "It's SAC Frank Lowie, idiot!"

Wedick mumbled an apology. *Holy shit, did I fuck up today,* he thought.

The incident quickly blew over—Lowie considered it one of Wedick's New York moments. And Jim Deeghan remained a solid ally. Dark-haired and in his mid-thirties, he believed in the case enough to push the bureau's comfort zone. The next time Brennan and Wedick were in Indianapolis, he pinned index cards to a conference room wall for each potential prosecution: Mucci's stolen bonds. The Shaker House scam. Nick Carbone. For each open case, the FBI allotted $1,500 in expenses. If they kept opening cases, Brennan and Wedick would have money to travel with.

Laid out in this way, the Kitzer investigation looked convincing. Nobody wanted to be accused of ignoring repeated criminal activity. Brennan and Wedick also had Richard Hanning in the U.S. attorney's office on board, which was key. After hearing that federal prosecutors believed that they had a good case, Lowie agreed to give them a chance.

They had flown off to their training in Quantico feeling excited. Wedick and Brennan even came up with a code name for the investigation. They called it Operation Fountain Pen.

Andrew D'Amato was forty-five, with a Mediterranean complexion and a head of curly black hair that spilled across his forehead. In contrast to Kitzer, who preferred business suits, D'Amato dressed casually, in looser-fitting, open clothes with wide lapels, as if he'd just arrived from Monaco. When he joined the others in Cleveland, he presented a card identifying him as chairman of the board of Hotel Fontainebleau International, Ltd.; he said he was in the process of acquiring the massive Miami Beach resort. He was also the U.S. representative of a large London-based trust run by the Martini family (of Martini & Rossi) that spread its largesse around underprivileged countries, often through long-term loans.

D'Amato claimed that the European trust, headquartered in Liechtenstein, was a masterstroke. He'd cooked up the idea with Alexander Martini, a con man with a criminal record going back two decades who was actually unrelated to the famous wine family. What's this thing called? Kitzer asked.

The Euro-Afro-Asiatic Trust, D'Amato said.

Kitzer burst out laughing. You don't want to do any deals with that, he said—the name is so bad. D'Amato said they called it EAAT or the Eurotrust.

"Wait," D'Amato said. "Let me show you something."

He opened his briefcase and took out copies of certificates of deposit. One Crocker Bank CD had a face value of $4.5 million. From First National City Bank, London, were CDs for $5 million and $1 million. All were made out to the Eurotrust.

Kitzer examined the CDs. "You're renting the money," he said.

This was an old game that required a friendly banker. You go to, say, Wells Fargo and ask your insider for a $20 million CD. You pay the banker an under-the-table fee, and he creates a CD. But it's good for only five days.

You then go to the Bank of Hawaii to do Kealoha's takeout commitment, and the banker there wants to check out the CD. He calls Wells Fargo, reaches a teller, and says, "We have a certificate here," and gives the number.

"And she'll say, 'Okay, just a minute,'" Kitzer later explained. "And she hits her machine and it comes right up on her screen and she says, 'Yeah, that was purchased so-and-so day. We have it here, no problem.'

"It's confirmed. Now, if the Bank of Hawaii wants to go further and they say: 'Well, now, listen, tell us more about this. We want to know: How did this come about?' There's no way that girl knows. But on that certificate it's coded that this certain bank officer— the one that you paid off—is the one that handled the transaction. Normal course of business she says, 'I got to refer you to Mr. So-and-so.' She transfers that call into his desk. Bank of Hawaii says: 'Did you issue this certificate?' Well, this guy is in on the deal. He knows he's going to get a call from Bank of Hawaii." Your inside man confirms everything. "He never tells them," Kitzer said, "that the thing is going to cash out in two, three days."

To cover himself, the banker sets up the transaction as a loan. The money comes into a loan account, and from there it goes to a CD account, then to a collateral account. The money is like the pea in the classic shell game. D'Amato now appears to have opened a million-dollar account as collateral for his loan. The money never leaves the bank, and the banker will soon absorb it back into the coffers, but its movement through a CD account allows him to generate the carbon copy inside D'Amato's briefcase. "Window dressing," Kitzer said. "People see those types of certificates issued, they want to believe that it's really true."

A plan coalesced. D'Amato would go to a bank offering to provide a takeout commitment on Kealoha's project—that is, the Eurotrust would commit to providing the $10 million long-term. The CDs were the collateral. "What does the bank have to check?" D'Amato asked. "We've got real money."

"In real banks," Kitzer said.

"In real banks," D'Amato echoed.

"No Mickey Mouse."

Kitzer suggested they charge Kealoha $80,000 for a Eurotrust takeout—a phony letter guaranteeing that the trust would cover the long-term cost of the project. If Kealoha managed to use it to get the $10 million short-term loan, Kitzer would write in loopholes—trick language—that would prevent the Bank of Hawaii from ever collecting from the Eurotrust. He would insert a line near the end of a long, wordy contract mandating that all work had to be done "to our satisfaction." It sounded innocuous enough, but then D'Amato would endlessly ask for more paperwork, work orders, appraisals—and find fault with it. Not "satisfactory."

Later, Kitzer said, "you use that with the victim, saying, 'You didn't do what you said you were going to do, and that's the reason the deal didn't work.' And that is one of the best ways to cool a person down after they lost the money."

Not only would the Bank of Hawaii be defrauded out of $10 million, but its officers probably wouldn't say a word about it. "If they made a mistake and issued the funds," Kitzer said, "and later the bank attempted to collect, when the bank's lawyers got done studying that takeout, they would tell the bank: 'Keep your mouth shut.

Straighten it out, eat it. You were a fool, and don't go to court and admit that.'"

Kitzer had another idea. They could create a shell corporation to acquire the project from Kealoha—then *they* could take the $10 million from the Bank of Hawaii. The group loved this. Bendis suggested a name for the new shell corporation: Island Investments. For the officers, Kitzer volunteered two new associates, Jack Brennan and Jim Wedick, who were en route to Cleveland.

As for how to "cut up" the money: Kitzer and D'Amato would split the fee and pay a share to anyone they brought in to help. The promoters routinely picked up people to play certain roles, like characters being written into a play.

Kitzer left to make a call. When he returned, he announced that everyone should book flights to Miami. Kealoha could meet them there the day after next.

8

The Junior G-Men

MARCH 3, 1977

The early-morning chill was beginning to lift on what would become an unseasonably warm day when Brennan and Wedick caught their flight out of the nation's capital. Wedick quietly brooded. He was still furious about the way Jack had sprung this trip on him.

Brennan figured that once they got started, Wedick would forgive him. Jim's heart is in this, Brennan thought. The agents boarded a train to downtown Cleveland and headed for the bureau office. Deeghan had helped by calling ahead to his buddy in Cleveland to put in a last-minute request for surveillance help.

Still, Wedick hated the thrown-together nature of this trip. He, too, was happy to flout the FBI's calcified ways—he found the organization maddening at times. He'd once received a letter of censure for failing to provide a six-month report on a fugitive case. Two months later, he collared the fugitive in a dramatic arrest involving a closed freeway ramp and received a letter of commendation. Same case. "In one letter I'm the stupidest asshole of all time, and in the next one I'm the greatest agent on the face of the earth," he said. He framed both in his bathroom. But if he and Brennan were going to barrel ahead and ignore the usual protocols, he understood, they would need to do it thoughtfully. They needed to treat these rare opportunities with great care.

Wedick was pretty sure that their FBI colleagues in Cleveland wouldn't be impressed with Brennan's aw-shucks southern mannerisms—not with the two of them storming in at the last minute, asking for the world. They needed recording equipment and a surveillance team of five, including two women, so they could blend in at a bar. Those agents would have to push aside their own cases and cancel their Thursday-night plans. All for some white-collar case from Indiana no one even understood.

I wouldn't like us, Wedick thought.

Sure enough, they arrived in late morning to an icy reception. Brennan and Wedick recognized agent Walter Setmeyer from their trip to the Cleveland airport two weeks earlier, but no one else. Someone gave Wedick a Nagra and pointed toward an empty stenographers' room where he could take his clothes off so he could put on the recording rig.

"This does not feel good to me, Jack," Wedick said, closing the door behind himself. "How could you think that this was a good idea?"

"I had an afternoon to kill," Brennan said, shrugging, not wanting to engage.

"Then you put your name on this thing. Let them know you're the son of a bitch."

Wedick had just dropped his pants when a female steno walked in; he stammered an apology. They moved out into a back hallway, behind a filing cabinet. Wedick, now flustered, told Brennan that since this was his idea, *he* should wear the Nagra and held the recorder out to him.

Brennan threw him a look that said *Fine, whatever,* and stashed the recorder inside the breast pocket of his sport coat. He was brawnier than Wedick and figured the device would be visible on his back. He also dropped a wireless transmitter into his shirt pocket, similar to the one Wedick had worn in the airport. Setmeyer would sit in his car and record the transmission—both as a backup for the recorder and for security. If someone pulled a gun, he could alert the others.

When Brennan and Wedick met the Cleveland team for a briefing, the lack of enthusiasm for Operation Fountain Pen was palpable. There were no conference rooms available, so they all wedged into a hallway cul-de-sac, the undercover agents and a semicircle of unfamiliar faces wearing blank or annoyed expressions. After walking through the plan, Wedick and Brennan asked where they could store their guns. In Washington they'd just been issued Walther PPKs—the handgun James Bond used in the 007 movies—and they realized by the reaction that their colleagues hadn't seen the new weapons yet. This added to the impression that they were divas. Now they were flashing their special new toys.

Wedick, rattled, couldn't get out of there fast enough. None of this was going to help him feel more comfortable with Kitzer. It was like trying to stretch a twin-sized sheet over a king-sized bed. There were so many places where they might be exposed.

The agents arrived at the Sheraton Beachwood by midafternoon and tried to check in. But here was their first speed bump: In their rush, they hadn't made reservations, and the hotel was full. Unsure what else to do, they called Kitzer's room and headed up.

Kitzer, resplendent in a fitted suit and tie, greeted them warmly, then excused himself to answer the phone. While he was talking, there was a knock on the door, and Wedick answered it. Armand Mucci stood outside next to a smiling, curly-haired man, and Wedick stepped into the hall to meet Andrew D'Amato while they waited for Kitzer to finish his call. Eventually Kitzer hung up and asked Wedick to invite everyone in.

D'Amato peppered Brennan and Wedick with questions: where they were from, what deals they'd done. Brennan said that he was in commodities and had a source who gave him tips to come out ahead—a fictional college buddy who possessed inside information on certain commodities. This was the story he and Wedick had come up with to explain where their money came from and provided the financial engine for Executive Enterprises. The agents felt that it was important for their credibility to establish that they had their own angle they were playing. And this story was ideal in that in addition to linking Wedick and Brennan to illegal activity—which helped them fit in—it was also hard for any of the promoters to confirm, in the event they wanted to find out more about the two newcomers.

But they were still novices at this, and the stress of meeting someone new—enduring the scrutiny and the initial waves of natural curiosity—was as intense as when they'd met Kitzer. Each introduction was a fresh test. Wedick felt they had to be rock solid as young promoters, or one of these guys would sniff them out.

He mentally ticked through the safeguards they had in place, much like the way his mother rubbed her rosary beads. They had Howard and now Kitzer vouching for them, and the Executive Enterprises business cards. The promoters had no reason to expect the FBI to send agents to live among them. There was no precedent for that. The longer they hung in, the easier it would get. Or so Wedick hoped.

Kitzer explained the Kealoha plan, and D'Amato seemed enthused about Brennan and Wedick. They always needed more operators, he said, and these guys were so young and fresh-faced, they would make solid front men. Kitzer recalled that, in fact, the first time they'd met, he'd said they looked like FBI agents because they were so clean-cut.

Everyone chortled, and D'Amato bellowed, "They're the Junior G-Men!"

The room exploded in laughter, and Wedick and Brennan gamely joined in, even as they both pondered how surreal this was. They were surely the first undercover operatives ever to be teased by their targets for their uncanny resemblance to undercover operatives.

Fortunately, as with the other promoters, D'Amato didn't cede the spotlight for long. He handed them a Fontainebleau Hotel business card and explained about acquiring it. Warming up, D'Amato launched into a round of strenuous name-dropping. He was friends with Spiro Agnew, who'd been Nixon's vice president, and Chuck Colson, the Watergate lawyer. Did they know Sophia Loren and her husband, Carlo Ponti? They were D'Amato's friends, too. And he knew powerful people in Italy. In fact, his daughter was one of *very* few people on a list to get married in the Vatican.

The men peeled off their jackets and settled in to talk business around the small hotel room table. Brennan hesitated. The Nagra was in his coat. He decided it would be worse to be conspicuous than to lose the recording—plus, the transmitter still sat inside his shirt pocket, looking like a pack of cigarettes—so he peeled his jacket off and hung it up with the others. Bob Bendis arrived, and Kitzer made his announcement about entering into a conspiracy and unpacked the Hawaii deal. The promoters loved the idea of taking the $10 million loan, maybe even building part of the complex and selling all the units before bailing out with the rest of the cash.

When happy hour arrived, Kitzer popped up and herded the others toward the lounge. Brennan walked past the jackets in the closet, stanching a geyser of anxiety over whether someone would rifle through his pockets. He hadn't even had the chance to turn the machine off.

Wedick, meanwhile, mentioned that they'd been unable to get a room, and D'Amato said that as chairman of the Fontainebleau, he would speak to the management. He marched off as everyone took seats in the lounge and ordered drinks: Scotch for Kitzer, Jack Daniel's on the rocks for Brennan and Wedick. Mucci sat next to them and repeated the Junior G-Men joke, and everyone smiled and nodded. Apparently the nickname was going to stick.

Around then D'Amato reappeared and, with a triumphant flourish, presented Wedick with a room key. He had somehow induced the sold-out hotel to find an available room. Then Bendis piped up: If the Junior G-Men were playing a role, they would have to be able to pass a credit check.

Brennan replied that this wouldn't be necessary; their credit was fine, he said, smiling, laying on the southern accent. The word came out *fahn*. But Bendis insisted. As an attorney, he could easily run a check—because what was the point of putting them out front only to learn later that they'd declared bankruptcy five times? Brennan nodded. This was ripe with irony, that a group of con artists were concerned about their credit scores, but he and Wedick were unamused. If Bendis researched their Social Security numbers, he would unearth personal information: home addresses, and maybe their employers.

Wedick and Brennan exchanged looks. They needed to call Deeghan. But then the promoters dropped that topic and launched into a discussion of how they would defend themselves if questioned about the Hawaii scam. This was part of orchestrating any deal, Kitzer explained.

The promoters turned to Brennan. As a front man, he would tell the FBI that he'd had no idea what was going on. He was a legitimate businessman and hadn't intended to defraud anyone, and his lawyer, Bendis, had told him the deal was legitimate. To prosecute him, they pointed out, the government would have to prove that Brennan "willfully and knowingly" conspired to defraud.

D'Amato chimed in that all Brennan had to say was "I don't know nothing."

Worst case, if they were prosecuted, Kitzer continued, federal white-collar prisons were cushy. An acquaintance had recently been sentenced to three years at the facility in Danbury, Connecticut. "He calls me [from prison]: 'You can't believe, they got a gymnasium, a swimming pool . . .'"

"I'm from Connecticut," D'Amato said. "We call it the Danbury Hilton."

"If I go, that's where I want to go," said Brennan.

They could appeal any sentence and go free on bail while the lawyers argued. All of this was merely an "occupational hazard," D'Amato said.

Outside in the parking lot, agent Walter Setmeyer listened in, a Sony cassette recorder on his front seat capturing the feed from the transmitter in Brennan's pocket.

The promoters then began a mock trial, with Kitzer playing

the judge and D'Amato the collared con man. "The judge gets up, whoever he is," D'Amato said. The atmosphere in the room is tense, D'Amato explained, because everyone looks at the promoter and decides he's "gotta be smarter than we [are] 'cause he just ripped off $3 billion."

The swindler is facing just one to three years in prison, and the judge, D'Amato said, starts asking himself, "Am I crazy? I should talk to the lawyer to see how much is in this for me for him not to do" *any* time behind bars.

Kitzer interrupted: "I get up and say, 'Good morning, Mr. D'Amato, I don't wanna waste your time. Marshal, take him into custody, we have given [him] fifteen [years]."

Everyone laughed at Judge Kitzer's harsh sentence. Breaking out of character, D'Amato told the Junior G-Men, "You have to know when to keep yourself outta trouble when you're walking the tightrope bordering the illegal."

He added, "There's three principles in life. You do what you do, do what you know, but equally as important, be goddamn sure you know who you're doing it with."

Kitzer chimed in: "And if you don't know, be very careful what you do."

Brennan's brain ached as he sat in the Sheraton lounge. Howard had described the depth and complexity of the promoters' schemes, but none of these accounts had prepared the agents for the experience of being embedded inside one. Kitzer wasn't just carefully plotting out his cons. He was anticipating what the FBI might do and taking evasive steps in advance—all while blending seamlessly into crowds of businessmen in their three-piece suits and fat neckties.

Kitzer saw his targets through different eyes. Take Jimmy Kealoha. To most people, he was an ambitious but unlucky businessman—someone who'd overreached on a project. But they would sympathize at some level: He was chasing a dream. Kitzer, by contrast, saw a man who still had money he could afford to lose: *He's still got $80,000. What do I need to say to convince him to give it to me?*

More drinks arrived, providing enough lubrication that the conversation hopped the tracks into past exploits—mostly Kitzer and D'Amato arguing about who'd taken more money in cons. The stories became increasingly outlandish. D'Amato's Eurotrust increased in value over the course of the evening from $30 million to $50 billion. Dinner plates appeared. Kitzer had ordered hundred-dollar bottles of wine, steaks. Wedick cringed; Setmeyer was probably eating fast-food burgers in his car, if anything at all.

Someone new appeared: a promoter from Boston named John Calandrella. Kitzer had told the others to be guarded when Calandrella arrived; he didn't know whether he could trust the guy yet. Calandrella looked to be in his early forties, with a round face and dark hair that was far shorter than the shaggy haircuts popular in the day. He chatted briefly and scheduled a meeting with Kitzer for the morning before disappearing.

After Mucci and Bendis headed home, Kitzer and D'Amato continued their friendly rivalry, switching to the topic of women. D'Amato bragged that he knew Shirley Eaton, the blonde who wore gold body paint in the James Bond film *Goldfinger*. Several key scenes in that movie, in fact, had been shot at the Fontainebleau—where, D'Amato hastened to mention again, he was chairman of the board. They talked about prostitutes, then women in the hotel bar, debating who would try to pick up whom. Scanning the room, the promoters discussed two women sitting together at the bar (whom Brennan and Wedick knew to be FBI agents conducting surveillance). Success with the opposite sex—real or imagined—seemed central to the promoters' world, so Wedick and Brennan began to play along.

"She's nice," Brennan said. He elbowed Wedick. "She wants to talk to you, Jim."

But Brennan himself stood and walked over to them—using

the moment to check in with the agents instead of flirting. The promoters loved it, and praised the gameness of the Junior G-Men, and ordered another round. Wedick and Brennan saw that the pace of the drinking was a problem. Kitzer and D'Amato seemed to possess a Herculean tolerance for liquor, while Wedick—at six-two but barely a hundred and sixty pounds—had gotten buzzed fast. He headed to the men's room, leaving his drink on the bar, and on the way back ordered a club soda. Brennan deposited his drink across the room and pretended he'd misplaced it—but Kitzer, hearing this, ordered him another.

Wedick and Brennan also faced a more immediate problem. Kitzer was now also buying drinks for the female agents and trying to draw them into conversation. Brennan and Wedick attempted to deflect his attention, but it was as if a periscope had risen from his head and zeroed in on the women, and he seemed oblivious to the possibility that someone might reject his overtures. They smiled and waved but declined to come over. Two male Cleveland agents hovered nearby, seeming uncertain, and Kitzer noticed them looking over. Wedick shifted uncomfortably as Kitzer asked D'Amato whether he thought the guys across the room were watching them. Every operation possesses a surface tension for the undercover agents involved. Puncture it, and disaster can follow: Assumed identities begin to feel flimsy; scripts become hard to follow.

Seeing the way things were trending, Wedick felt a jolt of unease. He wrestled with a sense that he should do something, only he had no idea what. They might have anticipated that bringing female agents in was unwise with such a libido-driven, relentlessly social target. Too late. Wedick was at once deep inside the moment and floating above it, aware that the evening was on the verge of detonation but unsure how to defuse it. He couldn't tell Kitzer that the women weren't interested, nor could they ditch him and leave; they were on duty. Kitzer seemed determined to either win them over or drive them, exasperated, out of the bar. Time began to slow down for Wedick as his mind raced. He and Brennan worked furiously to change the subject, but Kitzer waved them off.

Around midnight, everything finally unspooled. Brennan headed to the men's room, and Setmeyer, having left the parking lot, followed him in. "Hey, you gotta get out of here," Setmeyer said. "Break off the meeting. We're going home."

Brennan paused. Break off the meeting? How were they supposed to do that? It was Kitzer's show. Setmeyer told him that was their problem.

Brennan saw no way to move the whole group, so he decided to splinter it. He would pretend to leave with the female agent he'd chatted up, which, hopefully, would discourage Kitzer's advances. He came out and waved good night, grinning triumphantly at the others. The rest of the surveillance team departed immediately after, as if the two groups were not quite together but also not *not* together.

Kitzer watched with dismay. "Did you see that? Those people weren't part of a group, and they suddenly leave together?" he said. "And those guys kept looking over here? Don't you think that was strange?"

Confused about what was happening with Brennan and the Cleveland agents, Wedick tried to pivot the conversation back to Kealoha, and D'Amato, for one, played along. He beckoned Wedick to follow him to his room—leaving Kitzer sitting in the saloon—then took the rented CDs from his briefcase and asked whether Kitzer had ever showed him anything like that.

Eventually Wedick excused himself and found Brennan in the parking lot with the Cleveland agents. Everyone was tired. Brennan and Wedick were distraught about Kitzer, angry about the way the surveillance team had bailed out, their whole facade nearly crumbling in front of their target. Wedick had sensed all along that attending the meeting was a bad idea, and now he cursed himself for going along with it. But he was also disturbed by the Cleveland agents' lack of professionalism, which might have compromised the investigation.

"How screwed up can you guys be?" Wedick barked. "We're undercover agents. We're still collecting information. How is it that *you* can decide we're done?"

Wedick said they had just come from headquarters and were heading up a new undercover initiative that the local agents had nearly blown up. "Hey, guys, if you didn't think this was big, it *is* big, okay?" he said. "You guys are in trouble."

The Cleveland agents were disinterested in any sort of post-mortem analysis. Minutes later, Wedick and Brennan were standing alone outside the Sheraton Beachwood, wondering how things had fallen apart so fast, and whether it was going to be possible to pick up the pieces.

9

The Poodle Lounge

MARCH 4, 1977

Wedick and Brennan rose at six, before the first slate-gray light of the late-winter Ohio morning could slither around their blackout shades. They showered and dressed and tried to feel good about Operation Fountain Pen, but the previous night had rattled them. They'd gone to bed buzzing from bourbon and stress, unsure whether Kitzer's suspicions had mushroomed into something worse. They were also worried about the ramifications within the FBI. Lowie and Cleveland's SAC would have to try to iron out the events of the previous night. FBI politics were such that if the Cleveland boss was exceedingly bent out of shape—about the last-minute incursion or the way things went down—Brennan and Wedick would have to deal with the fallout. He could go to Washington with his beef. Worst case, they could get pulled back home. Later, the FBI would require agents to submit proposals for undercover work and create a committee to scrutinize them before anyone went out in the field. But that process didn't yet exist.

Wedick was still furious with Brennan and the Cleveland team, and livid that the operation had nearly collapsed for no good reason. His name was attached to the case, so he was risking more than anyone else. If this went badly, it was his career dangling over the precipice. The previous night's debacle validated his more deliberate, calculated approach. He didn't want bureaucracy holding him up—but they had to be sure, now more than ever, that they did this right.

Everything about their undercover operation seemed like a minefield. By some hideous luck, their flight to Miami that day included a two-hour layover in Washington—at almost exactly the time their FBI colleagues would be heading home from their training in Quantico. Brennan and Wedick feared that someone wearing a .357 Magnum would tap them on the shoulder while they were sitting with Kitzer and say, "Hey, Jim and Jack!" Even their airline tickets were wrong. Wedick gazed in frustration at the letters *GTR* stamped on his. Kitzer was probably savvy enough to decode the acronym—for "Government Transportation Request"—so the Junior G-Men would have to try to hide them.

They had to make changes. The first one they instantly agreed on: no more surveillance. The promoters posed no obvious physical threat, and Brennan and Wedick didn't want to have to worry about more disruptions. They would still, however, meet field agents wherever they traveled, to hand off leads. As for their dynamic? Wedick told Brennan that he had to stop pushing too fast. Later that morning, Bendis asked for Brennan's and Wedick's Social Security numbers and birth dates so he could run a credit check. They handed over their information—but as soon as everyone split up to head for the airport, the agents dialed Deeghan to ask whether he'd been able to erase important information in their credit history. Deeghan said he was working on it, and that they should head for Miami and hope for the best.

Much of the country was grinding through the last of a brutal winter. In the weeks leading up to president-elect Carter's inauguration, the nation had endured a cold snap so severe that it had snowed in Miami Beach. But now spring loomed, and for Brennan, the return to southern latitudes improved his mind-set. He and Wedick joined Kitzer and D'Amato in a three-room suite on an upper floor of Kitzer's favorite Miami hotel, the Sheraton Four Ambassadors. For the agents, this represented a significant upgrade from the usual government-budget rooms—not that they expected to enjoy it. In fact, they felt anxious about the arrangement, all of them packed inside the same walls.

Kitzer turned in early the first night, leaving the others lounging in the suite's living room. D'Amato declared that he was happy that Brennan and Wedick were "paying their dues" to the Fraternity, which he described as a loosely connected group of fifty-plus promoters spread across four continents. The idea behind their schemes was to create a mutually reinforcing illusion. A mark might not believe one con man—but if he hears the same story repeated by three others, all of whom appear to be connected to legitimate banks on different continents? The scheme sounds far more plausible.

D'Amato never tired of recounting his exploits, but he eventually conceded that he wasn't actually the chairman of the Fontainebleau. He had been—for about three days. The previous November, he'd been introduced as the new owner—the Associated Press even published a story about it. But the *Hartford Courant* followed up with a story about D'Amato's central role in the largest bank scandal in Connecticut history. That investigation was still pending when the Fontainebleau deal was announced. Hotel owner Ben Novack flinched after the *Courant* exposé came out, declaring that D'Amato was "not involved anymore." But D'Amato didn't give up, securing the legal services of Carl Ajello, Connecticut's sitting attorney general.

After absorbing D'Amato's verbal stylings for several hours, Brennan and Wedick said good night. In the quiet of their room, they contemplated what to do. They had no surveillance equipment, so they scribbled some notes to drop into the mail. Although this way of conducting their business had its limitations, the agents were relieved to be untethered from a surveillance team.

The events of the next day only reinforced their thinking. Wedick and Brennan slipped away to meet Miami-based agent Mike

Douglas, who seemed confused by the case and annoyed that he'd had the unfortunate luck to have picked up the phone when Wedick called the local office.

"I'll do what I can, but . . . ," he said, looking around for the nearest exit.

A jangle of phone calls and revolving-door meetings filled the next day, March 5. Kitzer and D'Amato met with the contractor for Kealoha's project, and squeezed in another Hawaiian developer trying to build a hotel addition. Kitzer was a blur. When he traveled, he said, he always had one headliner deal involving a client who paid the expenses for his trip. He usually had a couple of other, smaller propositions under way, and after the word had spread that he was in town, local brokers—lower-tier con men selling Kitzer's paper, like Arthur Murley in Charlotte—emerged with proposals. His phone service in Minnesota included a forwarding mechanism, so people could always reach him. By the second morning in Miami, Kitzer had a stack of messages waiting, and his phone rang incessantly.

Brennan and Wedick did their best to keep track of the various threads, hoping to generate leads they could report back to the bureau, but Kitzer didn't include them in every conversation, and he went alone to meetings where he was collecting money. Several times he emerged from his room or a corner of the lobby tucking away a roll of cash.

Kitzer clearly relished the role of the sage. Going into one meeting with a binder two inches thick, he said, "Hey, Jack, this is how this is done." He flipped to a random page and pointed out a paragraph about the liability rate for a proposed loan, telling Brennan to pay attention. Five minutes into the meeting, he interrupted: "You know, I was wondering about the liability rate." The mark was now thinking: *He's really scrutinized the details.*

Kitzer used these methods to confuse victims or coax them into handing over money. Alpha-dog businessmen in high-stakes negotiations generally avoid appearing not to understand something. It weakens their position. And if someone tried to put Kitzer on the spot—say, about whether he had enough assets on hand to write a performance bond—he might reply, "The performance bond and such-type instruments, they are related to the capital surplus of the company, and $1.1 million in cash does not mean you will have it in policyholders' surplus, and the ratio is ten percent to policyholders' surplus. And even if the $1.1 was in policyholders', ten percent would give them the authority to write a $110,000 bond on any one obligation. That's by federal law."

The guy would think, *Did he answer that? He must have.* Or he'd forget the point of the question.

Amid the hive of activity, Bendis called Kitzer from Cleveland to say that Wedick and Brennan were clear: Their credit scores were excellent. (Deeghan had succeeded in altering their personal information.) Kitzer put down the phone and turned to his two protégés. This was such good news that he decided they should change their Hawaii plans. He didn't want to risk exposing the Junior G-Men on a midlevel deal like Kealoha's. To have two pristine, unknown young promoters like them? They were a precious resource that had to be spent wisely.

The next day, after their meetings, Brennan and Wedick ran into Kitzer with a slight, attractive blonde. He shocked them by introducing her as his wife. Audrey Kitzer was in South Florida taking a break from the rugged Minnesota winter. They flitted off, leaving Wedick and Brennan exchanging looks of surprise. Kitzer was *married*? They had avoided conversations about their personal lives. Kitzer knew only that Wedick was single and that Brennan had some sort of situation but was coy with the details.

Otherwise, the Junior G-Men focused on fitting in. Brennan listened generously and laughed at everyone's jokes, and Wedick played the chatterbox New Yorker, telling animated stories in which he acted out different characters, some with cartoonish Bronx accents. They were relieved to find that they didn't need to adopt entirely new personas. D'Amato kept pulling them into side conversations about *his* schemes, unsubtly trying to recruit them away from Kitzer. That afternoon, he asked Brennan to accompany him to the Fort Lauderdale airport. He explained on the drive north that he'd called a contact in Connecticut about advancing some money, and in the airport lounge, D'Amato told Brennan to watch carefully. Soon a woman entered, looked in their direction, and exited.

"Come on," D'Amato said.

They followed her to a parking lot, where the woman stopped by a car. As the two men passed, she reached out and handed D'Amato an envelope, then drove off. Brennan tried to memorize the license plate. D'Amato smiled and said they were like characters in a spy movie as he opened the envelope and pulled out ten hundred-dollar bills.

The agents strained to tease apart the layers of this kind of pulp-fiction intrigue, the shifting cast of characters. Their third morning in Miami, a knock at seven o'clock woke everyone. A diminutive Chinese man entered and laid several framed paintings on the floor. Kitzer called Wedick and Brennan, and they all stood around in their underwear and gazed blearily at the artwork. Their visitor claimed the paintings had been stolen from the People's Museum in Beijing and were national treasures.

"If you say so," Kitzer replied, shrugging.

The art thief said he also dealt weapons to various nation-states, including North Korea, with a mutual acquaintance named Jack Scharf. He wanted Seven Oak letters of credit to fuel these enterprises, but Kitzer declined. Missiles and despots were like taking a guy's last dollar: nothing but trouble.

Jimmy Kealoha was a no-show in Florida. No one knew why, but Kitzer shrugged it off: He was juggling a dozen deals at any given moment, and inevitably some fizzled.

When he was in Miami, Kitzer liked to punch out at five and head to the Fontainebleau. The Junior G-Men were struck by the scale and grandeur of the place. Built in 1954, the massive, sickle-shaped hotel boasted more than twelve hundred rooms, the best of which loomed over the Atlantic Ocean. Painted white and fronted with sculptures of centaurs and bathing maidens and a massive fountain, the place had been featured in a 1960s TV detective series called *Surfside Six*. Frank Sinatra regularly appeared onstage in the La Ronde Room, entertaining Mafia dons and cocaine traffickers. But the hotel had recently fallen on hard times, flirting with bankruptcy and sending off the kind of distressed-animal sounds that attracted predators like Andy D'Amato.

Kitzer loved it. D'Amato had been boasting earlier about taking over the hotel when Kitzer had cut him off. "Remember, to pull that off, *you* need *me*," he'd said. "If the bankruptcy court takes your offer, it's going to be because of my paper."

That afternoon, he walked briskly into the Fontainebleau and greeted the concierge by name, calls of "Hello, Mr. Kitzer" echoing around the lobby. Passing a gift shop, Kitzer stopped at the window display.

"Hey, Jack, J.J.," he said. "C'mere. Watch this."

Kitzer entered the shop, pointed toward a teddy bear on display, and told the salesclerk he wanted every one the store had in stock. He peeled several bills off a roll he was carrying and began piling stuffed animals onto Brennan's and Wedick's arms. They strode out clutching more than fifty of them and wobbled to the Poodle Lounge.

The place was easy to spot. The bar featured portraits inspired by the French artist Jean-Honoré Fragonard in which all of the subjects had poodle faces. The room hummed with happy-hour traffic: fashionable snowbirds and young couples and people there to people-watch, men with shirt collars turned out over white sport coats and women in feathery strapless tops. There were sideburns and chest hair and flower-patterned dress shirts. Kitzer led Wedick and Brennan around, approaching each woman and offering a teddy bear with a hello and a smile. After they'd given one to every female in the room, they moved to the entrance and passed out the last of them to women walking in.

Kitzer then headed to the bar, and Brennan and Wedick watched everyone watching him. He was five-eight and scarcely a hundred and forty pounds, but he had a Wilt Chamberlain presence. The room grew louder and more energized as people showed around the teddy bears and Kitzer announced he was buying drinks for everyone in their vicinity. For himself and his two friends, he ordered an Aggravation—a cocktail made with Scotch, Kahlúa, and cream—and he pulled out his wad of cash when he was sure people were looking.

Brennan and Wedick figured that within fifteen minutes, Kitzer had managed to get every one of the hundred-plus patrons to notice him and puzzle over who he was—he had to be *some*body. There was some Clark Gable in there, Wedick thought. Kitzer said that he loved old movies; he'd studied the way Humphrey Bogart smoked with Lauren Bacall in *To Have and Have Not*. He appreciated how Cary Grant made moves on Doris Day or Grace Kelly or Eva Marie Saint.

Kitzer laid his gold Dunhill lighter and cigarettes on the bar and grinned at his companions. The lighter, made in Geneva, was among his favorite possessions. It was his icebreaker. He scanned the room, alert for any woman—even if she was with someone—pulling out a cigarette so that he could swoop in, flame flickering. Phil explained that the lighter provided a means of instant connection, and he wielded it the way a woman might showcase a string of pearls. He kept it ready. He didn't want to miss opportunities.

Kitzer chatted with everyone who entered his orbit, explaining that they were financiers who had just hit on a big deal. He was a ballroom dancer, so he would sometimes, if the music was right, grab a girl and take a few steps and spin her, and he clinked glasses and reveled in the attention radiating from the room, most of all from his two new friends.

Kitzer was dressed at eight the next morning, looking casual in a short-sleeved button-down. Wedick and Brennan were exhausted. Wedick stood in the shower and tried to clear his head enough to divine what Kitzer might talk about that day. He'd resolved to spend some time each morning moving through a chess match in his head: *If Kitzer says this, I should say that. Then what? How will he respond?*

Although he and Brennan were growing more relaxed in the con man's presence, they tried to remember that every word, every conversation carried the potential to dynamite the enterprise. They had agreed on several rules: Don't stretch the truth much. Tell stories that mirror something that actually happened so it's possible to remember later. Don't try too hard. Though no one had taught them how to act undercover, they instinctively grasped that they were most likely to succeed by playing versions of themselves.

Brennan tried to do what came naturally: He listened. He'd found that informants—like many people—enjoyed an audience. They tended to fill uncomfortable silences, and when they started talking, he would nod sympathetically: *I can see why you'd feel that way.* His eyebrows and forehead scrunched into empathetic expressions that matched his ingratiating conversational style. He folded his hands and laughed easily and said self-deprecating things. With the promoters, in particular, his strategy was: Ask questions, be dumb. Divert attention if they're getting personal. People with big egos always want to describe the great things they're doing. "Oh, man," Brennan would reply. "Wow."

Wedick, for all his verbal fireworks, also knew when to clam up. A prosecutor friend later described his demeanor "as father confessor . . . a rabbi with all the characters he deals with."

They had to be ready. Kitzer often tested them, probing their willingness to participate. When they checked out of the Sheraton, he playfully asked for Wedick's American Express card. Both Wedick and Brennan had one, and Kitzer, who paid in cash, always, to avoid leaving any kind of trail, was fascinated with the concept of plastic. "You know what you guys could do with those things?" he'd say.

He didn't mean pay for their rooms. The idea behind a credit card—pay me now and I'll pay you back later—was a core concept underpinning his scams. The card could serve as a portal into American Express, with its vast lines of credit, and Kitzer felt he could vacuum mountains of money through that window.

"Phil, I know you," Wedick replied. "I ain't giving you my card."

Heading to the airport, Kitzer told his apprentices that they would meet John Packman there. "London John," who ran Seven Oak's daily operations, had the previous day been served an order by Scotland Yard freezing all funds and transactions. Kitzer had told Packman to empty the coffers of whatever cash was on hand and fly it to Miami before the government could seize it. Packman and Kitzer had then drafted a letter dated the previous Friday, March 4, in which Kitzer ordered an $8,000 withdrawal.

They spotted Packman in the international terminal, signaling from the customs area. He explained that he had visa problems—not to mention $8,000 cash in his bag—and couldn't enter the country. Kitzer pondered this while gazing at the departures board. He noted that a flight to the Bahamas was leaving soon. Packman would have no trouble traveling to an island in the British Commonwealth.

"You guys wanna go to the beach?" Kitzer asked the others, grinning. They could be there in less than an hour.

Wedick and Brennan hesitated, their brains straining to calculate the cost of this snap-of-the-fingers plan change. They'd originally expected to be in Quantico for a few days, and they'd already been gone for a week. Jack thought about Becky, his kids. And they'd need to contact Deeghan, obviously. This was a new complication—another test of the tensile strength of their tethers to their everyday lives. The agents didn't know it yet, but this was only the first of many.

They couldn't equivocate for long. They had no plausible excuse for passing up the offer, and they wanted Kitzer to believe he could count on them. Maybe this was a test, his way of gauging their level of commitment.

Minutes later, Brennan and Wedick were buckling their seat belts for a flight to the Caribbean with no idea how long they'd be gone.

10

Mr. Mutt and Mr. Jeff

MARCH 9, 1977

Wedick stared at his watch, wiped the sweat off his forehead, and cursed. The line he was standing in snaked around the corner and out of sight. Every few minutes he shuffled forward a few steps, but it seemed to him that the ocean's tides might rise and recede again before he reached the front.

It was their second day in Nassau, in the Bahamas, which they'd found to be a prototypical Caribbean backwater. Everything happened on island time, including, apparently, the installation of the kinds of utilities folks back home took for granted. Such as telephones. When Wedick and Brennan had arrived at the Sheraton British Colonial the previous day, they'd been eager to report that their trip had lurched off course unexpectedly. But the room phone was a relic: It lacked any way to dial a number. To make a call, a guest lifted the receiver and told the hotel switchboard operator the name and number of the party he wanted to reach. To call the States, the operator then had to reach *another* operator, one capable of accessing an international line—which might take ten minutes or more. The Bahamas was ideal for honeymooners, but not for marooned undercover agents.

Brennan and Wedick quickly dismissed the hotel phone option. Phil might wander into the room before the operator reached Deeghan, or he might be friendly with a hotel employee who might note an incoming call from the FBI. The agents figured the only way to reach Indianapolis safely was via Nassau's public phone bank. Wedick told Kitzer he was heading out for some sightseeing.

"Sightseeing?" Kitzer said, grinning incredulously. His idea of relaxation was sitting at a bar on a beach, chatting with everyone in the vicinity. Wedick, feeling like a high school senior sneaking out his bedroom window, figured he had two hours to take care of business before Kitzer wondered where he was. But he'd burned through that time without coming close to reaching a phone. Apparently, half of the island's population needed to make a call.

Wedick pondered his options. If he left without calling, Deeghan and Lowie would probably begin to wonder whether their bodies were floating somewhere in the Everglades. The FBI was a highly regimented organization. Under Hoover, agents had been expected to be at their desks every morning at eight. The boss would leave you alone if you were established and productive, but otherwise he'd sit on you. For Wedick and Brennan to be not only out of the office for so long but also incommunicado was an affront to bureau culture.

They would undoubtedly be censured for this later, but they were at a loss for what else to do.

Wedick shuffled a few more steps forward, then looked at his watch again and started back toward the Sheraton.

A group of three women were talking to the concierge in the Sheraton lobby, asking about dining options, when Kitzer overheard them. He stopped and bantered with them in a way that Brennan and Wedick recognized as being as effortless as breathing for him. *Where are you from? Canada, really? Why don't you join us for dinner? We're just on our way out!*

The Junior G-Men exchanged looks: *Here we go.* It was their third day there; Packman had returned to London. Brennan and Wedick had both checked the phone bank again, but the line only seemed to lengthen. Their anxiety about their situation was gradually intensifying, and, vexingly, Kitzer wouldn't say how long he wanted to stay. Maybe he didn't know yet himself. He was too busy digging a hotel sewing kit out of a drawer and running a thread through a Bahamian hundred-dollar bill, then dangling it off the balcony of his second-floor room. Phil would let it sit on the ground or appear to flutter in the breeze and watch passersby lunge or jump for it before yanking it away. Part of the fun was predicting who would go after the money—and he was uncannily accurate.

He harbored no grand ambition otherwise. Jimmy Buffett's hit "Margaritaville" had been released as a single a few weeks earlier, and Kitzer was happy to join the throngs of tourists eager to waste away now that they'd finally tunneled out of winter. That year's deep freeze had overlapped with another paralyzing natural-gas shortage, which, after years of inflation and a wallowing economy, had left Americans feeling cynical and frustrated. *All in the Family* was among the most popular shows on TV, and later that year Carroll O'Connor would win an Emmy for his role. Archie Bunker was alive and well.

Kitzer was intent on spending the Seven Oak windfall, and he'd told Wedick and Brennan to get ready for a big dinner. At his behest, the three of them squeezed into a cab, their new acquaintances from Canada sitting on their laps, giggling. Kitzer directed the cabbie downtown to the historic Graycliff Hotel. The property, according to legend, had been built by a pirate in the 1700s, only to be captured, along with the rest of Nassau, by the American navy in 1776. It later became an exclusive private club—Al Capone visited during Prohibition—before being purchased by British royalty in the 1960s. The new owners jammed the place with antiques and high-end decor for visits from the Duke and Duchess of Windsor. Then, in 1973, the property was turned into a hotel with a five-star restaurant, complete with a humidor, overlooking downtown and the Caribbean beyond.

The Graycliff was the kind of place where Kitzer's proclivity for flashing rolls of hundreds would not go unappreciated. When they arrived, he instructed the cabbie to keep the meter running and wait outside: He didn't want to have to hail another one when they were finished. Inside, a crowd redolent of old money packed the room, forming a sea of white hair and starchy dinner jackets. Brennan and Wedick felt underdressed in their blazers and slacks, but Kitzer headed straight for the maître d' and pointed toward a corner table with expansive ocean views.

The maître d' shook his head: That table was permanently reserved for a regular. Kitzer waved a hundred-dollar bill. The maître d' smiled in a pained way and shook his head and instead settled them near another table of six—all of them older, highborn Brits, whom Kitzer greeted like childhood friends. As the courses rolled in over the next two hours, he led a conversation across both tables, his stories triggering cascades of laughter. As the meal wound down, he waved the maître d' over and pointed toward the still empty corner table.

"Hundred bucks," Kitzer said, smiling. "You missed out."

The three men fired up enormous Cuban cigars from the humidor and ordered Drambuie. A pianist began to play. Kitzer perked up and signaled again to the maître d'. This time he requested Tony Bennett's signature song, "I Left My Heart in San Francisco."

The pianist knew that one, and also the Sinatra song Kitzer asked for next, and the show-tune requests that followed. Kitzer smiled when he heard the first notes of "Hello, Dolly!," then rose to his feet and burst into song, signaling for everyone at the table to join him. Brennan and Wedick and the Canadian girls began to sing; then the neighboring table chimed in. The crooning spread like a torch passed from hand to hand, lighting up their surroundings, until the entire place was belting out lyrics and clinking glasses. Brennan gazed across at a septuagenarian British matron wearing a string of pearls, her face beatific and lifted skyward as she sang. Amid it all stood Kitzer, a huge grin creasing his face, the maestro at the height of his powers, fully in control of the room.

———

Between songs, the maître d' approached with a familiar-looking figure hovering behind him. It was the cabbie. His meter had been running for more than two hours; anxious about the ballooning fare, he was asking for partial payment.

Kitzer was irked by the interruption, as well as the implication that he might welsh on the fare. Nearby diners watched as the cabbie haltingly explained that he'd been victimized before, but Kitzer held up a hand, dug into a pocket for his gangster roll, and peeled off enough bills to pay the fare, then dismissed the driver. The wide-eyed cabbie quickly backpedaled: He was happy to wait. He'd just gotten nervous.

Kitzer waved him away. The spell was broken. He asked the maître d' to call another cab.

Once they were rolling again, Kitzer told the new driver to take them to an after-hours bar. The overstuffed cab sped out of town, eventually stopping at what seemed like a distant fishing port. The six of them emerged from the car and looked around. The only place in sight was a dingy lounge that was clearly a world away from the tourist schlock of Paradise Island. The bar's entire clientele turned to stare as they walked in. The Junior G-Men nonchalantly led the way into a billiards room, settled around a table in the corner, and ordered drinks.

Wedick and Brennan exchanged wary looks. It was amazing how quickly things could turn in Phil's company. Not an hour ago, they'd been singing "Oklahoma" with British aristocracy. Now they sensed an unwelcome vibe in a dive bar beyond American jurisdiction where they'd gone without the knowledge of their U.S. Department of Justice employers. With three Canadians. The situation had all the ingredients of a spectacular international incident.

The women passed around a large, decorative ceramic Paradise Island ashtray they'd found on the table—they thought it was a cool souvenir. The six of them did their best to chat unself-consciously and sip their drinks even as a patron approached and asked what they were doing there. At that point, Brennan convinced Phil that they should leave. They were all hustling toward the exit when someone yelled, "Hey, you!"

Everyone stopped. The group turned toward the unhappy-looking figure standing behind the bar—probably the owner. He was looking at Phil, who grinned and said, "Who, me?"

"Yeah! Put it back."

Phil stood there for a moment, motionless. Everyone looked from him to the owner, confused.

"You know what I'm talking about. Underneath your coat."

Phil said, "Oh, this?"

He pulled a small plastic ashtray from his blazer and held it aloft. "Oh, I was just taking this for the girls," he said. He placed the tray on a table, and then they turned and left.

Outside, Wedick turned to Phil. "Are you crazy? We were gonna get killed in there."

The six of them circled up outside the cab. Phil grinned and reached into the other side of his jacket.

"Fuck those guys," he said. He produced the larger ashtray the girls had coveted. Everyone stood there, stunned, as he handed it to one of the women. They all stared at it while the girls giggled, and then everyone hurried back into the cab and the driver peeled away into the sultry night.

Becky Brennan was cold. That year's pitiless Indiana winter was particularly punishing for a child of the Deep South.

After returning to the Midwest, she'd rented a small apartment in Chesterton, outside Gary; she'd felt awkward about going back to Crown Point. She settled in with beanbag chairs and a card table, and took the boys sledding on a tiny hill in the middle of the apartment complex, with just enough slope to harness some gravity. "I had never experienced snow like that," she said. "[Jack] would be gone and I would be shoveling. . . . It becomes ice, and I didn't know how to do it, and it was just *miserable*." She watched the boys for as long as she could stand before rounding them up and retreating inside. She prayed a lot. She prayed for spring. She prayed for things to work out with Jack.

The couple talked about reconciling, but at first Jack was immersed in a demanding trial, and after long days in court he needed to strategize with the prosecutors, so he often slept at Wedick's or with another buddy. "He was," Becky said, "just doing his thing still."

Becky had forgiven Jack, but Jack was not so clear about where they stood. The heart wants what it wants—but sometimes it takes time to figure things out. "It just took quite a while for him to trust I was really not going to walk out," Becky said. "If I was the same person, he wasn't really interested in trying to work it out."

Becky was intent on showing that she was committed. She was relieved when Jack finished his long trial, figuring they would have time to explore a détente. So she was surprised when he started in on an undercover case and couldn't tell her what it entailed, for her own safety and his. Initially it had just been a couple of meetings, nothing more. But now the travel and duration were open-ended. This time, he left for a few days of training, then started into his case and had been gone for well over a week. "It's just not an easy thing to repair the marriage when he's gone all the time," she said, "plus not knowing where he was, what he was doing."

She understood that this was part of the deal. That didn't make it less hard.

Jack had never taken on a case like this one before, nor had anyone else she knew, and Becky wondered about its dimensions, its risks. Playing with the boys, she found herself distracted by questions of where he was and whether he was safe.

Now she prayed for him to come home soon, because even though he had to keep his work secret, she had so much to share—in particular, one piece of news that reached to the core of everything they were trying to do and figure out together. She was pregnant.

The agents didn't know it yet, but Kitzer's life was filled with similar complexities—with the same kind of conflicting forces and tensions. His parents had emigrated from Hungary when they were quite young; his father, Fulop, was in his teens when he arrived in Chicago and Americanized his name to Phillip. He found work as a bricklayer and married; his wife, Helen, raised their kids. Although the family grew fast, Phillip's mind was too hungry to settle for manual labor. As they sank taproots into the city, he mined an entrepreneurial vein. The 1940 census lists him as the operator of his own real estate agency. Shortly after that, he would morph into a bail bondsman.

Phillip Karl Kitzer, the fifth of seven children but the first son, was born on March 5, 1933. When he and his father went into business together, people called him Junior to avoid confusion. Junior was a fast learner who had little use for school, preferring to put his mind toward making money. He was only seven when he started selling magazines and working as a shoeshine boy in South Chicago—but he soon upgraded from polishing wingtips to renting out kits to others.

He dropped out of high school after the tenth grade to join his father's bail-bond business. One afternoon, a friend brought Kitzer along to Woolworth's to pick up a girl he was dating who worked an after-school job there. Helen Braun had dark, wavy hair and a bright, attractive smile. A few days later, Kitzer called and asked her out. She initially said no because she was seeing their mutual friend, but Kitzer kept calling, and finally she caved. He was fun to be around and exuded an irresistible charisma, and they were seeing each other regularly in 1953 when he was drafted into the army.

While stationed at Fort Gordon, near Augusta, Georgia, Kitzer phoned Helen to pitch a crazy idea: He wanted her to quit her job and move to Georgia to get married. Again she resisted, but again she eventually caved in. During a seven-day leave that Fourth of

July weekend, he flew home for a ceremony and a brief honeymoon. He was twenty; she was nineteen. "It was stupid, stupid, stupid," Helen would say later. "But at the time it was the normal thing to do."

When Kitzer was discharged in March 1955, they moved back to Chicago, and Helen gave birth to their first son, Phillip Michael, later that year. Kitzer, now a father at twenty-two, became a licensed bail bondsman, following his father's path. Then he found a book published by the state of Illinois that covered the requirements for becoming an insurance broker. "I bought the book," he later recalled, "read it four or five times, took the test and passed it."

Kitzer took a job as a door-to-door salesman with State Farm Insurance in 1956, solely to find out how the agents there obtained their business. After four months, he split off on his own and became an independent agent selling casualty, life, and auto policies, among others, on behalf of various insurance companies— collecting commissions along the way. Then he became what's known as an attorney in fact—a person authorized to perform transactions on another party's behalf—for a handful of insurance companies. He wrote surety bonds and fidelity bonds and was eventually given power to commit the companies for expensive policies. One agency authorized him to write policies for as much as half a million.

Soon Junior expanded his role in his father's business, which had blossomed. From early on, the elder Kitzer knew it was possible to profit from the Chicago Police Department's rampant corruption. A bond agency he worked for in the 1950s was one of two investigated by a grand jury for apparent monopolies in federal narcotics cases. The bail-bond agents were thought to be giving kickbacks to the cops in exchange for business referrals.

In 1959, a Cook County grand jury investigated Phillip Kitzer and his sons, Phil and Joe. At the time, the Kitzers were writing more than half the bonds posted in Chicago's federal court. Jimmy

Hoffa was among their clients. But the father deflected guilt by spreading the story that, to the contrary, *he* was the honest businessman treading water in a sea of venality. "I've been telling a lot of people who are now in trouble over this what would happen to them," he told a *Chicago Daily Tribune* reporter, "and it has happened. . . . It has gotten to the point where a man who wants to run his business according to the law, and with a little self-respect, has got the choice of going broke or changing his morals."

Junior and Helen welcomed two more children into their brood. Phil Kitzer was a solid, stable husband and father. Helen sometimes suffered from debilitating migraines, so he took over the chores of cleaning the house, feeding the kids, packing them off to school.

But on the job, Kitzer had fully grasped the nuances of the insurance game, and in the summer of 1961, a newfound ambition began to take hold. He and his father and brother sought to open an automobile-insurance firm in Chicago. They filled out a loan application at Exchange National Bank in Chicago for the $200,000 they'd need to get started. But the bank officer demanded a $25,000 kickback.

"So I said, 'That's all right,'" Junior later recounted. "So I gave him $25,000. He gave me two hundred [thousand]. Then I wanted to borrow more money from him. It became a steady thing. Every time I borrowed money I had to pay him. At that point I didn't know how to reverse it any longer." In total, he said, he kicked back around $70,000.

"From then," he said, "I learned how bankers think."

Phil Kitzer was then asked: Did those events force him into a life of crime?

"I won't say I was forced into it," he replied. "I'll just say that it happened."

Down in the Bahamas, Kitzer greeted his protégés on March 11 with some welcome news. Captain Jack Elliott had called from Los Angeles reporting that the Jimmy Kealoha deal was back on, and they needed to hop on a flight to California. Brennan and Wedick, enormously relieved, quickly packed their bags.

But when they climbed into a cab, Phil pointed out that they had some time to burn before the flight and suggested they stop for a last Yellow Bird. This had become a running joke. Everyone in Nassau seemed to be drinking the orange-juice-and-rum drinks named after the Harry Belafonte song. "Let's have a Yellow Bird" was their shorthand for going out, even if they never ordered one. Brennan and Wedick didn't care to go partying—it was barely past noon—but there was no talking Kitzer out of it.

Kitzer ordered the cabbie to stop as they reached a large resort. Climbing out of the cab, they could hear music shuddering and saw tourists carrying towels through the lobby. Kitzer nodded to Wedick and Brennan to follow the crowd, and rounding a corner, he stopped and smiled. A band was playing, and besotted patrons were lunging into the pool and sitting under umbrella-shaded tables, clutching drinks from the poolside bar.

Kitzer viewed his first moments walking into scenes like this one as critical. His primary objective was to find an open seat next to a table full of women. That wasn't an option here—the room was packed—so he settled on a barstool and laid out his lighter. Then he began his routine of buying drinks, lighting cigarettes, pulling two strangers together to dance, or escorting someone onto the floor. Recently he had started incorporating Wedick into his act. Kitzer would approach a woman and say, "My friend likes you." Or he would tug Wedick into a crowd and say something outrageous or provocative. Wedick disliked this, but he found it challenging to escape.

Now Kitzer leaned toward the others. "You know, we don't have to catch this flight," he said. It was Friday afternoon, so they could stay at the beach until Sunday, then fly to Los Angeles in time for work on Monday. Wedick smiled tightly. Two more days AWOL would be slow torture. But it wasn't so easy to come up with a compelling reason why they needed to leave: He and Brennan had no families or jobs to get back to, as far as Phil knew.

Wedick blurted out the only thing he could think of: "This scene is over, Phil. Southern California has even more women and places to party."

Kitzer conceded that they could use a change of venue. Seizing the moment, the Junior G-Men hauled him to the taxi he'd kept waiting, saying they could still catch the flight if they hustled.

When they reached Miami, Wedick slipped off the plane ahead of the others and sprinted to call the office. Brennan, tasked with the role of distracting Kitzer, would have no chance to call Becky. By then she was getting used to his enigmatic travel schedule, but he still would've embraced the chance to let her know that they were okay. He reminded himself to focus on the next task. That was all he could do.

Wedick reached Bowen Johnson, who'd recently replaced him as Operation Fountain Pen's case agent. After the Cleveland debacle, Wedick had asked out of the administrative work, saying it was too much to juggle with the undercover role. His bosses had chosen Johnson, an unflappable southerner who had recently transferred to Indianapolis after several years as the senior resident agent in Terre Haute.

Johnson sounded both apoplectic and sick with worry. Wedick had expected this, of course, but he and Brennan were lucky: It was late Friday afternoon, which meant that even though Indianapolis was furious, Johnson and the others would be ready to start their weekend.

Wedick's time working as a clerk in New York had taught him a few administrative tricks. He knew that Hoover-era supervisors told their wives never to answer the phone on a Friday night, in case it was the office—whoever was calling would just find a different supervisor. Orville Watts would be unreachable by now.

Wedick just had to let everyone know they were okay and ward off any kind of communication to headquarters indicating they were missing.

Johnson started shouting questions and orders: Where the hell had they been? What did they think they were doing? They better get their asses back to the office immediately.

"Look, Bowen," Wedick said, cutting him off, "it's almost five o'clock on Friday, and nobody gives a shit until Monday morning."

"You have to come back now!" Johnson bellowed.

"Listen. Former case agent to present case agent: We'll be there at eight o'clock Monday morning, guaranteed, but it ain't happening right now. We can't."

"I'm *ordering* you!"

Wedick glanced at the gate. Brennan and Kitzer had emerged from the tunnel and were looking around.

"Bowen, I'm hanging up the phone, but we'll be there," Wedick said. "I promise."

"Don't hang up!"

Johnson was still shouting as Wedick plunked the receiver down and walked over to join the others. Sure, everyone would still be apoplectic on Monday morning, but that was a problem for Monday—for now, they had plenty to worry about with Kitzer. And anyway, Brennan and Wedick and some of their colleagues had a running joke. Whenever they pushed up against the rules, they would shrug and say, "What are they gonna do, send me to Gary?"

Kitzer went to the counter to get their tickets for their next leg. In 1977, air travel was a more casual undertaking than it would become in the era of Homeland Security. All you needed was a valid ticket for whatever flight you were taking.

When Kitzer returned, Brennan and Wedick looked at their National Airlines tickets and chuckled. According to their boarding passes, they would be flying to Los Angeles as Mr. Mutt and Mr. Jeff.

Rip Off Hawaii

MARCH 22, 1977

The elderly couple murmured appreciatively as they toured the penthouse suite in the Fontainebleau Hotel. Andy D'Amato made sure they saw every square foot; the foyer alone was nearly as big as many hotel rooms, he pointed out. There was a kitchen and a dining room with a chandelier and a living room with couches, and there were several bedrooms. The terrace overlooked Miami Beach and the Atlantic Ocean. Eventually Jimmy Kealoha and his wife, Miulan, who insisted that everyone call her Mama, settled on a set of circular couches across from D'Amato and Kitzer.

The Hawaii scam had come back together with a thunderclap abruptness. About a week after Wedick and Brennan had finally flown home from their zigzag journey through the Bahamas and on to Los Angeles, Kitzer had received a call from the Kealohas. The couple, who also ran a papaya farm, apologized for having missed their earlier meeting in Miami and said they still wanted to get together. They were still seeking financing for the Waikiki Beach development. Kitzer called around, located D'Amato in Miami and the Junior G-Men in Indiana, and suggested they again try to meet in Florida.

Once they arrived, Kitzer kept Brennan and Wedick downstairs, out of concern that the Hawaiians would be overwhelmed by too many new faces. But after asking about the Kealohas' flights and the weather in Hawaii, D'Amato introduced someone Kitzer had never seen before. Mark Iuteri was brawny, in his late thirties, with a thick head of puffy dark hair and a mustache. D'Amato said he was an appraiser, but he didn't look the part.

The Hawaiians began to detail the project, handing out a bound proposal that included an appraisal from John Child & Company, a large and reputable firm. Kitzer had warned D'Amato that this presentation was interminable. D'Amato held up a hand. "Listen, Jimmy," he said. "I know all about your project. I've checked it out. . . . We're late into this thing already two weeks."

D'Amato said there was one issue: He first needed to do an on-site inspection. The Kealohas would have to pay his travel expenses to Honolulu, plus $1,500 a day regardless of whether the takeout came through. Also, the appraisal the Kealohas had acquired was inadequate. Fortunately, he said, Mark Iuteri was certified by the Master Appraisers Institute and the Eurotrust would readily accept his work—which would cost the Kealohas $25,000 plus travel and expenses.

Jimmy Kealoha asked for information about the trust, and D'Amato handed over a brochure detailing its background. Kealoha thought it sounded impressive. He turned to his wife. "What do you think of this?"

"Well, Jimmy, we're into this so far, what are we going to do?" she said. "We have no other way out."

In an article the *Hartford Courant* had published just three months earlier, two investigative reporters had looked into the Eurotrust and turned up "phony claims of connections to a famous Italian wine firm, an obscure Liechtenstein prince and supposed missionary investments that couldn't be traced."

But there was no Google then, and the Kealohas had no time to commission a lengthier investigation.

"Yeah," Jimmy said. "Okay. Let's do it. I finally want to get this thing done."

On paper, at least, the Kealohas did not appear to be easy marks. Jimmy had been chairman of the county of Hawaii before becoming lieutenant governor. But he was now close to seventy, had never translated his political success into the business arena and was now more desperate than ever. Kealoha was, in fact, the prototypical desperate man.

He had sunk more than $400,000 into the project and had only a blank slab of beachfront land to show for it. He was too far in to extract himself cleanly, and the urge to move forward overwhelmed any semblance of common sense. In that mind-set, he wouldn't blink at spending another $25,000 to get his hands on $10 million in financing.

The Kealohas agreed to everything. Mama wrote down flight information for first-class tickets to Honolulu for Kitzer, D'Amato, and Iuteri. D'Amato asked to speak to Kitzer privately. "Let's hit them up for a few days' advance," he said behind one of the bedroom doors.

Kitzer shook his head. "No, Andy, that's not fair. You just met these people, they're going to lay out thousands of dollars right now for plane tickets, expenses. You can't conceivably ask them to give you money here in Miami."

"Mark and I don't have any walking-around money when we get to Hawaii," D'Amato protested.

"I have cash on me," Kitzer said. "I can take care of that."

While Kitzer reconnected with Kealoha, Wedick and Brennan had been busy with damage control in Indiana. They'd finally flown home from Los Angeles on Sunday, March 13, after two weeks on the road, then left Gary at five-thirty the next morning, battling bone-marrow-deep weariness, jet lag, and a monster Phil Kitzer hangover.

As fatigued as they were, they wanted to get to Indianapolis before everyone else showed up for work. They hoped to avoid a scenario where the rest of the office was sitting there talking about the prodigal sons—how they'd been off doing who knows what in the Bahamas—when they walked in. Everyone arrived by nine, and Brennan and Wedick filed into a conference room with Johnson, Deeghan, Lowie, and a few others. Wedick started to explain what had happened, but Lowie held up a hand to stop him.

"I've got my ass out hanging here," Lowie said, "and there was a period of time where I didn't know where you were. You know how that looks if headquarters calls me?"

Wedick and Brennan nodded. Next time, Lowie said, they'd better wait on that phone line. The agents agreed that they would. They had been in an impossible situation, but in this moment they grasped the dynamic: The worst-case scenario for Lowie and Deeghan was to be asked what was going on and not be able to answer. People up the chain of command would seize on Brennan and Wedick's disappearance to score points: *Look what's happening there. I was the one who said this would be a problem.*

The undercover agents spent the next fifteen minutes expressing contrition and letting Lowie and Deeghan vent. They promised to do things differently next time. They knew that these two supervisors were their most important allies, along with Johnson.

Once Lowie felt adequately understood, the conversation shifted to the scams Brennan and Wedick had learned about. They added more index cards to the wall, officially turning the conference room into OpFoPen headquarters.

Even though it was a tricky topic under the circumstances, Wedick felt he had to point out the high likelihood that Kitzer would again hijack their plans. Plotting out moves with him was like trying to steer a rudderless boat through a whirlpool. For Kitzer, the lack of scheduling was the point. His priorities were scamming money and spending it. He saw no point in planning for next week when tomorrow might bring a new customer paying cash for paper—if tomorrow arrived at all. In the days of open-return airline tickets—you didn't need to give a date for the back end of your round trip—that sort of spontaneous travel was easier.

Wedick and Brennan felt as if they were shuttling between two planets that loomed just out of each other's field of view. They understood why the FBI would be reluctant, as well as flummoxed.

The bureau wanted numbers: How much money was Phil stealing, and how much could they recover? But Kitzer didn't plan any one huge heist. He'd taken $60,000 from Kealoha and might swindle the Hawaiian out of $80,000 more—and that was just one deal. There were dozens of others at any given moment, only some of which Phil had told them about.

Then there was the loss-recovery problem. The agents recounted how Kitzer had spontaneously decided to spend the $8,000 from Seven Oak. There was no stockpiling cash to buy weapons for the IRA or to prop up some idealistic cause. Kitzer mostly seemed interested in partying and traveling and showcasing his powers to whatever audience he could find.

And all of it *right now*. It was the ideology of dopamine.

This confused everyone as much as one of his complex deals did. Who takes all that money, then just burns right through it? Jack and J.J. could see that the bureau's befuddlement made it ill-equipped to pursue him. "The average person, you have your mortgage, your car payment, your whole list of things you need to take care of," Wedick said. "He has no list. All he has is, *Where do I have to go to make money?* That's it. Otherwise, he's going to do whatever he wants, whenever he wants."

Brennan thought about his early twenties, his own focus on making money just so he could burn through it, the full-on sprint toward the next experience. He'd grown out of that life within a few years and now instead had mountains of paperwork awaiting him: transcriptions and reports and expense vouchers. In a certain mind-set, it wasn't so hard to see why Kitzer did what he did.

And those were just Brennan's responsibilities at the office. Back home in suburban Gary, Becky delivered her news that Jack was about to become a father for the third time. He spun through a whorl of conflicting emotions—confusion and excitement and fear and anxiety and joy, all of which he worked to compartmentalize. Jack took pride in his serenity, in his ability to focus on the next most urgent thing. The baby was due in October. Between now and then, he was going to have to be able to focus. When they weren't with Kitzer, Wedick wanted Brennan in Indianapolis, dictating reports and catching up on paperwork and talking to the U.S. attorney's office. So even when Jack was home, he often wasn't home.

In the meantime, Brennan had absorbed an important lesson: When he left to travel with Kitzer, he would no longer try to guess for Becky when he'd be back. If that seemed cruel, it was better than the alternative, which was making promises that Kitzer would almost certainly force him to break. It was better not to disappoint.

After locking down their Hawaii plans, the promoters spent the next couple of days in Florida on other business. Sitting in on a meeting on March 24, Wedick and Brennan caught something important: Kitzer said he wanted to introduce them to a promoter named Jean-Claude Cornaz in Denmark the following week.

The agents huddled on this development. In Indianapolis, Frank Lowie had won the authority to approve the agents' travel anywhere in the United States—a hard-fought victory. The only thing the headquarters disliked more than FBI employees traveling was having their power decentralized. The higher-ups essentially told Lowie: *You want that authority? Fine. But when they fuck up, we're coming after you.*

Foreign travel was a whole other matter. To travel to Copenhagen, Brennan and Wedick would need the U.S. ambassador and the FBI's legal attaché to Denmark to sign off, and they would have to obtain permission from a high-ranking Danish government official—preferably someone in law enforcement.

The Copenhagen request triggered calls up and down the chain of command and into the diplomatic community. Some officials were concerned about trusting Danish authorities with the case's sensitive banking and financial components. But the FBI's legal attaché in Denmark knew someone trustworthy who could secure permission for them to travel without being classified as government agents.

Working steadily over the next few days, slipping away to make calls, the agents lined up the necessary approvals. The promoters checked out of the Sheraton Four Ambassadors on March 26 ahead of the next leg of their journey, to Hawaii. In the lobby Kitzer chatted up a woman named Candy and convinced her and her friend to join them on their ride to the airport. At the check-in desk at Miami International Airport he cashed in his first-class ticket for two coach tickets, one of which he pressed into Candy's hands.

Wedick parked the car and reached the terminal after Kitzer and the others had boarded the plane. He found Candy standing alone, gazing at the ticket, trying to make sense of what had just happened. Wedick sometimes played along on Kitzer's pursuits, but Candy looked to be in her twenties and she was considering flying halfway around the world to meet Kitzer. Wedick waved her over to a quiet spot near a phone bank. "Look," he said. "This is going to sound strange: You need to forget that you ever met us and hope that you don't meet us again. You don't want to get involved with us. Trust me."

He took the ticket out of her hand, ripped it up, tossed it in the trash, and headed for the gate.

The itinerary included an overnight layover in Los Angeles. The group checked into the Marriott Airport Inn and settled in at the rooftop bar. Iuteri was excited to order a Coors, a beer about which he'd heard lots of buzz but couldn't find back home in New Haven.

Iuteri puzzled the agents. He didn't sound or dress like a promoter. He wore gold chains and was far less verbally gifted than Kitzer and D'Amato; there was too much street in his sentence construction. Wedick had instantly picked up a New York accent.

As he sipped from his bottle of Coors, Iuteri mentioned an odd coincidence: That morning, at the Miami airport, he'd spotted the owner of a boatyard where he'd once stored a thirty-foot cabin cruiser. In 1969 he'd burned the boat for insurance money, he said, and the fire raged out of control and razed half the boatyard. This was a surprise because he'd firebombed other places—including a few factories—but firefighters had knocked those down quickly.

Still, Iuteri recounted this as if it were the funniest pratfall he'd ever heard of. He also described his connection to a northeastern drug ring and asked Brennan and Wedick whether they might want jobs in that organization.

They drank and gabbed until two a.m., a chill gradually descending on the California night. Wedick, who tended to get cold quickly, shivered. Kitzer offered his fashionable thigh-length leather jacket. Wedick shook him off, but Kitzer insisted: "Come on," he said. "I'm telling you to wear it." The jacket fit pretty well even though Wedick was six inches taller.

Everyone overslept the next morning. After hustling through a shower, Brennan called Deeghan and was updating his boss in Indianapolis when he heard a knock. Wedick opened the door to find Kitzer outside with Iuteri. Jack abruptly hung up, and Kitzer strolled in and asked who he'd been talking to. Brennan pawed at his sandy hair, still wet from the shower, and blurted out that he'd been making arrangements with his commodities broker.

Kitzer didn't question this, and anyway, they were running late. By the time the men reached their departure gate, their flight to Honolulu had left, so they jogged to catch the next plane. As they boarded, Kitzer asked Iuteri, who was sitting in first class, to bring some champagne back to them. Iuteri delivered a bottle once they were airborne, and the three of them toasted the day and all that awaited them in Hawaii.

Brennan and Wedick sipped the bubbly—they had no way to

dump it out—and tried to relax. Wedick thought about how Kitzer had handed over his jacket. As a threesome, they had started to develop a certain rhythm and cohesion. The agents now knew not to check out of hotels too early; Kitzer routinely flouted the check-out times when they had a later flight. Brennan and Kitzer both had stomach issues on occasion and passed rolls of Tums back and forth. Kitzer had started calling Wedick by his nickname, J.J. They sometimes called Jack "the Golden Bear" because he was burly, the sun had lightened his sandy-colored hair, and he often wore a light blue Jack Nicklaus golf shirt with an ursine figure emblazoned on the breast. One of them was always making the other two laugh.

As the champagne took hold, Kitzer explained Iuteri's presence. Iuteri was a "button man for the Outfit"—a made man in the Mafia. Kitzer said that several months ago, D'Amato had borrowed money from a crime family and hadn't paid it back on time; he had subsequently been called to a sit-down.

"Andy," the mafioso had said, "when you wanted the money, we told you we would give you the money at three o'clock, and we gave it to you at three o'clock. But a payment was due at four o'clock."

Apparently, D'Amato didn't know the time.

"You don't have a watch, Andy—you didn't know it was four o'clock," the mobster said. "We've got to give Andy a watch. Andy, here's your watch."

And he pointed at Iuteri. Now, wherever D'Amato went, Iuteri went. Any money D'Amato scammed, Iuteri took a cut for his bosses.

Kitzer, who appreciated a good nickname, had come up with one for Iuteri: He called him the Watch.

As the sun cracked the horizon over the yawning Pacific Ocean, Brennan lowered himself to his knees in room 1011 of the Ala

Moana Hotel. The previous night they had checked into the massive Honolulu property, where the Kealohas had made reservations for everyone. Brennan gazed under the bed, then studied the walls and ceiling.

The Junior G-Men weren't sharing a suite with the promoters, but they were just down the hall on the tenth floor—and Kitzer's presence permeated their days. He now treated Wedick and Brennan as buddies, constantly entering their space. The agents wanted him to trust them, but these newfound invasions of privacy created stress and presented pressing logistical challenges. Kitzer burst in with no notice and pawed through the agents' possessions, asking to borrow Wedick's nail clippers or wanting to check out Brennan's new shirt.

They reacted cautiously to this newfound familiarity. They didn't want to seem upset, which might suggest they were hiding something. But Kitzer's behavior made gathering evidence a challenge. Concealing a recorder was already out of the question; everyone in Hawaii wore bathing suits and aloha shirts. Wedick and Brennan were left to write notes by hand late at night, then mail them to Indiana at their first chance. But it was almost impossible to keep up—and Kitzer always wanted them to go out with him at night.

Still, the agents resisted asking for surveillance help. Too many risks and complications. At the Ala Moana, they brainstormed another solution: They bought a mini recorder that used tiny cassettes; they could dictate reports into it at night or whenever they could slip away. Brennan's inspection eventually brought him to the room's thick, heavy curtains. He found a hem at the bottom, which he carefully cut open and probed. The fabric formed a pocket just large enough to hide the recorder.

Kitzer knew plenty about hiding things, about moving in shadows. His early-life bail-bond work and the bank kickbacks—all of it fed into the narrative that the system could be manipulated behind the scenes, that people who seized the controls of a business ought to pull the levers for their own gain.

In 1961, Kitzer and his father and brother formed their new insurance company, which they called Adequate Mutual. From there, Junior talked the others into starting up a second firm, Bell Casualty, in Chicago, to reinsure part of Adequate Mutual's risk. The father and brother largely left the operations of both companies to Phil. Though still only in his twenties, he took to the leadership role without hesitation.

In 1962, they took over American Allied Mutual Insurance Company in Minneapolis, a floundering high-risk car-insurance firm, acquiring it for $25,000 in cash and a car worth $1,200. And in a flash, the Kitzers' business metastasized. They added more firms with nearly identical names—for example, American Allied Insurance Company on top of American Allied Mutual Insurance, and Bell Mutual Casualty to go with Bell Casualty.

Within a few years, they controlled a spiderweb of fifteen businesses: eight insurance companies in Illinois, six in Minnesota, and a reinsurance firm across the Atlantic in London. They employed more than twenty-five thousand brokers and took in many millions in premiums. What had started with a single low-six-figure bank loan had morphed into a conglomerate in which a single firm was taking in $180,000 in premiums in a single month.

The sudden influx of money triggered profound changes in Kitzer. Helen had already sensed something when he'd come home and announced that he and his father and brother had bought an insurance company in Minnesota. "I had a very bad feeling about that," she recalled. "I said, 'Don't do that—it's going to break up our family.'"

By the time his fourth child, Richard, was born in 1963, Phil was traveling constantly and had become flamboyant with cash and evasive about where it had come from. "They started making a lot of money," Helen said, "and he was Superman. He could do no wrong."

He started coming home less, until his appearances dwindled to once a month. "He would say, 'I have to leave again in a couple of days, I got a lot of business going on,'" she said. "I didn't know where he was, and he never discussed any type of business with me. I was in the dark all the time, and he would always say, 'You'll never have to worry about that.'"

Phil was busy managing his companies' dizzying growth, which he insisted followed a certain logic: As his insurance companies' business grew, so did their potential liability. He bought and formed new insurance firms to spread out the risk, so that if one business began to sink from excessive claims, the others could prop it up.

But his actions suggested another motive: More insurance companies meant more premium money to siphon out. Kitzer soon developed a system for withdrawing cash from their firms. In August 1963, they set up Allied Realty of St. Paul, Inc., the stock of which was owned by American Allied. Allied Realty was a real estate holding company, ostensibly created as a vehicle for investing profits. The scam was simple: Acquire an unwanted piece of property and pay an assessor to artificially inflate its value. Then assign the property to Allied Realty and withdraw from the business the equivalent amount in cash—a classic con man's ploy also known as asset substitution. On the books, it looks like an even swap.

The foundation of this overnight empire began to spring leaks in 1964, when it came under the scrutiny of George Head, an enterprising thirty-eight-year-old postal inspector who wore oversized glasses and punctuated his sentences with exclamations like "dad bust it!" That year, Head's boss told him about the Kitzers and said, "The U.S. Attorney in Minneapolis thinks these people are committing a crime. But he doesn't know what the crime is, and the FBI hasn't been able to find out."

The U.S. attorney, Miles Lord, handed Head stacks of records from the Kitzers' fifteen interlaced companies. Head was baffled, and sought out accountants who had worked their entire careers in insurance companies. None of them could penetrate the Kitzer labyrinth either, but one contact referred Head to someone who had himself committed insurance fraud. "If you steal money from an insurance company," this source told Head, "you steal it by taking out good money—cash or other assets—and hide it by putting in bad or worthless stuff. Take a look at the assets. They can cover a multitude of sins."

Head holed up in a hotel room and studied the array of million-dollar assets in American Allied's records. Some looked highly suspect. He telephoned the state examiner who had audited the Kitzers' books. "Have you checked their securities?" Head asked.

"Didn't have to," the examiner replied. "The National Association of Insurance Commissioners certified them as okay."

Head then queried brokers in Chicago and New York and discovered that the stocks were a mirage. The daily Wall Street listing of over-the-counter stocks, called the pink sheet, described two of them as "no bid," meaning worthless. A third stock sometimes sold at one cent a share. The entire portfolio, the state of Minnesota later discovered, was worth no more than $750. But the Kitzers had swapped out more than $500,000 in company cash for it.

Head subpoenaed the broker who had sold the Kitzer stocks. Under oath, the broker conceded that the Kitzers didn't even own the stocks—he had, in fact, rented them the inflated assets. The $478,000 worth of real estate the family claimed was another facade: They didn't own much of that, either. After swapping out cash for these phony assets, the Kitzers then mailed false statements and misleading letters to insurance agents to assure them that they were on solid footing. The decision to expand to Minnesota had been calculated. The Kitzers knew that state regulators would look only at companies within their borders. When it was time for Minnesota to scrutinize the insurance companies there, the family would transfer assets over from Illinois.

Head's investigation triggered alarm bells in both states. In June 1965, the Illinois insurance commissioner ordered the Kitzers to temporarily stop issuing policies. In July, a policyholder filed a lawsuit asking the court to order the company to restore nearly $600,000 in missing U.S. Treasury notes. A month later, Minnesota declared the two-year-old American Allied Insurance Company—one of the many spinoff firms—insolvent. That agency had one hundred thousand policyholders in thirty-two states but carried more than $1.2 million in debt and far fewer assets than the Kitzers had claimed. Head finished his investigation that summer and handed the findings to the U.S. attorney in Minneapolis.

Federal prosecutors targeted the entire Kitzer enterprise in an indictment announced on October 29, 1965. Both Phillip Kitzers and Minnesota insurance commissioner Cyrus E. Magnusson were among seventeen people—including bankers, attorneys, and a securities broker—from five states charged with mail fraud, wire fraud, and conspiracy. The government contended that the Kitzers had built a sham empire off a single firm, Adequate Mutual, that was itself insolvent within a year—and that the recently collapsed American Allied had been a shell game from the start, having been created with $150,000 borrowed from two *other* firms, one of them bankrupt. If convicted, Junior faced as many as fifty-five years in prison. "A proper investigation of this transaction at [that] time would have shown that American Allied Insurance Co. was insolvent the day it commenced business," said Minnesota's attorney general.

The Kitzers were living in high style on the $4 million in premium payments they had vacuumed out. The family had recently acquired lake homes and speedboats and had renovated those houses, filling them with new furniture. They hosted huge parties at the Blue Ox nightclub in Minneapolis. Phil traveled to Miami, Las Vegas, San Francisco, Acapulco, and Honolulu. The charges contended that insurance commissioner Magnusson had overlooked all this, having been promised a job with the Kitzer companies.

On November 10, the defendants all pleaded not guilty and were freed after posting bail. But the following January, the state of Illinois sued the Kitzers and others for fraud related to Bell Casualty and Bell Mutual Casualty, claiming the family had misappropriated $650,000.

The Kitzers were suddenly living under a microscope. Minnesota prosecutors charged Phil with writing an illegal $2,000 check from one of his companies for the reelection campaigns of Minnesota's Governor Karl Rolvaag and Senator Walter Mondale. The scandal resonated so widely that Vice President Hubert Humphrey, a resident of Minnesota, came to the politicians' defense, charging that their opponents had distorted the facts about their relationship to the Kitzers. "Phony charges and personal vilification never have been acceptable to our voters in the past, and they won't be today," the vice president inveighed.

Only a few decades earlier, the elder Phillip Kitzer had been an anonymous Hungarian immigrant on the streets of Chicago. Now the Kitzers had made millions of dollars, adopted an opulent lifestyle, and were a topic of discussion in the White House.

Instead of conceding defeat, the Kitzers went on the offensive. In June 1966, they sued the National Association of Insurance Commissioners, claiming that the agency had falsely described the stock of three Kitzer companies as worthless. Six months later, in December, they filed a $3 million libel lawsuit against *Reader's Digest* for a story about Head's investigation, titled "Riddle of the Vanishing Insurance Companies." They also sued George Head.

Young Phil Kitzer's life was by then unrecognizable to people who'd known him a few years earlier. Helen learned that Phil was seeing Audrey Jensen, a stewardess he'd met during one of his trips, whom he would soon marry. "I don't know what happened to him," Helen said. "He just changed completely."

By late 1966, he had fully moved out, and Helen and the kids hardly ever saw him again. "He walked out the door," she said, "and he never looked back."

Fortunately for the agents, who sometimes couldn't get enough space from Phil, Kitzer had plenty of distractions in Hawaii. He was often locked in his room with a woman named Ruby, whom he knew from previous interludes; they had registered at the hotel as Mr. and Mrs. Phillip Kitzer. He asked the Junior G-Men to hold his address book and had his calls routed to their room to avoid having Ruby become entangled in his business.

Kitzer's extracurricular romantic activities were now a familiar sideshow on their travels. For every lost cause like Candy, whom Wedick had quietly intercepted, Kitzer added another trophy to his case. He liked the thrill of the chase—as a king dealmaker, he was constantly practicing his trade—and by now Brennan and Wedick were accustomed to him disappearing during their evenings out. He would show up a couple of hours later, flushed and smiling, ready to continue partying. Kitzer had made a point of calling Wedick a few weeks earlier to say he had someone he wanted J.J. to talk to. It took Wedick a minute to remember Cheryl, the young woman they'd sent flowers to on their first trip together. Kitzer wanted to make sure that Wedick knew he had hooked up with her. Other times, Kitzer, short on time or energy, suggested that they hire a couple of high-class escorts. Wedick wiggled out of those situations, saying he didn't want to miss out on the pursuit.

On the business front, Kitzer had meetings lined up on the third-floor swimming pool deck. The hotel's architects had designed the pool area as a gathering place, with lounge chairs and a neighboring bar with tables shaded from the withering sun.

The Kealoha deal was proceeding steadily. Kitzer instructed Iuteri to raise the amount in the original appraisal slightly, to $9.75 million, so that Kealoha could ask for a large enough loan to justify Kitzer's $80,000 fee. Inside the hotel coffee shop, the promoters gloated about how smoothly things were going. "The marks in Hawaii say 'thank you' after you take their money," D'Amato said, triggering laughter.

That sparked a debate about whether it was easier to rip off Hawaiians or Floridians. D'Amato insisted that Hawaii was the softer target.

"It's like a candy store," Iuteri agreed.

D'Amato had other pressing business but planned to stick around until they "popped the deal" and cut up the proceeds. As they left the coffee shop, Brennan began singing a song they'd heard at a show at the Ala Moana the previous night that featured the phrase "aloha Hawaii."

"No, you have the words wrong," D'Amato said. "The words are 'rip off Hawaii.'" He sang a bar substituting those lyrics, and they cracked up.

Back at the pool, Iuteri and D'Amato belted out the revised song, breaking into a jig by the poolside and snapping their fingers. The ecstatic mood carried over into the evening. The agents felt a kind of awe for Kitzer's stamina and alcohol tolerance, the way he could stay out drinking until three in the morning and rise and be dressed for meetings at eight. At times they thought he'd passed out in his room and figured that they were safe to slip out and work on their reports—but the next morning Kitzer would ask them, "Where did you go last night? I couldn't find you when I got up from my nap." His memory was remarkable—who had been sitting at a table, and where, and what had been said—even after four or five Scotches.

During the daytime, the promoters combated the heat with steady poolside rounds of cold beer. Brennan and Wedick experimented with different strategies for handling the constant drinking. Brennan told the waiter to take away half-full pints. Wedick wandered off and deposited his beer on a table on the far side of the pool. Other times they dumped their brews anyplace that was convenient and inconspicuous. The agents joked that the government would later face a lawsuit over the number of plants they'd killed by flooding them with alcohol.

Everyone kept a wary eye on Iuteri, who evinced little interest in the promoters' careful preparations. When Kitzer asked him a question, drilling each actor for his role, Iuteri would pause and say "Okay" before hesitantly replying. He used words like *anywheres*. The contrast with Kitzer, whom Brennan thought of as "an artist at talking," was vivid.

Once, sitting by the Ala Moana swimming pool, the promoters watched a pair of young women settle into lounge chairs nearby. The men wore flowered shirts and bathing suits that, according to the fashion of the day, covered only their upper thighs. A shirtless Iuteri walked into the girls' field of vision, dropped to the deck, and knocked out a set of push-ups. Kitzer and the Junior G-Men snickered; they started calling him "Bimbo" and "Bimbo Boy."

Beneath the booze and banter, Brennan and Wedick couldn't shake a simmering tension. The FBI's lack of oversight and rules for undercover agents left open the question of what kind of crimes they could participate in or observe and ignore. But at the start of OpFoPen, Wedick and Brennan had decided that they would interrupt any crime in progress. This might mean warning banks not to accept Seven Oak paper or finding other ways to discourage marks. The previous October, after learning of Kitzer's new vehicle from Howard, the agents had contacted Scotland Yard about Seven Oak.

The trick was to avoid triggering Kitzer's suspicion that someone was ratting him out—and the Kealoha scheme was particularly challenging in that regard. If they asked local FBI agents to come and start asking questions, the promoters might suspect that Wedick and Brennan were snitches. But if they did nothing, Kealoha would lose another $80,000.

At nine-thirty the next morning, Kitzer was sitting at a poolside table with Brennan and Wedick when Iuteri appeared, looking bleary-eyed. He and D'Amato had been out late partying, and Kealoha had roused them at six a.m.

"Did you do your appraisal?" Kitzer asked.

"Yeah. I went out there and kicked some dirt around."

Brennan asked whether he'd purchased new boots for the job, and Iuteri laughed and said he'd poked at the concrete with his shoes and waved his hands around. He and D'Amato had admired the location, across from the beach. Kealoha had offered to make the architect available, but Iuteri had said that wouldn't be necessary. He had asked just one question: "This is the site where the building is supposed to come up?" After less than thirty minutes, Iuteri recounted, he'd said, "Okay, Jimmy, it's done."

Iuteri had appraised the property at $9.75 million, as instructed. Squinting in the morning sun, he told Kitzer and the others that he would've spouted out any number Kealoha had asked for in order to get his $25,000.

"That's the extent of your appraisal?" Kitzer asked. "[For] $25,000?"

"Yeah, that's it."

"When are you going to write it?"

"I'll get it done later," Iuteri said, plopping onto a seat. "Get me a drink."

Kitzer cringed and exchanged looks with the Junior G-Men: *Bimbo Boy is at it again.* Kitzer had vouched for the guy. "That's a good price for an MAI appraisal," he'd told Kealoha. "The man is not robbing you, I'll tell you that. That's a hell of a good price."

Kealoha had gone along with everything the promoters asked for, and D'Amato had in return given him a "pre-advice letter" from the Eurotrust—a document recommending a $10 million long-term loan. This was a promoter's confection—a meaningless document that appeared to move Kealoha a step closer to a loan. Still, he might be able to use it to delay foreclosure.

Iuteri said D'Amato was at Kealoha's bank, First Hawaiian, making a presentation about the Eurotrust. The four of them sat for a while, and as the hour tilted toward noon, D'Amato arrived by the pool with Kealoha. Kitzer sat up and asked how it had gone.

"Fantastic," D'Amato said.

They looked pleased. Kealoha excused himself to make a call, and Kitzer eyed D'Amato. "Tell me what happened," he said.

D'Amato recounted that he'd delivered his full spiel at First Hawaiian—including, of course, flashing the phony CDs in his briefcase. "Their eyes got big," D'Amato said.

The First Hawaiian bankers had tentatively agreed to provide short-term financing.

"All right," Kitzer said. "Let's see what happens."

The agents were developing a grudging admiration for Kitzer's operation, in which, they now understood, there were three tiers of participants. Kitzer himself formed the top level, as the operator of Seven Oak or whatever vehicle he was running at the time.

The second tier of the operation included the brokers—people who sold his fraudulent paper. The brokers lived in cities like Charlotte and Miami and New York, connecting with victims and taking their money and forwarding half of it to Phil. Brokers swarmed Kitzer because of his unique ability to make a vehicle stand up. Sometimes brokers even put up seed money to help him start a new briefcase bank, once an old one had been "blown out" by overexposure or an investigation.

The third tier comprised the people who paid for the paper, and that was where things got interesting. Some were unwitting victims: Jimmy Kealoha types. But many others who bought Kitzer's paper were co-conspirators of a sort.

John Kaye was one such person. A septuagenarian from Marietta, Ohio, Kaye ran a company called Globe Natural Gas and had recently paid $10,000 for a $100,000 certificate of deposit from Seven Oak through a broker, Tom Bannon. Kitzer had instructed Bannon to tell Kaye that he should never present the CD to a bank—it was to be used on his balance sheet only. Kaye had to know that he was getting a fraudulent certificate: No legitimate bank would hand out a $100,000 CD for $10,000. The idea was that Kaye, in turn, would try to victimize a bank—to obtain a loan that he otherwise would be unlikely to obtain.

Kitzer's meetings with brokers had three purposes: First, everyone involved needed to understand what they were trying to do, and how they were going to do it. Second, he would have "a more or less pep talk on what they're going to have to tell bankers whenever they start dealing with banks about this letter of credit," Brennan later recounted. And third, they planned their cover story—which would start with a declaration of how eager they were to cooperate with the FBI because they certainly hadn't intended to do anything wrong.

Kitzer made countless thousands of dollars providing a "reader" service, or a phony reference. Say Kealoha wanted to check out Seven Oak before Kitzer used his letters of credit to buy up the condos. Kitzer would produce a list of bankers who would tell Kealoha, "Yes, we have done business with them, and they live up to their obligations." Kealoha would have no idea that he was speaking to other promoters. For a fee, Kitzer would also send Chase Manhattan a telex falsely informing the bank that John Kaye maintained an account of $200,000—to try to jiggle loose a loan. He could also arrange for confirmation from a major European bank—the more you were willing to pay, the more credible the reference. For $3,000, Kitzer could obtain the imprimatur of the venerable Union Bank of Switzerland—a real institution he had "wired" with a corrupt banker.

"What is your price?" Kitzer would ask. "If you've got the money, we will give you confirmation. How much do you have? How important is it to you?"

Kitzer's careful planning aside, there was something maddening about how gullible Hawaii's former lieutenant governor was. Iuteri's appraisal was laughable, and D'Amato's promised takeout letter was scarcely more believable. Kitzer knew from his years in the insurance business that an authentic takeout commitment involved extensive underwriting that required three to six months of work. The agents believed that anyone who possessed the common sense of a houseplant could have detected a problem. But Kealoha didn't just *want* to believe what the promoters were telling him—he *needed* to.

Later that day, D'Amato brought Kealoha the letter promising a long-term loan. Kealoha planned to go to his home in Hilo the next day to pick up a cashier's check for $80,000. Iuteri groused that he'd done his part and wanted his $25,000, even though he hadn't written the appraisal yet. The others told him to be patient, rolling their eyes at Dim Lightbulb Boy—Brennan had thought up that nickname—and explained that running a successful scam was about knowing when to push and when to sit and wait.

The promoters awoke on March 29 anticipating a payday. They gathered at the pool just after noon and ordered beers in advance of a meeting with Kealoha at one p.m. But at 12:45, the overcast sky opened and rain pummeled the pool area, scattering the group.

When the downpour relented, Kitzer and the Junior G-Men decided to go find Iuteri and D'Amato. The threesome strung out as they walked the hotel's hushed, carpeted hallways toward their room, Brennan a few paces ahead of the others. Brennan knocked when he reached room 1022, and Iuteri instantly snapped it open. Bimbo Boy stared at them for a beat, then stepped into the hall.

"Get lost," he said in a hoarse whisper. His face was flushed. "The feds are here."

They looked past him, into the room. Phil saw two men talking to D'Amato.

"And don't go to your rooms," Iuteri hissed. "In case the FBI is looking for you, too."

12

The Parking Lot Fugitive

MARCH 29, 1977

The rain had not been part of the plan. All morning, Wedick and Brennan had tried to think through every potential glitch in their plot to derail the Kealoha deal. A tropical storm on the cusp of the day's big meeting hadn't entered their thoughts.

The question of how to disrupt the scam without dynamiting Operation Fountain Pen had preoccupied Brennan and Wedick for days before they finally hit on an idea: What if local FBI agents turned up at the Ala Moana—but pretended to know nothing about the flimflam in progress? They just needed to rattle Kealoha enough to coax him into calling off the deal. Their thunderclap of inspiration had been the Fontainebleau Hotel. Newspapers back east had covered D'Amato's potential acquisition, so the Honolulu agents could credibly claim they were looking into the suspicious-sounding European trust. To backfill the story, Brennan and Wedick called the mainland and requested that their colleagues in Miami, Cleveland, and Southern California seek out anyone they knew connected to the fraternity and ask about the Eurotrust. The undercover agents figured that D'Amato would hear that the FBI was poking around and would assume that someone had told the bureau he was in Hawaii.

Wedick had slipped away that morning to meet with Gerry Lonergan, a Honolulu-based FBI agent, in a shopping area of the Ala Moana Hotel. Lonergan was dumbfounded that Wedick and Brennan had managed to persuade the FBI to fly them to Hawaii in

Kitzer's company. The bureau famously forbade agents from traveling to Hawaii and Las Vegas because of the likelihood that they would turn their trip into a vacation. "This is incredible," Lonergan said after listening to Wedick's description. "They're gonna make a movie out of this."

They formulated a plan for several agents to appear at the meeting with Kealoha—but Wedick stressed that they should not say a word about the ongoing scheme to defraud the former lieutenant governor.

The plan seemed watertight, but Wedick and Brennan spent the morning feeling queasy with angst. Wedick felt like a GI hunkered down across enemy lines, about to call in air strikes on his own position. He had no idea how the promoters would react, or if they would buy the Fontainebleau story.

And then the skies blew open and everyone scattered after making loose plans to regroup when the weather cleared. Exasperated, Brennan and Wedick huddled to figure out their next play, and Wedick slipped away to find Lonergan. When they ran into each other near an elevator bank, Wedick handed over D'Amato's room number.

Back at the pool, Kitzer and the Junior G-Men discussed the potential reasons for the FBI visit. Kitzer seemed unperturbed—but he looked closely at Wedick.

"You know what's weird?" he said. "One of those agents looked exactly like you."

Wedick had noticed it, too. It was eerie. The three of them had taken one long look inside the room before Iuteri shooed them off. One of the agents could have been Wedick's twin—the same mustache, dark hair, lean. Wedick felt a twinge of exasperation. He and Brennan had gone through endless contortions to avoid suspicion, but a Wedick doppelgänger? How do you game-plan for *that*?

There was a lilt in Kitzer's voice—a question, maybe a challenge. Wedick shook his head and pulled on a tobacco pipe, popular in the day, that he sometimes puffed on. A wave of agitation spiked through him—a sensation that had grown familiar over the past six weeks. But he reminded himself that this was just a strange coincidence. A weird, irritating one, but still. He was J.J. Wedick, president of Executive Enterprises of South Bend, Indiana.

"Yeah, Phil, well, you know," he said, smirking, "I haven't decided to join the FBI just yet."

They all chuckled and sat back. After a half hour, Kitzer said, "I'm going to call and find out what's going on."

"It's all clear," D'Amato told him. "Come on up."

He and Iuteri looked wan when they answered the door.

"I think it's my deal in Miami, the Fontainebleau, that's bringing the heat," D'Amato said.

Hearing this, Wedick and Brennan felt a wave of relief that they tried not to show. The five of them walked back down and resumed their places by the pool while D'Amato elaborated. The Honolulu-based agents had wanted to know about the Eurotrust and the Fontainebleau. D'Amato said he'd referred the feds to the trust's lawyer in Boston and had blown some smoke—claimed he didn't know the backers. He said he'd done lots of work for the Eurotrust before and believed it was legitimate, and he'd asked the FBI to tell him if they knew otherwise.

Kitzer sat quietly for a few moments, blowing streams of smoke from a filtered Pall Mall. Then he said that regardless of what the bureau knew, the promoters should now assume that a couple of things would happen. Those agents would eventually find out what D'Amato was doing in Hawaii; then they would go see the Kealohas—and when that happened, Phil said, "Jimmy and Mama will tell them everything that we ever told them."

He proposed that they reach the Kealohas first and tell them that the FBI was trying to kill their deal—to prey on their anxieties about losing the commitment. That way, he might be able to control them. Kitzer also pointed out that those same FBI agents would probably get search warrants for their rooms, which jolted the promoters into action. D'Amato turned to Iuteri and said, "Let's go up and get the papers."

They scrambled from the lounge chairs. Kitzer stood and left as well, and all three returned minutes later with piles of papers. Iuteri, in a fit of paranoia, had unbuttoned his flowered shirt, tucked some documents into his pants, and rebuttoned his shirt over it. Kitzer handed the Junior G-Men some Seven Oak letters of credit and stationery, telling them to rip everything up. On the other side of the table, D'Amato and Iuteri shredded Eurotrust stationery. The promoters destroyed their phone messages, too, and then everyone dumped the torn documents into the trash bin by the pool. Kitzer gave his address book to Brennan to hold on to. He figured that since his protégés hadn't yet assumed roles in the Kealoha plot, the FBI wouldn't hassle them.

But he was still working over the situation. Kitzer turned to D'Amato. "I don't know," he said. "It seems funny to me that just a half hour ago you were over in this bank in Hawaii. You leave that bank and everything is supposed to be so grand and great there, and the next thing we turn around and have the FBI here. I think maybe that bank brought down the FBI based on your trust coming out of [Europe]."

Kitzer said the FBI had been circulating flyers encouraging bankers to report any contact with foreign banks doing business in the States. "They put one out on me on Mercantile," he said.

Then he proposed a darker theory: Someone in the group was an informant. As that thought sank in, the Kealohas arrived. The agents felt grateful for this respite as they all stood and moved to a shaded area behind the bar.

"Jimmy," Kitzer began, "how well do you know this bank that Andy was just at this morning?"

"I know that bank, I've done business with them. They're nice people."

"Is there any reason, Jimmy, that bank would want to hurt you or kill your project or anything?"

"No, I can't imagine anything."

"Listen, I want to tell you what just happened here. A half hour ago, the FBI was here in Mr. Iuteri and Mr. D'Amato's room. They came in, they want to know about this trust. Now, Jimmy, there must be something wrong with your project. There must be something wrong with you. Is the FBI investigating you?" Again, Kitzer was deploying his skill with gaslighting, deflecting blame.

Kealoha blanched and shook his head. Kitzer suggested that instead maybe Ronnie Yee, the real estate lawyer, had tipped off the bureau.

Kealoha didn't necessarily believe that, either, but he was at a loss. He finally said, "Well, I'll call the FBI."

The promoters exchanged looks. "Wait a minute," D'Amato said. "Don't."

Kitzer pointed out that the FBI would undoubtedly contact *him* if they wanted to speak to him. Then he proposed that they go over what Kealoha should say if the agents returned.

Kealoha agreed to parrot Kitzer's version of events. Wedick and Brennan were again struck by the spell Kitzer held over him, through some alchemy of need and desperation and salesmanship. The couple eventually departed, and the promoters moved back into the sun and ordered drinks. Kitzer sat with his back to the bar, facing the pool, the others spread out around him around a circular table.

They were puzzling through their next steps when Kitzer stopped talking. He was watching a knot of middle-aged men in flowered shirts—everyone, including FBI agents, dressed that way in Hawaii—wending through knots of tourists, heading in their direction.

"Okay, fellows," Kitzer said. "Here they come. Don't move."

Iuteri swung his chair around to look, then popped up. D'Amato did the same, and both of them hustled toward the hotel's cavernous interior. Brennan, acting instinctively, also jumped up. The herd was moving.

"Where are you going?" Kitzer said.

"I'm going to the parking lot."

"Oh, you're going to be the fugitive in the parking lot, huh?" Kitzer said, laughing. "You don't think they can find you over there?"

Kitzer and Wedick stayed put and watched while Brennan hovered uncertainly near his chair. The mystery men came within fifteen feet of the table and stopped. After looking around, they turned and walked back out. Wedick stifled an urge to laugh: Whoever those guys were, they had nothing to do with the FBI; they were probably just newly arrived tourists who had taken a wrong turn. D'Amato and Iuteri, watching from a distance, crept back.

"I thought that was it," Iuteri said. "I thought we were gone."

"Yeah," D'Amato said. "I thought they were back."

"What did you run for?" Kitzer said, chortling. "Where did you think you were going to run to on this island? It's only ten miles wide."

"That's the natural reaction back in New York," Iuteri said, and everyone laughed.

"I'm getting off this island and going back to Los Angeles," said D'Amato, now clearly rattled.

Kitzer noted that, as far as the U.S. government was concerned, there was no difference between Hawaii and California. "Andy, you don't think the FBI can arrest you in Los Angeles?" he said, chuckling.

If they were going to be arrested, he said, it would look better in court if they weren't trying to flee. In fact, if an arrest seemed imminent, they should just surrender, because then they would have an easier time posting bail and mounting a defense. Kitzer then began teasing Brennan about running away. The Golden Bear now had a second nickname: the Parking Lot Fugitive.

Kitzer called Kealoha the next day and asked to meet to go over the former lieutenant governor's statements to the FBI. Then he pulled Wedick and Brennan aside and told them that since they weren't participants in the deal—they were just there to learn—they were better off not taking part. As far as the FBI knew, they had nothing to do with it.

That night, the promoters' festive mood seemed to have lifted away on the whispery South Pacific winds. Iuteri was upset about the recent developments and said that if the FBI arrested them, Jimmy and Mama wouldn't live to testify against him. Ronnie Yee, either. He believed Yee was the rat.

Kitzer stopped him. Look, he said, Jimmy Kealoha is seventy—he and his wife would probably die of old age before they had a chance to testify. And there were plenty of other ways the promoters could wiggle free.

That wasn't Iuteri's way. In 1965, he said, he'd been indicted in New York for the murders of three New Jersey men at an after-hours drinking club he co-owned. He spent eighteen months in jail awaiting trial but beat the charges when his employees told the police that the men had been robbing the place. He also claimed to run a shylock-loan business in New York City that netted millions. On one occasion, he said, he drove to the house of someone who owed money, tossed gasoline into the foyer, then held up a box of matches and demanded payment.

Some tourists took seats nearby, interrupting Iuteri's grim monologue. Brennan excused himself to call his commodities broker, a ploy he frequently used to phone Indianapolis to call in the kinds of leads Iuteri had just provided. Over time he'd expanded on this ruse, weaving in details from his work at Lind-Waldock about trainloads of pork bellies headed out of Chicago. His contact kept him on the winning end of trades. The promoters appreciated these anecdotes.

Kitzer, meanwhile, headed out to meet with the Kealohas. Sitting across from Jimmy, he adopted a serious demeanor. Now that the FBI was involved, he warned, no Hawaiian bank would fund the condo project. "It will not happen," Kitzer said. He added, "If any-thing scares a banker, it's the FBI."

Kealoha looked crestfallen. "Phil, what can I do?"

Kitzer flipped to good cop. All was not lost if they found financing elsewhere—and, fortunately, he had a Swiss-banker acquaintance, Jean-Claude Cornaz. "I have reason to believe that with Andy's takeout, he would fund your project," Kitzer said.

Kealoha quickly agreed, not knowing, of course, that Cornaz would only produce more fraudulent paper.

"Now, Jimmy," Phil said, "if you took this money from the Bank of Hawaii, they would charge you a fee."

"Absolutely."

"Mr. Cornaz will want a fee, too, for funding."

"Oh, I can appreciate that."

"Okay. Just a minute."

Kitzer excused himself and called D'Amato, who loved the new angle, partly because he'd wanted to work with Cornaz, a long-time con man who had a stellar reputation within the Fraternity. This was a particularly elegant outcome for Phil; John Calandrella had already offered to pay his airfare to Europe to work on some other deals. Kitzer then confirmed everything with Cornaz, who requested that they all meet in Frankfurt.

The Kealohas left to book flights for themselves, D'Amato, and Iuteri.

D'Amato was giddy. "You *sprechen Sie Deutsch*?" he said to Phil.

The agents were significantly less enthralled. They'd worked to get clearance for Copenhagen, and once again Kitzer had zigged when they'd expected him to zag. They would leave in less than forty-eight hours—far too little time to work out diplomatic clearance with West Germany. And they had no plausible excuse not to go.

———

They sat by the pool at around ten the next morning, March 31. Hotel guests drifted to nearby chairs with towels and tubes of Coppertone. Kitzer explained why Cornaz was the perfect solution: When the deal went bad for the Kealohas, Kitzer would claim he'd had no idea the Swiss banker was a fraud. And Cornaz, of course, was outside the FBI's jurisdiction.

Brennan and Wedick nodded, suppressing their dismay. They were sure they'd be able to spook Kealoha into abandoning the deal. Still, they couldn't help but admire Kitzer's resourcefulness.

The group scattered as the day wore on. Iuteri and D'Amato left Hawaii, having made plans for Frankfurt. Kitzer, set to depart the next day with the Junior G-Men, disappeared with Ruby. Brennan and Wedick, who'd barely stepped outside the hotel during their time in Hawaii, decided to take advantage of a rare afternoon to themselves. They barreled off in a rental car and pretended to be tourists, sweeping through Pearl Harbor and kicking some sand on a few beaches. But they felt distracted and uneasy amid the throngs of lei-wearing vacationers. When it came to tripping up Kitzer, they were stumped.

The agents split up at around six the next morning. Jack took off with Kitzer's address book, which was filled with scraps of paper, notes, and messages. He planned to copy as many entries as possible—and needed to do it somewhere away from the Ala Moana because of Kitzer's tendency to burst into their room unannounced. Wedick's task was to dictate an update on the Kealoha situation and mail the cassette to Indianapolis before they left town.

They'd developed a system for their 302s, reports detailing what they'd learned from their subjects that could later be useful as evidence. They roughed out what the report should include together, and then one of them either recorded it or called it in to a stenographer. Deeghan cleaned up the language and passed it on to Lowie. The 302 would then go to all relevant FBI offices around the country: *This is OpFoPen. We're in Honolulu. This morning we met with Andy D'Amato and Mark Iuteri and discussed fraud against Jimmy Kealoha. D'Amato will provide a phony takeout commitment.* Each respective FBI office—for example, Miami for Iuteri's firebombing incident—would pursue the fresh leads. All of this helped validate what the undercover agents were doing.

Wedick was distracted by the day's travel plans. The bureau still had no idea of Kitzer's itinerary change. The agents had held off on telling anyone back home, hoping Kitzer would change his mind about going to Frankfurt. As government agents conducting business in a foreign country, Brennan and Wedick were required to notify the host nation by, at minimum, presenting customs officials with maroon government passports. But with Phil, the agents carried only blue civilian passports—and would be breaking the law by violating West Germany's sovereignty.

Worse, West Germany was roiling with domestic terrorism: A leftist militant group called Baader-Meinhof, or the Red Army Faction, had recently been hijacking airplanes and kidnapping businessmen and politicians. The West Germans were particularly vigilant about screening for anyone in the country illegally, and the agents feared that this extra layer of scrutiny would lead Frankfurt airport personnel to identify them in front of Kitzer. Wedick and Brennan had few good choices.

Wedick figured he had at least a couple of hours of quiet before heading off to the airport to begin that journey. He entered the elevator, figuring he'd hole up somewhere outside the hotel complex. But when the door opened in the lobby, Kitzer was waiting to get on.

"Phil!" Wedick blurted. His hand reflexively brushed the pocket where he'd stashed the recorder.

Kitzer's eyes widened. He stepped into J.J.'s personal space. "Oh my God, I was just going to find you," he said. "Brennan was arrested."

Wedick stared at Kitzer, trying to read him. His mind churned. *This could be bad,* Wedick thought.

"Come on, we've gotta make a call," Kitzer said, waving him out of the elevator. "We've got to get some bail going." He suggested they strategize in the Ala Moana coffee shop.

Wedick watched him. Kitzer looked worried, his eyebrows knitted close.

But at the coffee shop entrance, Kitzer spun toward him and roared, "April Fools'!" Then he laughed and pointed at Wedick in a way that said, *Gotcha!*

Wedick stood there shaking his head. He hadn't realized it was April 1.

13

The Cold Plunge

APRIL 1, 1977

When they reached the ticket counter at the airport, Kitzer suggested that they book a flight on Lufthansa that circumnavigated the globe en route to Frankfurt, stopping in Asia and the Middle East. Although he'd been almost everywhere, he'd never returned from Hawaii by flying west, and he thought it would be a fun three-day adventure.

The agents were stuck. It was Friday evening back in Indianapolis, and the chances of getting the wheels of bureaucracy creaking to life were nil. Without any other option in sight, they bought their tickets and settled in for the first leg to Tokyo, which offered the kind of coach-class comfort and festive spirit that no longer exists in modern aviation. The 747 featured a bar in the back where stewardesses hovered, so Kitzer naturally gravitated there to chat and buy drinks. Soon the strangers around them became new-old friends, pulling out pictures of their kids and laughing at Kitzer's stories.

Wedick and Brennan tried to relax. Tapping into Phil's joie de vivre, they chortled about Dim Lightbulb Boy and the Parking Lot Fugitive. Phil imitated how Brennan, when he was trying to remember something, squinched his right eye while simultaneously raising his left eyebrow. They roared about the way Kitzer drew Wedick into barstool conversations with women, even though—or especially because—he resisted it.

Brennan had on his Golden Bear shirt, and Wedick wore a blue Fire Department of New York shirt with a hook-and-ladder emblem his father had given him. It was a favorite, and Kitzer teased him about the fraying seams—Wedick was literally wearing it out.

Wedick, in turn, called Phil "Phillip," in a mock scolding-parent way, and slipped into his gravelly-voiced Bronx persona: "Ay! Not for nuttin', but I told youse to move that freakin' car already." They called out his malapropisms—"An apple doesn't fall from the tree" and "I was very squirmish about that."

They headed out to stretch their legs after checking into a hotel in Tokyo, and Wedick handed someone a camera for a picture. He was wearing Kitzer's leather jacket, something he did frequently after finding that the coat was comfortable and looked good on him. The image snapped that day shows the three of them back-dropped by spring greenery, Kitzer between the two younger men, their arms wrapped around one another's shoulders. Brennan is wearing a wide smile and a white button-down, his hair spilling across his forehead, and is leaning into Kitzer. Phil looks dapper in his other leather jacket, his hair combed rakishly, a hand draped over Wedick's left shoulder, index finger slightly raised. They look like three friends in the throes of a rollicking adventure.

When they headed out that evening, Kitzer was electrified. His plan was to plunge into the Ginza district, which was legendary for its nightlife. The agents, who'd never been to Japan, blinked at the city's incandescence—the sheer volume of neon pushing back at the darkness. There were bars stacked atop bars along the packed streets, and Kitzer's face both reflected and amplified the city's wattage. Brennan wore a plaid blazer; Wedick and Kitzer had on shirts with oversized collars layered over the top of their leather jackets, per the fashion of the time.

The agents spotted cops everywhere, which made them nervous. They had zero sense of Japanese customs—and spending time with Kitzer was like skiing a few miles per hour faster than your abilities dictated, constantly hovering on the edge of a stupendous wipeout. Brennan and Wedick had heard a story about when Kitzer lived in Florida in 1970. He'd bought a forty-foot Thunderbird Formula 400 speedboat and took a friend out the day it was delivered. He knew nothing about boats, and the friend offered to peruse the manual, but Phil snatched it and threw it into the water. Then he gunned the engine, ignoring the NO WAKE ZONE signs. Once they hit the Atlantic, he pushed the throttle to its limit, the boat skittering over the open water, Kitzer looking ecstatic. Somewhere out on the Atlantic, the friend noticed a red light pulsating on the control panel. Had Kitzer checked the engine fluids? Should he ease up?

"Ah, don't worry about it!" he bellowed, smiling rapturously.

The red light glared as the boat hammered over the chop, and the friend began to wonder about how far a distress signal could carry. Kitzer, sufficiently sated, eventually steered the craft back to its slip. Hours later, back home, he took a call from the harbormaster. His expensive new toy was resting on the harbor's sandy floor.

Kitzer didn't blink. He told the harbormaster to hold the line, saying he wanted to set up a conference call. He then dialed in his insurance agent and introduced the two men, saying they had something in common and needed to talk. He then told the harbormaster to explain what had happened with the boat and hung up. Kitzer seemed no more put out than if he'd discovered a hole in his sock. On to the next toy. He was a present-day version of Edgar Allan Poe's Imp of the Perverse, giving in to the compulsion to do something wrong simply for the rush of doing it.

Phil picked a bar, and they squeezed in around a table adjacent to a woman sitting alone. The agents felt stretched far beyond their comfort zone. Wedick and Kitzer ducked into the bathroom and were shocked to see both a man and a woman inside. They stopped abruptly, thinking they'd walked in on something, but the couple barely noticed them while they washed their hands. Apparently, the restrooms were coed. Kitzer and Wedick looked at each other and laughed.

Back at the diminutive table, they squinted at their surroundings. Brennan's shoulder was pressed against that of a guy in a business suit at the next table who spoke some English. On the opposite side, Phil tried striking up a conversation with the neighboring woman, who was gorgeous: long hair, high cheekbones, stunning smile. But she spoke only Japanese.

The waiter tried to help the foreigners along with his few words of English. The three men attempted to order Scotch, which was an ordeal of loudly pronounced words and pantomimes, but the waiter brought them a pitcher of some other alcoholic beverage. Kitzer rejected this as plainly wrong—he wanted a highball with ice. He shrugged in mock outrage, and the beautiful woman, watching, smiled back. Then she leaned over and poured three drinks into their glasses.

Kitzer now no longer cared about his Cutty Sark. Seeing this act of neighborly kindness as an invitation, he reached for her hand. She offered it up, and he kissed it with a small bow. The waiter hovered nearby, seeming eager to communicate something but incapable of doing it. Kitzer ignored him. The tables were so close together that he merely had to lean to enter the Japanese beauty's personal space. After more failed attempts at verbal communication, he moved in for a kiss.

At that moment, the room erupted. The maître d' came running over, yelling in Japanese, and chased the woman out. The three of them looked at one another in astonishment.

"Hell, that's not right," Kitzer said. "Let's go over there. Who is that guy?"

Brennan's neighbor bumped his elbow. "That girl," the man said, leaning toward Brennan. "She was a *he*."

Jack looked at him, puzzled for a moment; then it hit him: The woman was a transvestite, and probably a prostitute—which explained the staff's reaction. Jack told the others, and he and Wedick exploded with laughter.

Kitzer joined them, but less enthusiastically. Wedick was already grinning at him and shaking his head, and Kitzer knew that it would not be the last he would hear of this.

Hong Kong was merely a refueling stop, so they hoped they'd have an opportunity to explore Bangkok, but when they touched down the airport seemed to be sliding into chaos. Several months earlier, Thailand's military had responded to student protests with a massacre, then staged a coup, leaving the economy in a slag heap and the nation palpably tense. Airport employees stood around, listening to a loud, shrill speech being piped in. Kitzer and the agents looked at the scene uncomfortably, not understanding a word of the diatribe but surmising that it would be wise not to venture out.

Karachi, Pakistan, was another refueling stop. As the plane prepared to leave, the final passenger to board dropped to his knees and kissed the floor. When Brennan asked for his story, the guy explained that he worked for a transport company in New York that had sent a cargo ship. The Pakistanis wouldn't unload it because of a labor dispute, so the guy had been dispatched to try to settle it. But then someone put a knife to his neck and he was held hostage for eighteen days; his captors had just released him ahead of their flight.

It was as if Kitzer and the agents had signed up for a tour of the world's testiest geopolitical squabbles. They next flew to Athens, where airport officials were on the alert for hijacking attempts by the Popular Front for the Liberation of Palestine (and, indeed, six months later, the terrorist group would take hostages on another Lufthansa flight). Brennan watched armed guards in jeeps surround the plane as it pulled up. They hadn't expected to leave the aircraft, but airport personnel refused to refuel the plane until everybody on board had exited. The stewardesses piped up with instructions: *Do not stand in large groups inside the terminal.* Clusters of people made more attractive targets for gunmen.

The terminal was eerily empty, and the counters were mostly unattended. Kitzer, Wedick, and Brennan split off from the other passengers and hunkered in a recessed corner, their senses alive and alert, as if they were Neanderthals clustered around a fire, listening to the sounds of an incomprehensible new world. Airport employees on a balcony pointed down at them. As they kept vigil, the conversation tilted toward the personal, Phil revealing some details about his life off the road. His wife, Audrey, was a farmer's daughter from southern Minnesota who'd been a stewardess on one of his flights to Miami in the 1960s. She was nearly a decade younger, but he was fun and dazzling. Soon after they were married a son, Jeffrey, arrived. They lived in an old run-down farmhouse in tiny Ellendale, near where she grew up, south of Minneapolis. She taught Sunday school and competed in a bowling league.

Audrey was near her parents there, which was important because Kitzer was gone most of the time. Kitzer tried to blend in, but that was tricky for a Chicago guy who traveled the world, meeting with bankers and businessmen, not to mention high-finance swindlers. Ellendale folks noticed when, in a bar, he flipped through a wad of hundred-dollar bills—one local would later describe it as "big enough to choke a horse"—then asked for change. People talked about the time he went to buy a TV and pulled out his money and a roll of thousand-dollar bills spilled onto the floor.

He'd told Audrey's father, Lawrence Jensen, that he was a broker in the finance industry, and no one pressed him beyond that. Jensen believed that if a man didn't want to tell him his business, then he wouldn't ask. Kitzer tucked a telex machine into an upstairs bedroom closet and otherwise projected to this modest middle-American world the image of a successful businessman. When he was around, Kitzer was good to Audrey and Jeffrey and was a steady provider, and he spent every Christmas at home. She appreciated that he'd agreed to live in her beloved hometown.

Kitzer didn't tell them about the dark secrets lurking in his past.

A decade earlier, on March 20, 1967, the central characters in the collapse of American Allied Insurance went on trial in federal court in Bismarck, North Dakota. The Kitzers had successfully petitioned for a move from Minneapolis, where, they'd argued, they couldn't get an impartial jury. A local newspaper described the pending drama as "sensational" and noted "an air of excitement" for the "big-city trial."

The prosecutors aimed to portray the Kitzer empire as an exotic pyramid scheme, one insolvent firm propping up another for the purpose of getting rich. "This case involves bribery, blackmail, payoffs and corruption," U.S. Attorney Patrick Foley told the jury. He described one of the Kitzers' businesses as their "personal checking account."

"They stole, they gypped, they plundered, they took," he said.

Several young women testified that Kitzer had invited them on trips to Florida, Puerto Rico, and Mexico. Audrey Jensen said he flew her to Miami twice and bought her a fur coat. Foley charged that the Kitzers took at least $3.7 million in cash from Allied and replaced it with worthless securities—and were "bad people" who had abused the "great concept of social justice" that insurance represented.

The government's chief expert witness, a U.S. Treasury employee, spent more than fifty hours on the stand, trying to explain the dense thicket of Kitzer companies and transactions. The prosecution stretched across a sonorous six weeks. For the Bismarck jury, which the New York Times described as "six North Dakota housewives, three nurses, and three laboring men," this was a lot to digest.

The Kitzers built their defense around one concept: Confuse everyone even more.

When the defense team took its turn, lawyers walked the jury through a jungle of contradictory accounting data. Witnesses opined that the government had declared American Allied insolvent based on a capricious set of accounting principles, arguing that Minnesota's insurance examiners had pointedly undervalued or disregarded legitimate assets to justify crushing the firm. Given more time, they said, the company might have blossomed.

The trial took a bizarre turn when, one day, the lawyer for David Kroman, the president of an American Allied affiliate, informed the judge that Kroman had been discovered by police at four a.m. in a locked car pulled off a road outside Bismarck. Kroman was hefting a loaded shotgun and claimed he'd been forced off the blacktop at gunpoint because he was transporting documents proving that someone other than Lee Harvey Oswald had assassinated John F. Kennedy. The judge declared a mistrial and dispatched Kroman for a mental exam. The four other defendants continued to stand trial, though Magnusson, the insurance commissioner, interrupted the proceedings for a three-day stay in a Bismarck hospital after a fainting spell in his hotel room.

Frank Oliver took over from there. A flamboyant and blustery lawyer representing the younger Kitzer, Oliver sometimes defended mobsters in Chicago while wearing a cape. He claimed the Kitzers were collateral damage in a high-level political plot led by former U.S. attorney Miles Lord. The conspiracy, which included Minnesota's governor and attorney general, had had two goals: to damage Lieutenant Governor Alexander Keith, a former Kitzer employee who harbored ambitions to challenge Governor Karl Rolvaag in a primary, and to get Lord appointed as a federal judge. To accomplish all this, Lord had needed to destroy American Allied. One defense lawyer even gave it a name: Operation Get Kitzer.

To bolster this theory, Oliver, known by some in Chicago as the "Caped Crusader," dragged virtually every key Minnesota political figure to North Dakota to testify, including Rolvaag, who had lost his reelection bid the previous year. When Junior himself, then thirty-four, took the stand, he mesmerized the jury for eight days, portraying himself as a scrappy and striving young businessman who'd been ensnared in a net of political intrigue that reached all the way to the White House.

Kitzer said Lord once sent FBI agents to Chicago banks to inquire into loans made to his businesses, causing the banks to shut down lines of credit and call in loans and forcing the insurance empire to spiral toward receivership. He described a meeting in April 1965 in which Lord, determined to follow through on his plot, grew "very, very angry. He was red hot."

"He asked [David] Kroman, 'Where's the money?' " Kitzer testified. "Kroman asked, 'What money?' Lord said, 'The money of the insurance company.' The questions started coming thick and fast and finally I said, 'Wait a minute.'

"Then [Lord] came out of his chair, slammed the table, and said, 'Don't *wait a minute* me. If you don't like the way I'm running this investigation, you can get out of here.' He said that at the top of his voice. I fell back in my chair. I was scared."

At another point, Kitzer said, Lord "came up to me, took his finger and drove it against my chest." Lord said, "You're going to jail, kid."

Kitzer asked Lord why.

"I don't know, but you're going there."

Kitzer testified, "At that point my mind went blank."

He also claimed that he jokingly offered Lord a job, and Lord replied, "No, kid, I've got bigger things in mind. I'm going to be a federal judge and you're going to be my stepping stone."

Two days later, Kitzer testified, Minnesota Insurance Department examiners began investigating Allied.

Lord also ordered that certain correspondence be destroyed to protect both Rolvaag and Vice President Humphrey, Kitzer claimed.

His richly detailed yarns, told with an air of Shakespearean outrage, pulled the jury's attention away from his financial skullduggery. "You won't let me explain," he complained to Foley. "I thought that's why we came to Bismarck, so we could tell our side of the story. You don't want to know the truth, do you?"

Kitzer bantered, parried, blustered. At times he turned the attorney-witness dynamic upside down. "What is wrong with borrowing money?" Kitzer asked Foley.

When Foley pointed out that the web of businesses was built entirely on loans, Kitzer questioned his patriotism. "Borrowing money to start a business is the American way of life. The only place you can't borrow money to start a business is Russia."

After a grinding, bewildering, often surreal fourteen weeks, the jury began deliberating on Wednesday, June 21. After two and a half days, the jury returned late on Friday afternoon to a tense federal courtroom. The unanimous verdict: not guilty on all counts. The room "erupted into tears and shouts of joy," one reporter wrote.

Kitzer sobbed, covering his face, then triumphantly walked out with his father and attorney.

The state of Minnesota later reduced the campaign-contribution charge for the illegal campaign check and fined him $100. There would be more difficulties to contend with—lawsuits and millions of dollars in claims. But such nuisances were eventually settled for whatever assets remained when the family's companies were liquidated. Kitzer skated off unharmed—if anything, his reputation was burnished by his having survived a showdown with a cast of powerful and prominent politicians. He had even gone out drinking one night in Bismarck, wrecked a rental car, and walked away from it.

Kitzer picked up several lessons from his battle with the government: Confusion is useful. Sleight of hand works. But mostly what he absorbed was that given the chance to tell his story, he could win over the regular folks in the jury box.

In the end, he was the one they believed.

Phil, Jack, and J.J. finally reached Frankfurt on April 4, to yet more heightened security. Soldiers with machine guns marched around the terminal, ready to suppress another terrorist incident. Jack and J.J. were also on high alert. In those pioneering days, the few long-term undercover FBI agents espoused the idea that if they got into a jam and got arrested, they should avoid telling the arresting officer what was going on. To avoid getting exposed, you simply went along with the bust and let FBI officials running the investigation figure out the next move. But they hoped it wouldn't come to that. Acting as nonchalant as possible, the threesome moved through customs, handing over their passports and blending in with tourists and businessmen. They entered West Germany without incident and checked into a suite at the Intercontinental Frankfurt—Phil in one room, J.J. and Jack in another—jet-lagged but exhilarated by their harrowing, epic journey.

J.J. wanted to shake off the mental fog from their travels. He didn't feel up to a run, which would involve navigating unfamiliar foreign streets alone. He flipped through the hotel directory and found a listing for a spa facility. They could sweat out their journey. He pitched the idea to the others and was surprised when they agreed to it, because Phil was not one to exercise (not that the spa required him to elevate his heart rate).

Within minutes they were wrapped in towels and headed into a wood-lined sauna, the stocky Jack next to the reed-thin Phil and J.J. At first, Phil seemed skeptical: Sitting in a hot room with other guys was not an activity he usually sought out. Then a woman walked in, also wearing only a towel, and sat down nearby. The two younger men watched Phil's face light up: *Okay, now this has possibilities.* They hadn't realized it was a communal facility. Phil appeared to be formulating an opening line when the woman stood up and left. He nonetheless joked that the spa was a fine idea, and it was a good thing he'd thought this up. The door opened again, and a tall, blond, and powerful-looking woman wearing a hotel uniform entered, and—in brusque, broken English—ordered them out of the sauna. They weren't following the spa protocol, she said—the specific order in which to do things.

Phil tried to brush her off, but she was having none of it, and she divined from this interaction that he was the leader of their little group. She snatched his arm and led him toward the shower, their next designated stop. Phil began calling her "Sarge" and gave a sarcastic salute. After they'd showered and pulled on bathing suits,

Sarge led them to a small plunge pool. Phil dipped a foot in and yanked it back.

A brief standoff ensued while Phil and Sarge debated the merits of enduring the full spa experience. Jack, meanwhile, studied the pool. It looked shallow enough that if he slipped in, the water would come only to his navel; he could quickly dunk his head and pop back out. *That doesn't seem so bad,* he thought. He broke the impasse and hopped in.

Within a millisecond, he realized his miscalculation. He was immediately fully submerged, and the water was as frigid as anything he'd ever felt—an icy thirty-eight degrees. Jack surfaced like a shipwreck survivor clawing for floating debris, gasping, eyes bulging. He lunged for the ladder and clambered out.

His two friends laughed, and in this moment of inattention Sarge saw her chance. She grabbed Phil and shoved him into the pool. He, too, exploded to the surface, moon-eyed, sucking air into his lungs, yelling that Sarge was going to give him a heart attack.

J.J. wasn't about to wait around to be manhandled. He followed Phil in, leaving Sarge satisfied that her work was done. After the men spent more time in the sauna and showered again, she wrapped them in enormous towels and settled them onto chaise longues, where, within minutes, their skin tingling, the three of them surrendered to a deep, baby-like sleep.

14

The Ha-Ha Certificate

APRIL 5, 1977

"Did you ever find the train station?"

Jean-Claude Cornaz smirked at Phil as he asked the question. They'd just located each other inside the Intercontinental, and both men laughed. Phil turned to Jack and J.J. and told the story. During a previous trip, he'd arrived at Cornaz's office in Geneva to find a handful of Swiss federal police interviewing Cornaz about a recent scam involving the City of Los Angeles. Phil and Cornaz had helped cash a forged $902,000 municipal check, moving the money through a series of European banks before a Lebanese co-conspirator withdrew it in Amsterdam. Phil and Cornaz each collected more than $300,000 for that one.

Seeing the police, Phil, without skipping a beat, asked, "Can anybody tell me where the train station is?"

A cop gave him directions, and Phil walked back out.

As one of Phil's top cronies, Cornaz was the marquee attraction in Frankfurt. A distinguished-looking gray-haired gentleman in his mid-fifties, Cornaz brokered authentic deals for several banks, including the venerable Union Bank of Switzerland, for which, he boasted, he'd once served on the board of directors. He had a reputation as a lawyer who wielded awesome powers in Switzerland's famously lax banking system, capable of manipulating officials into verifying fraudulent securities. He claimed (rather preposterously) that he was the only attorney in Geneva licensed to practice in front of the Swiss Supreme Court.

He liked working with Phil. Their symbiotic criminal relationship had begun in 1970 and included many profitable capers. Whenever Phil opened or purchased a new vehicle, Cornaz provided a $20 million credit reference. And Cornaz could always provide a Swiss banking operative to say, "Yes, Seven Oak is a customer in good standing." Cornaz had made several hundred thousand dollars from Kitzer's Mercantile vehicle alone.

Cornaz's son Pascal, who was in his mid-twenties and had followed his father's career path, was also in Frankfurt, as was Harold Silverkur, a promoter operating a vehicle called Silver Pool in Copenhagen. John Calandrella had flown in, too, with a longtime promoter named Lucy Trajkovski.

The Kealohas hadn't arrived, and Andrew D'Amato and Mark Iuteri were missing, but Phil seemed unfazed. He introduced the Junior G-Men to everyone and explained to Jack and J.J. that he was pleased that so many operators had gathered under one roof—the gathering was a kind of promoter summit. A festive atmosphere pervaded the sleek five-hundred-room Intercontinental, which—as the largest hotel in West Germany—was Kitzer's platonic ideal: vast, showy, and anonymous. The promoters rolled out their latest anecdotes about bribing bank officials and pulling off cons around the world. Calandrella told everyone about two developers who had been sitting in Geneva's Hôtel Bristol for the past month, waiting for paper that would help them land a $14 million loan for a project in the Bahamas. Calandrella had already taken their money, and the financing, of course, would never arrive. Everyone found that hilarious.

The first night, Phil, Jack, and J.J. ran into Calandrella and Trajkovski in the Intercontinental's posh Silhouette supper club, its huge windows offering panoramic views of the neighboring Main River. An elegant woman in her mid-forties, Trajkovski said she was now president of an entity called Val-International and Associates, of Pacific Palisades, California. She claimed to have been secretary to the president of Mexico for several years, during which time she'd obtained an exclusive contract to export fish from nearly five hundred Mexican fishing cooperatives to Japan. This was how she'd met Calandrella, who had worked as a fish broker near Boston.

Trajkovski was intent on launching her fish-export enterprise with one of the more convoluted scams the agents had ever heard of: a "two-for-one deal." The concept was to simultaneously manipulate securities on two continents in order to trick Credit Suisse Bank in Los Angeles into lending her $5 million on zero collateral. On paper, the deal would be collateralized by Seven Oak and guaranteed by the Union Bank of Switzerland. Except for Phil and Trajkovski, everyone at the table struggled to grasp the mechanics of the deal. The agents felt like college freshmen who had wandered into a graduate-level microeconomics class, and they grimaced at the thought of having to explain this one back in Indianapolis.

Calandrella stood and left, and Jack followed. Outside the restroom door, Calandrella mentioned that despite the indecipherable nature of that deal, he was going to make a boatload of easy money in Frankfurt. Jack agreed about how great it was and laughed along with him.

The agents set off alarm bells at FBI headquarters when they reported in from Frankfurt, immediately shifting focus from the progress of the investigation to dealing with the diplomatic breach. Officials wrestled with when to tell the U.S. ambassador to West Germany and how best to avoid creating an embarrassing situation for him. FBI leadership decided to send word of the incident *after* J.J. and Jack had returned home—the United States would have to issue an official apology regardless, so the bureau decided to let the agents' work continue undisturbed.

Jack and J.J. settled into Phil's both-ends-of-the-candle routine. One night, they headed to the St. John's Inn, an English-speaking pub in Frankfurt's lively Sachsenhausen district, where they drank and danced and teased Phil. When Kitzer spotted a woman, J.J. murmured into his ear, "Nah, she's not your type, Phil—let's see, are there any attractive men here?"

They hit several more clubs, engaging in a tug-of-war over each check, before returning to the Intercontinental at one-thirty a.m. to find Calandrella in the lounge with John Packman from Seven Oak. The banker, who'd just flown in from England, was eager to see Phil. Packman said that a group of Seven Oak depositors wanted to withdraw $400,000, which was a problem because their money was gone. Packman was, for the moment, serving as a human shield. But British authorities were constantly sniffing around.

Phil told him not to worry so much. They tried to calculate how many weeks they had left before Seven Oak cratered, and Calandrella interjected that he wanted more paper before the window closed—he had $5 to $7 million worth of deals to push through. Calandrella also mentioned a Copenhagen bank for sale that Phil and the Junior G-Men might obtain for their next vehicle. Nobody wanted an interruption in the flow of paper, he said.

The conversation finally gassed out at around four a.m., but the meetings started again at eight. Brokers or corrupt bankers connected to one scam or another floated in. Jack and J.J. sat at tables with eight or more people, straining to remember conversations and faces and trying to parse the driving forces behind each. It was like puzzling through a Möbius strip of agendas and motives.

One surreal aspect of the proceedings involved the promoters' intramural rivalries. One evening, Trajkovski came downstairs to the dining room at eight. She was introduced to Cornaz and pitched her fish-to-Japan scheme as she ordered dinner. Cornaz agreed to take part and told her to get things rolling on her end—to ask her Los Angeles bankers to send an inquiry for the loan guarantee. Trajkovski left to make the call, and when she returned she said her man was on vacation, so they would have to wait a couple of days—but in the meantime, maybe Cornaz could start the process with Union Bank.

This, Phil explained later, was a ruse. Trajkovski was trying to play Cornaz—to scam him and UBS, too. Cornaz was too seasoned to fall for it.

This kind of *Spy vs. Spy* subterfuge seemed to be the norm. Phil commented that when members of the Fraternity gathered for dinner, everyone ordered extravagant meals and pitched $5 million deals. But when the check came, everyone got up to go to the restroom or to make a call and never returned.

Reeling with a glut of information for their 302s, Jack got a jarring reminder that he and J.J. were vulnerable, too—that Phil was fun, and they'd bonded in a way, but they were also locked into an adversarial relationship. He walked into his room at one point and found Phil on the phone. Phil hung up and said he'd been talking to American Express; he'd found a receipt showing Jack's credit card number among Jack's possessions and wanted to see what he could find out.

This was an ongoing worry for Jack, who was disorganized and prone to misplacing things. His desk in Gary was a scrap heap of paperwork and mail and coffee cups. The AmEx receipt had been a slipup—the kind of mistake he couldn't afford.

Phil said the AmEx representative had refused to divulge any details, but Jack didn't know how to respond. Did Phil suspect something, or was he simply curious about Jack's credit limit so he could mastermind some scheme with it? Jack sometimes felt a tinge of something: Phil seemed vaguely troubled about who he and J.J. were and how they'd suddenly turned up in his life.

Phil was hard to read, partly because he was a skilled, habitual liar. He lied to con his marks, of course, but in the past seven weeks they'd watched him fib to just about everyone else—including them. On days when he woke early, he sometimes roused J.J. and Jack to tell them there were people waiting to meet them in the lobby. After the agents got dressed and headed down, Phil confessed that in fact he'd just wanted company for breakfast. If he didn't want to go outside, he would say that it was raining. He routinely offered letters of credit for 10 percent of face value, and after a client agreed, he would say he'd forgotten an extra fee and jack the price up another few thousand dollars. One of his mottoes seemed to be: *Don't tell the truth if you can avoid it.*

Some part of Phil viewed everything he did as a lark, a massive inside joke. In his room at the Intercontinental, Jack and J.J. looked through a stack of fraudulent Seven Oak CDs Packman had brought to Frankfurt along with the "backup," or confirmation paper, they used to give a financial transaction the appearance of legitimacy. The CD contained the letters "ha" followed by a blank line.

"What's this mean, Phillip?" Jack asked.

Phil explained that the letters were meant to create the word *has* or *have,* as in: "John Kaye has_ deposited $100,000 with Seven Oak." But Phil said he sometimes left the "ha" intact, then wrote the same letters in next to it—making a ha-ha CD. They all laughed at this.

Phil had once considered naming a vehicle the Royal Overseas Bank so he could use the acronym ROB. He liked the idea of leaving clues in plain sight, dangling "little telltale jokes," as Wedick put it, that his marks would recognize later, in forehead-smacking moments, after it was too late. Like 219 Dearborn Corp., his taunt at the FBI.

Of course, the agents lied, too, with the counterintuitive purpose of winning Phil's trust. Maybe some part of him trusted them, as much as he was able to. Given the slippery there/not there quality of truth that permeated Phil's world, all they could do was play their roles as faithful subordinates—and hope.

These were challenging days for the truth. The country was still roiling from Nixon's Watergate lies. In New York City on April 7, as the promoters' meetings wound down in Frankfurt, the FBI faced its own crisis of credibility. A federal grand jury handed up a five-count indictment against John J. Kearney, an FBI supervisor who had overseen the activities of Squad 47, a unit that for years had conducted illegal break-ins and bugging operations during the Weather Underground investigation. (Kearney's indictment was dropped a year later on the grounds that his supervisors had sanctioned his activities.) Morale among many agents plunged. The *New York Times* reported the story on its front page. "It killed us," one agent later recalled. "It just killed us."

Early the next morning, John Calandrella knocked on the agents' door, looking upset. He'd just checked with the front desk and found that in four days, Phil had singlehandedly run up a tab of $1,600 (equivalent to roughly $6,300 in 2017). Calandrella had agreed to pay Phil's expenses through either Lucy Trajkovski or John Kaye, but he feared that both of them would stiff him. Trajkovski had vaporized after her two-for-one deal had fallen through, not even ponying up for a smaller swindle they had arranged involving a $200,000 letter of credit to be funded at the Banco Comercial Mexicano in Tijuana.

Like the other promoters, Calandrella had tried to recruit the Junior G-Men away from Phil with promises of highly profitable work. But Jack and J.J. stuck to their strategy of professing unflagging loyalty to Phil. In their hallway conversation with Calandrella, they pointed out that the Intercontinental was expensive and West Germany was pricey in general. They encouraged him to make good on his promise to pay.

But Jack wasn't surprised when Calandrella approached the table where he and the others sat drinking coffee later that morning. Calandrella asked whether Jack could cover the bill with his American Express; he would pay the money back when they returned to the States. Jack refused. Then Calandrella asked if he could use the card to guarantee a check he planned to present to the hotel. Jack again shook his head. With that, Calandrella packed his bags and said good-bye.

The three of them laughed that Calandrella had accomplished nothing in West Germany except annoying people. As they talked about the day's plans, a hotel manager approached to ask which of them would present his AmEx to cover Calandrella's bill. They all exchanged looks; then Phil told the manager that Calandrella was a business associate they'd only just met and there must have been a misunderstanding, because they weren't paying his tab. The manager stalked off, looking distraught.

The threesome left the next day, Good Friday. When the plane touched down in Chicago, they split up. Jack and J.J. didn't want to be near Phil going through customs. They had flipped through Phil's passport and figured there wasn't a place on the planet he hadn't been. A curious customs agent might take notice.

That turned out to be a prudent plan. About forty-five minutes after Jack and J.J. had cleared customs, Phil finally showed up, tucking in his shirttails. J.J. smiled wide under his mustache. "Did they ask you to take off your pants?" he asked.

Phil nodded and smiled. After three weeks, over ten thousand miles, several terrorist scares, more conversations about more schemes to defraud than anyone could count, and one strip search courtesy of U.S. Customs, they were back. None of them doubted that Phil would walk away free.

The agents had been on the ground in Indiana for only two days when Phil phoned from O'Hare, saying he was about to fly back to Europe to finally close the Kealoha deal. He wanted them to come along, but J.J. made up an excuse. The agents desperately needed to tend to their lives.

Problem number one was how to process all that they'd harvested on their travels. When they'd first started traveling with Phil, the agents had often felt overwhelmed trying to follow the details of the schemes—particularly when the machinations included a half dozen or more people. To cope, Jack and J.J. had come up with a system. At each meeting, J.J. would memorize who was there and where everyone was sitting, and Jack would focus on what was said. When they were preparing a report about Seven

Oak paper going to Mexico, for instance, they would compare notes: Jack would recite the plot and repeat what the third guy to his left contributed; J.J. would say, "That was Calandrella," then fill in anything else he recalled.

At one session in Frankfurt, nearly a dozen people had hashed out a major bank scam. The plot was intricate, and Jean-Claude Cornaz and a few others had occasionally lapsed into German or French. J.J. had missed most of it, and Jack had suddenly felt acutely aware of his aloneness. Harold Silverkur would chime in with a key element of the crime, and Jack would take note, but then Pascal Cornaz would suggest a different approach, and so on. With so many people chipping in with so many relevant pieces, Jack's mind locked up.

When they returned to Indianapolis, Jack recounted the story and expressed his frustration—and half-jokingly suggested that he should be hypnotized to see if he could pull back the details of that meeting. J.J. grinned at him. "You wanna be hypnotized, Jack? Really?"

They were astonished when, a few days later, Frank Lowie delivered the news: The bureau had signed off on a request for Brennan to undergo hypnosis. Lowie told J.J. to go along and take notes.

Deeghan suggested a psychiatrist who worked nearby, in a Victorian mansion. The doctor seemed to have been plucked out of central casting: bow tie, white shirt, tasseled shoes. He instructed Jack to lie on a couch and close his eyes, then cautioned him not to expect Frankfurt to flood back into his mind, as if on a movie reel. The goal was to gradually coax his memories to the surface.

Jack began talking in a faraway voice: "We're in the hotel. There are lots of men in the room, and Jean-Claude is sitting over there. There's a lot of people coming and going. There are deals."

"Can you focus on any one deal in particular?"

"There are lots of deals . . . everyone is talking about lots of money."

As the shrink probed, J.J. sat there with pen in hand, skeptical but hopeful, amused by the sight of his friend stretched out on a couch, mumbling dreamily. He wondered if Jack might start snoring. Eventually the psychiatrist instructed Jack to carry along any memories when he returned, then snapped his fingers.

The agents suspected that they'd made bureau history, regardless of the outcome. Jack was likely the first agent to use hypnosis to hunt for lost memories like surf-tossed treasure on the tide-swept shores of his brain. What his great-grandfather—a certifiable law enforcement pioneer—might have thought of this was hard to fathom.

Jack was able to recall only one thing with absolute clarity: his own despair as he'd looked around the table in Frankfurt and said to himself, "Oh shit, I'm not gonna be able to remember *any* of this."

Jimmy Kealoha called Phil around the same time to say that he still wanted to proceed with the deal they'd discussed and would pay for the principals to go to Europe to meet Jean-Claude Cornaz.

On April 12, Phil returned phone calls from O'Hare while waiting for the Kealohas to arrive on their connecting flight. He was trying to catch up on twenty other schemes he had going after having spent so much time abroad. He arranged to send a $100,000 letter of credit from Seven Oak to Spain in a scam with Cornaz involving Mexican notes. Another operation targeted a liquor purveyor, Heublein, Inc. A third, totaling more than $1 million, involved tractors imported from Brazil.

Eventually he departed for Frankfurt with the Kealohas, and the next day, in West Germany, they checked into the Park Hotel. After Andy D'Amato and Mark Iuteri arrived, the promoters met on a set of circular couches in the lobby. Cornaz joined them and ticked through a few of his past exploits. D'Amato was starting in on the Fontainebleau when Phil interrupted. "We can't just leave [the Kealohas] sitting upstairs," he said.

He called the Hawaiians to join them in the lobby, and as they made their way down he told Cornaz, "They have a presentation on their proposed building back in Hawaii. Just agree to fund this thing here. Let's not [let them] get into a two-, three-hour presentation, which they can make."

"Oh my God," D'Amato said.

"Yeah, I don't want to go through that again," Iuteri said.

When the Kealohas arrived, Phil explained that the group had spent an hour detailing the project for Cornaz. "The reason we waited before calling you," Kitzer said, "we knew that we could probably make a better presentation of the project than you yourself because we know so much about it."

Then he delivered the news: Cornaz had provisionally agreed to give them interim funding.

"Oh God, thank you very, very much," Mama Kealoha said.

Her husband smiled. *Finally*. The group discussed the steps involved in closing the deal. It was Friday, April 15; on Monday, after flying back to Geneva, Cornaz would telex the paperwork for a $10 million interim loan based on D'Amato's long-term commitment from the Eurotrust.

With that done, the ebullient Kealohas invited everyone to lunch in the hotel dining room. Afterward, Phil asked Cornaz to join him for a walk, and when they stopped at a coffee shop, Cornaz reported that he had heard from others about the Eurotrust.

"The whole thing is bullshit," Cornaz said. "They got trouble in Zurich. The police are chasing them there."

Phil was only mildly surprised. He'd obviously known that the Eurotrust was phony, but he hadn't realized that it was so close to flaming out. He hoped they could take the Kealohas' money before it happened.

Phil, having finished his part, headed home. But without him there to babysit the scam, it derailed yet again. D'Amato dragged the Kealohas to London to finalize the deal, then pressed the Hawaiians for more money, claiming that Iuteri had a high overhead in his appraisal business. Mama Kealoha wrote Iuteri a $1,000 check and—because her account was low just then—went to their hotel room and rounded up $1,500 in traveler's checks. Back in the States, with the paperwork tantalizingly close, she handed Iuteri another check for $12,500.

But D'Amato never delivered. The paperwork he eventually handed over fell short of what he had promised. Mama Kealoha called their bank to stop payment on the $12,500 check, but she was too late. By the time the bank located the check, Iuteri had already cashed it.

Not long after returning to Hawaii, the Kealohas filed for bankruptcy.

Jack and J.J. sensed a sea change back in Indianapolis. The chain of command no longer doubted what they were doing. The agents had been sending in daily fifteen- and twenty-page reports about the Kealoha rip-off; D'Amato's Miami Beach scheming; and Iuteri's alleged murders, arson, and other mayhem. J.J. and Jack had recorded conversations and charted patterns of fraudulent activity, and they could take the witness stand and say, "Andy D'Amato was trying to collect fees to arrange loans, but he said to me that the Eurotrust would never pay a thing." In many instances, a law enforcement agency knows more about a particular criminal enterprise than it can prove in court. But Operation Fountain Pen had cracked open a window into a world of financial crime the bureau had not previously understood or even glimpsed. Now everyone saw it.

The bureau responded with a sense of urgency. While J.J. and Jack were in Hawaii, the FBI had assigned six agents to help prepare summaries of each case and index relevant information. When the undercover agents returned to Indiana, they huddled with Bowen Johnson to try to deconstruct Phil's schemes and map out his business deals: where money was coming from, who was getting it, and what each promoter was doing. Three clerks worked full-time to keep a manual database of the various cases up to date, and the office's steno pool strained to transcribe all the audio coming back from the agents' travels. The agents converted one of the conference rooms into a full-time OpFoPen war room in which an entire wall was papered with index cards denoting various characters and schemes.

Still, the operation had not yet become a full-blown bureau priority. Lowie requested computer support to help with the indexing, but headquarters reported that no equipment was available.

And the FBI buy-in, while vindicating, brought new pressures. Jack and J.J. were no longer flying under the radar. They had to be ready to answer questions about what they were doing and how they were doing it. If Phil threw something away or specifically gave them something, the agents could keep it—but otherwise they couldn't take papers from him to use as evidence.

The stakes were higher now. If they screwed up and the cases got tossed out of court, their work would be wasted.

These weren't imaginary worries. Phil had described his Bismarck trial to the agents, the way he and Frank Oliver had turned it into a circus, blowing up years of prosecutorial work. Rather than a cautionary tale, his battle with the federal government was, as he saw it, a source of knee-slapping barstool humor. After his acquittal, Phil had been free to reinvent himself. He'd had a fresh shot at a quiet life of legitimacy.

But, instead of chastening him, the trial left Kitzer feeling empowered—as if the point of his trip to the edge of the abyss were to demonstrate his ability to hover over it.

He'd spent the past decade probing the ramparts and fortifications of the banking and insurance industries, and for his next act he would breach its soft spots.

In 1967, Phil Kitzer moved to Miami, where he purchased First American Insurance Company and began to write sham performance bonds. Florida's insurance regulators came sniffing around—a development he took seriously. "I knew what happened to me in Minnesota and in Illinois," Kitzer said later, "and I wasn't going to give the state of Florida the chance to do the same thing."

One morning about eighteen months after purchasing First American, he called the firm's stockbroker and told him to convert all of the company's securities into cash. Kitzer retrieved the money—about $100,000—at two o'clock that afternoon, then phoned the Office of Insurance Regulation in Tallahassee and said, "Do what you want with the company."

By the time the firm dissolved, Kitzer had lit out for Europe, where he was hired as an international loan consultant for the United Nations, working under Kurt Waldheim. The U.N. had launched a program to help foreign governments obtain loans, and Kitzer brokered deals between finance ministers and banks. He once arranged for Israel to obtain funding to purchase jets from the Nixon administration. Kitzer said he was told to ask for a "commission," which was actually a kickback sent to a blind trust fund in Liechtenstein; he took a percentage. The graft was eventually exposed and two diplomats were convicted of taking kickbacks, but neither Kitzer nor Waldheim was implicated.

While he was flitting around the globe, his ex-wife, Helen, was struggling to survive with four kids. Their oldest, twelve-year-old Phil, lied about his age to land a job washing dishes and cleaning toilets at a restaurant. Kitzer's specter haunted them. Helen had been happy in their modest Chicago bungalow, but before disappearing Kitzer had moved the family into a huge home in affluent Hinsdale. He'd filled the house with furniture, and only when the seller came after Helen for payment did she learn he'd never handed over a cent for it.

Helen sometimes spent her nights trying to harvest her memory of their lives together for clues that would explain his behavior: Possibly it was the money, or his hard drinking, or his family's dysfunction (his two oldest sisters had cut off contact with their parents and siblings). Maybe it was everything combined. She realized she might never fully know.

At times Kitzer stepped off the tail of his comet and the old Phil appeared. He would telephone Helen, penitent and vulnerable, alive to the cost of surrendering to his demons. He would tell her that he loved her and wanted to come back to her. In December 1968, he sent Helen some Christmas money and wrote that he was sorry for what he'd done to her and the kids, and that he hoped that she could forgive him someday.

In 1970, Kitzer opened a mutual fund called the Depositors and Investment Trust Company, or DITCO. The business was ostensibly located in the Cayman Islands, but he ran it out of Geneva. The idea was simple: Investors could send checks offshore and earn incredible tax-free returns. Kitzer mailed prospectuses around the world and advertised in *Time* and the *International Herald Tribune*. He sent statements to customers showing robust gains, when in fact he and a partner named Gabe Cicale were pocketing the money.

He opened First National City Bank and Trust of Grenada partly to provide false guarantees and confirmations of DITCO's deposits. (If investors became nervous, First National's bankers would reassure them with a phony statement.) This bank bore several hallmarks of a Kitzer operation. It was located in the Caribbean, thousands of miles from DITCO's headquarters, both of which were beyond the U.S. government's reach. He chose a name that would be easily confused with the long-established First National City Bank of New York (now Citibank). Opening it was simple. Kitzer rounded up seed money to pay an attorney for the corporation paperwork and to cover a government bribe, then ordered documents from a printer—letters of credit, cashier's checks, certificates of deposit. The law didn't prohibit him from having such paper, even though for Kitzer it was like printing counterfeit money. He rented a few sticks of furniture for a tucked-away office, where visitors who blew in on the Caribbean breezes would find nothing more than an empty room with a telex machine run by a sleepy factotum. One such establishment was located above a barbershop.

The magic was in creating the illusion of assets, and in this regard Kitzer's mastery of banking and insurance was invaluable. He knew how authentic documents looked and read. "I have the capability of putting together deals," as he later put it, "and making people believe something that is not there."

Kitzer learned how to manipulate banking terminology. He used "Corp." instead of "Corporation" when he created a holding company. By choosing this abbreviation, he avoided having to file incorporation papers.

Among his most successful phony institutions was Mercantile Bank and Trust, also in St. Vincent. Most nations had a central bank operated by its government, and Kitzer fed the perception that a Mercantile guarantee was equal to a guarantee from St. Vincent itself.

Over time, Kitzer became a favorite underworld consultant on counterfeit and stolen securities, advising the black market on how to extract the greatest value with the least risk. He developed ways to slip them into banks as collateral for loans or acquisitions, or into company coffers as assets. For several years Kitzer ran a scam involving prewar bonds the Nazis had stolen; he provided counterfeit ownership papers that could be used to trigger a reparation payment from the German government.

He learned from his mistakes in Minnesota: He moved around constantly, between jurisdictions, never accumulating substantial property or wealth the government could seize. And he meticulously sealed himself off from prosecution. Marks rarely met him or knew his identity, because the brokers "provide insulation from you and the victim," Kitzer later explained. "They will take the initial heat when the investigation starts."

If the FBI investigated a bank, the broker became a conduit of information, conveying what the agents were looking for. Kitzer never kept a diary, phone log, or documentation of his scams. Instead, he would type up phony records or self-serving letters he could later claim to have sent. "Sometimes, or many times," he recounted, "brokers will call and say, 'I got trouble with this deal. The FBI is going to come here in twenty minutes. They called me. I'm going to type this letter and backdate it five days and tear up the original. Here is what it is going to say and if you are contacted, you acknowledge that you got this letter.'"

Everyone involved knew that a fraudulent bank might last only eight or nine months—"and sometimes you can get as much as sixteen months out of one before it explodes on you," Kitzer said.

When that happened, "It is a matter of telling the brokers, 'Okay, drop that one. This is the new one now, and start operating with this.' And it is business as usual right into the new company."

Despite his fastidiousness, Kitzer was gradually becoming known in global banking and finance—which was partly why, in the autumn of 1975, he began working with Paul Chovanec, a young con artist who had called him to propose partnering on a deal. Kitzer liked the idea of bringing someone up through his system. Chovanec was fresh-faced and relatively clean, an ideal front man. This arrangement pleased Kitzer in another way, too—one that never occurred to his acolyte.

If things really went bad, Chovanec would be there to take the fall.

Phil knew about the demise of the Hawaii scheme by the time he phoned J.J. on April 25. He called his protégés constantly to give them updates and to inquire about their activities. J.J. had eventually given him his home telephone number, after Phil complained about the answering service.

"Have you talked to D'Amato?" J.J. asked.

"No, I didn't call him," Phil said. "Wait till I see him. I'll tell you what he pulled in Europe. Jesus Christ. They are so impossible."

"Was Bimbo Boy there with them?"

"Yeah, Bimbo was there." Phil recounted how he and D'Amato had had to explain to Iuteri that a German mark was legitimate currency: "Bimbo didn't know that was money."

J.J. burst out laughing. "Oh no. Did he show you he was illiterate or something?"

"Oh, yes," Phil said. "Even Jimmy [Kealoha] said afterwards, he says, 'You know,' he says, 'that Mark is not very smart.' Even Jimmy picked up on that."

They cracked up. "That son of a bitch," J.J. said.

"He is not very smart," Phil said.

"That goddamned son of a bitch."

Eventually Phil changed the subject: "What is your schedule this week?"

"We're down in Indianapolis right now again," J.J. said.

"You're down there again?"

"Yes. Brennan lost some bucks last week." J.J. laughed. "Remember when I last talked to you? We thought we were coming out ahead."

"Yes."

"Well, we had a position we didn't come out ahead on, man. We fucked up. . . . Fucked up not too good. So we are down here trying to save it again."

J.J. said they would wrap up by Thursday, and after that they would meet again.

A week later, the agents met Phil in Chicago for a flight to Miami. He was headed to Western Union to pick up money John Calandrella was sending, but all he wanted to talk about was their next big project.

The First National City Bank of Haiti would be his new vehicle—a crown jewel in his chain of fraudulent financial institutions. The briefcase bank would be a factory for fraudulent paper on a scale worthy of the potential of his two trainees. Jack and J.J. would be the bank's squeaky-clean directors, and Phil would pull the strings from offstage.

By the time banks around the world figured out what they were doing, they would have made millions.

Phil Kitzer, photographed on July 6, 1965, at age thirty-two, as president of American Allied, a Minnesota-based insurance company from which he was accused of fleecing millions of dollars.
Minneapolis Star Tribune

ABOVE RIGHT: Facing sweeping fraud charges, Kitzer (left) heads into a pretrial conference in federal court in St. Paul, Minnesota, on November 22, 1966, with his lawyer and sometime co-conspirator, Frank Oliver.
Minneapolis Star Tribune

Kitzer (right) and his father, also named Phillip, outside the federal courthouse in Bismarck, North Dakota, in 1967.
Bismarck Tribune

This Nagra recorder was the smallest device of its kind in 1977. Agent J.J. Wedick concealed it on his lower back on multiple occasions while traveling with Kitzer.
Courtesy of the Crypto Museum

Wedick took a few moments to relax with a pipe on the balcony of the tenth-floor room he shared with Agent Jack Brennan at the Ala Moana Hotel in Honolulu in late March 1977.
Courtesy of Jack Brennan

The FBI captured this surveillance photo of (left to right) Bob Bendis, Kitzer, and Armand Mucci in Cleveland Hopkins International Airport on February 16, 1977, during the FBI agents' first trip with Kitzer.
Courtesy of James J. Wedick Jr.

Brennan and Kitzer in a hotel in Tokyo, April 1977. On their round-the-world trip, Wedick bought each of them a Kodak camera, and they snapped more pictures on this trip than during any other point on their travels together.
Courtesy of James J. Wedick Jr.

Mark Iuteri, a con man and mob
henchman, traveled with the
agents and Kitzer to Hawaii.
This was his passport photo.
Courtesy of James J. Wedick Jr.

From left, Brennan, Kitzer,
and Wedick pose next to a
Japanese garden near their
hotel in Tokyo.
Courtesy of James J. Wedick Jr.

Brennan and Wedick pose—pretending to perform—in an
empty ballroom in their Tokyo hotel in an image taken by
Kitzer. Though Kitzer didn't like being photographed, he
embraced the role of documentarian as the trip progressed.
Wedick has cameras in his right hand and his right pocket.
Courtesy of James J. Wedick Jr.

Kitzer constantly carried this model of gold-plated lighter, using it as a conversation starter with women on nights out with the FBI agents throughout 1977.
Courtesy of the Black Swan Shoppe Ltd

Brennan on the group's next stop after Tokyo. Wedick asked him to stand in front of the sign to memorialize that stop.
Courtesy of James J. Wedick Jr.

Wedick commissioned this cartoon at O'Hare International Airport in Chicago while traveling with Kitzer and Brennan in July 1977.
Courtesy of James J. Wedick Jr.

Wedick and Brennan share a light moment during their stopover in Tokyo.
Courtesy of Jack Brennan

During happy hour at the Intercontinental Frankfurt hotel, Kitzer invited two women to join them, and he provided everyone at the table with roses. The agents put theirs in their lapels; the woman on the right is holding hers in her right hand.

Courtesy of James J. Wedick Jr.

Con man Fred Pro appears here at bottom center, wearing a keffiyeh, or Middle Eastern scarf, in the 1970s. Pro later told FBI agent Myron Fuller that he was planning to use the Arab motif as a new angle in his scams.

Courtesy of Myron Fuller

On this July night at the Mayflower Hotel in New York City, an inebriated Kitzer considered calling the FBI to find out whether he was under investigation.
Courtesy of Jack Brennan

A group of FBI agents gathered in Indianapolis in September 1977 to coordinate their efforts as the bureau moved into the prosecution stage of Operation Fountain Pen. Pictured at the lectern are Brennan, Wedick, and Allen Ezell; Jim Deeghan appears directly over Brennan's right shoulder; Phil Hanlon is the bald man kneeling just to the right of the lectern; Bowen Johnson looms directly above him. Gerry Lonergan, the agent Wedick met in Hawaii, is the second from the left, appearing to be asleep.
Courtesy of James J. Wedick Jr.

Because the Fraternity's scams circled the globe, the agents often worked with agencies from other countries. Brennan and Wedick (in back row, with Phil Hanlon) met with Swiss law-enforcement officials in Los Angeles after the undercover phase of the investigation was complete.

Courtesy of James J. Wedick Jr.

For his work on Operation Fountain Pen and Abscam, Myron Fuller (right) was presented with a $1,000 bonus by assistant FBI director Neil Welch.

Courtesy of Myron Fuller

The front-page headlines in the aftermath of the investigation reflect both its significance and its undeniably colorful backstory. This newspaper was published on May 9, 1980, during Mark Iuteri's federal trial in Honolulu.

Courtesy of Jack Brennan

Part III

FEAR CITY

Up to a brownstone, up three flights of stairs
everybody's pinned you, but nobody cares

—The Velvet Underground, "I'm Waiting for the Man"

15

Pilgrims in the Mayflower

MAY 6, 1977

Gabe Cicale was quiet. That was one of the first things the agents noticed when they sat down across from him in the coffee shop of the Mayflower Hotel in New York City. A leathery man in his sixties with gray hair and a potbelly, Cicale lacked the cartoonish braggadocio of most of the promoters they'd met. Even after greeting Phil warmly—they were old friends—Cicale seemed reserved, guarded. His eyes darted to Jack and J.J. as he talked, as if he were watching them watch him.

Phil and the Junior G-Men had flown to LaGuardia Airport from Miami the night before with one primary goal: to move First National City Bank of Haiti closer to becoming a reality. They had checked into the Mayflower, an unpretentious but elegant eighteen-floor hotel situated at 15 Central Park West, just off the southwest corner of Manhattan's signature park. One guidebook described it as "a good place to keep as your own little secret." It had become Phil's go-to spot in New York.

After the sit-down with Cicale, the threesome threaded their way south and east, through clods of tourists in Columbus Circle, then along Central Park South. It was unusually warm for early May, the temperature soaring into the eighties. New York City was like the Roman Empire in full tailspin: Eighteen months earlier, the city had teetered on the edge of bankruptcy. Central Park was weedy and brown; arson and crime were so rampant that the city had earned itself a new nickname: Fear City. About three weeks earlier, a serial killer with a .44-caliber handgun had gunned down two new victims as they sat in a car in the Bronx. He'd left a note near the scene identifying himself as the Son of Sam.

J.J. was within twenty miles of the buildings in the Bronx and Staten Island in which he'd grown up, and Jack was visiting New York for the first time, but there would be no family reunions or sightseeing. Before they reached their next meeting, Phil turned to his companions and mentioned that if the agents ever had any trouble with the Outfit, Cicale was a good guy to know.

The agents absorbed this. Until that point, they hadn't brushed up against organized crime, other than their travels with the menacing but hapless Mark Iuteri.

That was about to change.

Fred Pro was large. He was more than six feet tall and nearly two hundred pounds, his frame swallowing up a chair in the swank Marriott Essex House lounge, located on Central Park South. The Junior G-Men had heard Phil mention him frequently. He wore a brown toupee flecked with gray, and his voice came out a register higher than one might expect for a man his size. Both of the agents thought of Liberace.

Pro opened a box of Dunhills, the long, narrow British cigarettes favored by Hunter S. Thompson, and held one between manicured fingers coated with a clear nail polish. Then he passed around a business card identifying him as United States director of the Trident Consortium Funding Corporation, 128 Central Park South, just a few doors down.

It was four-thirty on a Friday afternoon, so Phil ordered drinks. Pro asked Phil whether it was okay to talk in front of the two strangers. Then they began a reminiscence of their colorful shared history of con artistry. A native of suburban Philadelphia, Pro claimed to have graduated from Temple with degrees in industrial engineering and electronic engineering. By the late 1960s, he'd become an executive at the Budd Company, a behemoth Philadelphia-based maker of railroad cars. In the seventies, he struck out on his own, creating a holding company in Florida called Parker West, with which he snatched up bankrupted or financially imperiled firms with names like Classic Motor Car, Custom Metal Products, and Plastic Dynamics.

Pro said he veered into a life of fraud after being swindled out of $160,000, a calamity that drove Parker West into bankruptcy. "I had a severe emotional shock," he later said of the incident. "I went through a traumatic emotional behavior pattern that got me into this con game." Also, during a visit to Paris, a woman gave him a blow job at the top of the Eiffel Tower that changed his life, he recalled. After that, a life of legitimate work no longer seemed an option.

He credited Phil with helping him learn the trade. Kitzer was "basically my teacher in a sense that I have learned an awful lot from him in the use of fancy paper from the fraudulent banks and so forth," Pro later said. "I considered him the top in the world."

In one instance, they used a letter of credit to "bootstrap" Rel-Reeves, an $18 million telecommunications firm. Bootstrapping meant assuming control of a company without investing a cent, by presenting paper that promised an ability to pay later. They talked their way past a heavy-hitting, court-appointed law firm; then Pro executed a classic bust-out: He liquidated the assets, diverted the cash flow into his own pocket, and increased business expenses until the company went belly-up.

Pro quickly became one of Phil's steadiest customers. He busted out a small airline called Span East using a photocopy of a check that Kitzer had given him, paying Phil $20,000 for a single mimeographed sheet of paper. Pro also bootstrapped Guyana Airways with a phony $250,000 Mercantile cashier's check, and he used one of the planes to fly to Geneva, where Phil, thanks to his old U.N. connections, had moved into a former embassy building. The two men threw huge parties there. Pro bought packages of Mercantile checks two or three times a month for $1,000 to $5,000 a pop.

Phil and Pro howled about a recent caper in which Pro had sent in one of Kitzer's Mercantile Bank cashier's checks for an IRS payment. When a revenue official asked why the government had been unable to collect the money, Phil said he'd never received the check, then subsequently explained that the mail boat carrying it had sunk on the way to St. Vincent.

Then there was Elvis Presley's Lockheed JetStar airplane.

Through another promoter, Pro had received word that Presley's father, Vernon, was looking to unload a private plane that Elvis rarely used. Pro, who had extensive work with airlines on his résumé, arranged for a meeting in Memphis, where he pitched a mutually beneficial deal. He engineered a $950,000 loan for a third party to buy the plane. The loan would pay off Presley's mortgage on the plane and leave a balance of $338,000 to upgrade the JetStar for commercial charter flights, which Pro's business would operate.

Presley would then lease the airplane back for $16,775 a month, and Pro would, in turn, lease it from him for $17,775. The bottom line: Elvis would make $1,000 a month, and Pro would make his money by operating charters.

Vernon Presley examined Pro's background and was impressed with his business acumen, a complimentary article about him in Dun & Bradstreet, his college degrees. Presley also received a telex from Phil's Mercantile Bank saying that Pro had the financial wherewithal to close the deal. (Phil and Pro had game-planned the transaction extensively.)

The closing took place in June 1976. Phil was home when Pro called from an air-to-ground telephone. "Fred, where are you?" Phil asked.

Pro sounded excited. "Phil, we got it," he said. "We got it, I'm in the jet. We got Presley's jet."

Vernon Presley had also handed over the $338,000 for upgrades, which Pro divvied up among his co-conspirators. "I didn't put one nut, bolt, or screw to anything [on] the JetStar," he later said.

Each of Pro's lease checks to Presley bounced. He provided a string of convoluted excuses over the subsequent six months—stalling an exasperated Presley while flying the JetStar around the country as a prop for other cons. Pro's only regret was that he and Phil never met the King of Rock 'n' Roll. Not because they were fans—just because it would have made the story that much richer.

About eight months passed before Vernon Presley finally sat down with the FBI. "You know what I got to thinking," he said to the agents. "Maybe that this guy, the reason he was wanting up-grading money was to use it himself, not to—this might have been a planned deal all the way through."

Jack was still dozing early the next morning when a loud knock rattled him awake. He cracked open the door of room 1103A and saw Phil waiting outside. "I'm gonna have to talk to Gabe about you guys," Phil said after stepping in. Cicale had called that morning about the Junior G-Men.

"He thinks you're too quiet," Phil said, "and you listen too much."

The agents dressed and went downstairs, and Phil told them to wait in the lobby. Jack and J.J. felt only mildly concerned. With each day together, Phil became more adamant in vouching for them—they were not only future officers of First National City Bank of Haiti, they were his friends. Phil told other promoters that if they refused to deal with the Junior G-Men, they couldn't deal with him. The agents were struck by the potency of his word. (Norman Howard would later be asked whether Phil had traveled with Paul Chovanec because he wanted an errand boy. "You want me to answer that truthfully?" Howard would say. "Phil Kitzer don't run with errand boys.")

J.J. sensed other dynamics bubbling under the surface. In New York, people seemed more wary of them. Cicale, for example.

Maybe he or Jack had asked a question that made Cicale wonder whether he'd said too much. There was a kind of culture clash between the promoters—always boasting about their exploits—and the mob, which operated much more on a code of silence. Joe Pistone, operating in the city in the same time using the name Donnie Brasco, noted that it was all about "playing this game of trying to be noticed without being noticed, slide into the badguy world and become accepted without drawing attention. You push a little here and there, but very gently. . . . You cannot seem eager to meet certain people, make certain contacts, learn about certain scores." Mob guys operated by the *omertà,* a code of silence and secrecy when it came to anyone in law enforcement, and breaking it was a death sentence. The previous night, Cicale had probably run the conversation through a finer filter in his memory, looking for a phrase or answer that was too revealing.

J.J. and Jack had to learn to calibrate accordingly. But by the time they met again, J.J. believed, Cicale had already crossed over to a different place psychologically. Cicale had said so much during that first meeting that he didn't want to believe his worst nightmare, which was that he'd run his mouth in front of an FBI agent. Now the agents' job was to help him get to the place where his mind naturally wanted to go, which was: *We're fine. These guys are fine.* J.J. hoped for an opportunity to look Cicale in the eye and say, "Yeah, if I'm an FBI agent, then everybody's busted. It's a damn good thing for your sake that I'm not."

Still. For the agents, these reassuring thoughts went only so far in New York, where everyone studied them a little harder, asked more questions about their backgrounds, and seemed less credulous. These anxieties churned through J.J.'s mind when Phil returned about ten minutes later to announce that he'd smoothed everything over.

When they sat down together again, Cicale seemed different. He and Phil talked about partnering on DITCO, the bogus offshore mutual fund, and First National City Bank of Grenada, which they ran from December 1974 through 1975. When they made plans to fly somewhere, they would run ads in a local news-paper in advance, claiming to be film producers holding auditions. They would then rent a room at a five-star hotel—like the Plaza in New York—and when women showed up, Phil and Cicale would invent a storyline and drop the names of a couple of Hollywood stars, then ask them to read lines. The ones they liked they would try to cajole into stripping before sending them on their way. The two men boomed with laughter describing it. Cicale clearly liked hitching onto Phil's portable party.

In 1975, they had laid plans for First National City Bank of Haiti, but they'd decided to shelve it for a while after the Grenada edition blew up. But Cicale still had the charter, which he had obtained through contacts·inside Jean-Claude "Baby Doc" Duvalier's gov-ernment. Phil said the next step would be to go to Haiti to get the bank up and running, which would mean bribing government of-ficials to ensure that the briefcase bank would run with minimal interference.

After Cicale left, John Calandrella entered the Mayflower's cof-fee shop. He'd called the previous day from Washington, D.C., where he was trying to raise money he owed Phil for Seven Oak paper. Calandrella had kept the entire $3,500 payment on a previ-ous deal, citing high overhead. Phil had subsequently heard only excuses for Calandrella's failure to pay up—the IRS had frozen Ca-landrella's bank account, and so on. And now Calandrella had ar-rived empty-handed.

The agents were surprised that Phil would still give him an au-dience. But Phil explained that, in fact, many brokers owed him money. "You can't expect to collect on each and every instance," he later explained. "You will win some, you will lose some. . . . I never dealt with a broker-promoter that paid you all the time he was sup-posed to pay. You keep hoping he'll get a deal, and you can even up. Stop doing business with him, you'll never get your money."

By this point, Jack and J.J. had grown accustomed to the bliz-zard of half-truths, deceptions, and outright lies the promoters told their clients and one another—and no one was more skilled at this than Phil. Instead of pressing Calandrella to pay up, he began to detail the exciting new possibilities of First National Haiti. He told Calandrella that, in fact, FNCB was a legitimate Port-au-Prince bank where he'd bribed an officer into issuing guarantees on Seven Oak paper. Calandrella was electrified: That was exactly what he needed, a genuine financial institution backing up the paper he'd been peddling, he said. He had a fat portfolio of potential scams, including a $5 million loan guarantee for the Color Chrome Corporation of Traverse City, Michigan. Calandrella once again promised that he would round up the money he owed.

The establishment was located at 128 Central Park South, one of the world's more expensive streets, in a row of apartment buildings and hotels overlooking Frederick Law Olmsted's masterpiece. Phil and his two companions stepped onto an elevator in the early evening and pushed the button for the fourth floor.

A sign on apartment 4B read TRIDENT CONSORTIUM. APPOINTMENT MANDATORY. The front door opened into a reception area jammed full with overstuffed furniture; two secretaries sat at desks. Pro, who was wearing an ascot, showed them around the one-bedroom apartment he'd converted into his office. There was also a kitchenette, a telex machine, some sophisticated-looking phones. Pro lived in the apartment across the hall, where he was in the process of installing a sauna.

The previous year, when he was casting about for new work, he had hit on the name Trident Consortium, basing it on the chewing gum. Having decided that he wanted to open an advance-fee business, he'd called Phil.

Pro paid for Phil and Paul Chovanec to fly to London to acquire Seven Oak, then flew over himself for a respite from Vernon Presley's increasingly urgent inquiries. Phil and Fred flew home from England together. Following the sun west through an endless afternoon, Phil walked his friend through the promoter business: how Pro would take money and create paper, how to talk to clients. "In the five-hour flight," Phil said, "I explained to [Fred] the best I could how that worked."

Trident Consortium would operate differently from Kitzer's vehicles. Pro would tell clients that the consortium was controlled by seven banks located around the world that sought to provide financing to a high-end clientele. Before making any loans, Trident required "good faith" payments up front—a phrase that in this context radiated irony. Pro called it a CIA business: cash in advance. The more common label for that type of operation—advance-fee scam—was beneath him. They didn't use traditional con-man language like "mark" and "grift." They saw themselves more as business professionals. "We are a little more sophisticated than that," Pro said. "We disguised that terminology."

Pro initially opened Trident in the Mayflower, where he rented a room and conducted business in the restaurant. He made a few contacts and printed some phony Seven Oak CDs to sell; Phil was happy to take a cut by sending confirmation telexes from England. Pro then began issuing pre-advice commitments, instructing clients that he had obtained preliminary approval for financing.

Trident Consortium launched at a fortuitous time. During the first half of 1977, after several years of economic hardship and inflation, banks were stingy with loans. Pro built a network of brokers to solicit clients and soon was overwhelmed, taking about 150 calls a day, the phone ringing from eight a.m. until midnight. In the early days, Pro called Phil nine, ten, sometimes twenty times a day, seven days a week, at all hours, asking what he should say to clients and how much money to ask for. Phil traveled often to New York to offer his counsel.

Pro claimed to have colleagues stationed in Geneva, London, the Middle East—whatever locale was "fashionable at the time." He intended to open branches overseas so he could have Trident representatives send confirmation telexes from around the world. Trident, he told people, "generally didn't deal in anything less than a million-dollar loan."

Pro moved into 128 Central Park South within a few months, spending lavishly on the offices and living space, though he rented everything—furniture, phones, even plants—figuring that he would leave it all behind when the business inevitably blew up. But money kept flowing in, and he hired a limousine and a driver, and as spring arrived he spent $100,000 to renovate his apartment and install the sauna. Female visitors flowed in and out.

Pro suggested they go to Studio 54, the celebrity-packed night-club and disco that had opened on West Fifty-fourth Street to great acclaim earlier that year. J.J. immediately said no way—the lines to get in were notoriously long. But Pro was insulted: "You think I'd invite you there and make you wait in line?"

He'd talked with Studio 54 management about financing and forged some kind of relationship. When a taxi dropped them off under the marquee, a bouncer greeted them at the velvet rope and said, "Welcome, Mr. Pro." Fred peeled off a hundred-dollar tip and waved his friends through. Inside, the place was all pulsing lights and throbbing music. The agents and Phil found themselves next to comedian David Brenner, a frequent guest on Johnny Carson's *Tonight Show*. Phil began dancing flirtatiously with his date. As the evening rolled on, Jack went upstairs and saw people sitting at tables snorting lines of cocaine.

Phil was proud of his pupil, that Pro "was able to take down this kind of money in New York so quickly after entering the business."

Pro, naturally, was interested in First National City Bank of Haiti and offered to kick in start-up expenses. That day in his office, he handed Phil $5,000 in fifties and hundreds so he could be the first promoter in line for paper when the vehicle got off the ground. He had a project in mind for the paper: For the past eighteen months, he'd been working with a mobster named Joe Trocchio to acquire the Brookhaven Servicing Corporation, a Long Island–based firm that originated and bought and sold mortgages. The idea was to help the Mafia take over the firm's $150 million portfolio of mort-gages so its thugs could burn down buildings for fraudulent insur-ance claims, run loan-sharking activities, and launder money for the Lucchese and Gambino crime families. When it was no longer useful to them, they would bust it out.

The higher stakes, the velocity, the voltage—all of it seemed to drive Phil to greater heights of grandiosity. When Pro boasted the next night about his successes, Phil stopped him. "Whenever we do a deal, Fred, the money always goes from you to me," Kitzer said. "It *never* goes from me to you. *Ever.* Don't forget that."

The same went for women they met. They *always* left with him, Phil said. Normally an indomitable braggart, Pro fell into a grumpy silence.

One night, heading out for dinner, Phil commandeered a horse-drawn carriage at the Plaza Hotel for a ride through Central Park to the Upper East Side. He had corralled several women to join them, and he decided in mid-ride that he wanted to hold the reins, so he sat up in front with the driver, chatting away. At the restaurant, the women couldn't settle on what to order. They fretted over the prices, even after Phil invited them to get anything they wanted. Finally, when the deliberations showed no sign of abating, Phil signaled for the waiter. "Bring us one of everything on this menu," he said.

The waiter fixed him with an inquisitive look. There were around twenty entrées, ranging in price from the mid-teens into the mid-twenties, plus a slate of appetizers, salads, and desserts.

Phil nodded and held up the menu. "One of everything."

The soups and salads came first, barely fitting on the table. For the entrées, the waitstaff dragged an empty table over and loaded it with full plates, as if Phil had arranged for his own buffet. The agents and the women ate, feeling conspicuous and awkward, while Phil picked contentedly at a chateaubriand, seeming oblivious to the stares from around the room. Eventually he allowed the plates to be removed to make room for dessert. The check would total $500 (equivalent to nearly $2,100 in 2017), but Phil was heedless. As he made a show of sampling a freshly torched crème brûlée, he called the waiter over. "I ordered one of everything on this menu," he said.

The waiter again looked lost.

Phil indicated the plates and said, "Do you see any spumoni out here?"

The waiter scanned the dishes and conceded that he didn't. Other waitstaff hovered now, and the agents tried to intercede. "Phillip, forget it," Jack said. "This is fine." As it was, much of the food sat there untouched.

"I *want* the spumoni," Phil told them. He took out a cigarette and loaded it into his filter.

Phil was also annoyed at a couple sitting nearby who kept glancing over with disdainful looks. Phil told Jack and J.J. he wanted them out of there.

"All right, Phil, whatever," J.J. said.

"No," Phil said. "These people are blowing up our operation."

Then, turning toward the offending table, he said, louder, "What, you don't like that woman?"

The couple looked over, startled.

Before J.J. could stop him, Phil pointed at Wedick and continued: "He doesn't like you, lady. He just said you're ugly."

The couple stood, the man red-faced but uncertain. He was a patrician gentleman who didn't look like the fighting type. They gathered their things, murmured their outrage to the maître d', and huffed out. The waiter returned, and Phil smiled and thanked him and turned back to the table, where everyone was now gaping at him.

"All right," he said. "Who wants some spumoni?"

Bernard Baker was thinking big. A dry-land farmer from Leoti, Kansas, he had, by his middle forties, mastered the intricacies of growing crops in arid climates. He planned to use that expertise to get rich.

The previous year, a Denver-based real estate agent had clued him in on an opportunity up north, in Idaho Falls, Idaho, called South Slope Farms. Baker saw in the farm's 7,570 acres the chance to become an entrepreneur. He purchased an option on the property, figuring he could install irrigation wells and pumps and sprinklers—creating conditions in which crops could be easily grown—then sell off parcels to other farmers. Baker had owned five or six farms before, but this was his first real business venture. That autumn he retained two Colorado-based brokers to help him locate $5.5 million to do the deal, but they struck out on conventional sources of financing.

In May, as Phil and the Junior G-Men roamed New York, Baker flew to Idaho Falls to meet Billy Hicks, an Arkansas resident who owned land in Idaho. Hicks said he had a source in New York City who had generated loans that had helped him build a multimillion-dollar salvage business.

Baker sent his financial statement and an appraisal of South Slope Farms to Trident Consortium Funding Corporation. Over the phone, Fred Pro told Baker that he could secure the loan for a fee of $330,000—6 percent of $5.5 million. And he required $110,000 up front.

In Kansas, Baker borrowed the $110,000 from the First National Bank of Tribune and bought a plane ticket to New York to personally deliver the money order. He hoped that after a year of chasing a loan, he was finally in business.

Pro had a term for people like Baker. He called them DMs, short for desperate men.

The evening of May 9, after leaving Pro's office, Jack and J.J. invented some errands so they could slip free of Phil. They headed across Manhattan to the FBI offices on Third Avenue and Sixty-ninth Street. Their four days in New York had exposed a hive of high-end con-man activity, and they hoped to find a local agent who might take the reins of an investigation.

New York was the FBI's largest, most aggressive office, and the brass there was pushing forward with new undercover initiatives. The previous year, Joe Pistone had assumed the identity of Donnie Brasco and begun the long, slow process of infiltrating the Mafia. To safeguard the operation, only a handful of FBI officials knew what he was doing—and several years would pass before his work bore fruit, though he occasionally helped agents in other parts of the country making early undercover forays into mob families.

J.J. and Jack were unsure how two upstarts from "Nowhere, Indiana," as one agent put it, would be received. But by chance, Myron Fuller was still in. Fuller had an unusual background: He was an Arkansas native who had attended Berkeley on a National Science Foundation grant in physics. Fortuitously, he was one of the few special agents there who could fathom what Kitzer and Pro were capable of. Several years earlier, he'd met an informant working with U.S. Customs who'd explained how con men traveled between countries, moving phony paper. This informant had later alerted Fuller to an airline passenger flying into JFK carrying stolen German war bonds. Fuller recovered a suitcase full of pilfered securities, and his mentor, an agent named John Hauss, told him, "Go through that. There's about twenty trips for you in there." Fuller emerged from that episode with a number of open cases and a newfound appreciation for the quiet way promoters swindled people out of massive amounts of money.

Over the past few months, Fuller had devoured Wedick and Brennan's reports and was astounded by their audacity. "Most people go through their careers only doing what's been done before, so they're kind of in a box," he later said. "These two guys, they saw the world as a candy store."

Now they were sitting across from him, describing Pro and Trident and the scheme to acquire Brookhaven. There's a gold mine on Central Park South, they said.

Fuller pondered this. The FBI in New York had recently begun aggressively pursuing the city's five major crime families, and Trident was a potential point of entry. Word was that Pro was an associate of Philadelphia crime boss Angelo "the Gentle Don" Bruno. And Fuller had heard of Joe Trocchio, a "knuckle dragger" henchman connected to four different families. Trocchio had been arrested in February for trying to sell $2.5 million in stolen federal treasury and mortgage bonds. He'd also been convicted in 1975 for possession of stolen Swiss traveler's checks.

The question for Fuller was: What was the best way in? Soon enough, Jack and J.J. would follow Kitzer out of town, so he needed his own method for probing Trident. Fuller had one creative, ambitious idea that would take serious effort, and weeks or maybe months would pass before it produced any results. But if any case called for thinking big, this was it.

Four months into her pregnancy, Becky Brennan looked forward to the times when Jack would roll in from the road. He hadn't fully moved back in, though it would've been hard to tell even if he had, he was traveling so much.

Sometimes Jack brought J.J. over and she spent time with them as they depressurized. Seizing the chance to relax away from the office, the agents played with little John and Chris, then drank Scotch after the kids went to bed and told stories about their travels, leaving out any meaningful details. They talked about Tokyo at night, and walking through the Frankfurt airport past guards wielding machine guns.

They also talked about what might come next. The Brennans dreamed of owning a farm, and J.J. called Becky "Sunnybrook," after the title character in the children's novel *Rebecca of Sunnybrook*

Farm. Sometimes, telling stories about the Bronx, he would panto-mime driving an eighteen-wheeler, bouncing in his seat and turn-ing a huge wheel and "talking New York," as Becky put it. "It was so real, we would just be in hysterics laughing."

Becky found it remarkable that the partnership Jack and J.J. had formed for the undercover operation had blossomed into a solid friendship. They were like television's iconic comedy pairing, Felix and Oscar. "The Odd Couple," she said, "is the perfect description."

When they left the next morning, Becky sat on the steps outside to wave as they pulled out. John pedaled a tricycle up and down the sidewalk. Inside the car, J.J. turned to his friend and said, "Jack, do you know what you're doing here?"

Jack stared back at him. The entire landscape of his life—Phil and the travel and the FBI and this shattered and reconstructed family—was too complex to map out in his head. There was no telling if, as with rebuilding a TV, the disparate parts could be made to fit into a whole. He turned away and buckled his seat belt, and J.J. started the car and pulled out.

Left on her own, Becky dug into her reserves of strength, push-ing through from one day to the next. Their younger son was now mobile, meaning that she was chasing two kinetic toddlers around. There was only so much of a brave face she could put on. Churned by the uncertainty of their situation and a roiling stew of hormones, she endured stretches of black loneliness. Sometimes she climbed into bed after the boys were down for the night and surrendered to tears.

When sleep finally came, it was a blessing.

16

The Rhinestone Cowboys

MAY 18, 1977

Phil Kitzer sat at the bar in the Shaker House Motor Hotel, chatting, drinking, and smoking. He'd been in Cleveland for several days, chewing over schemes with Armand Mucci, Bob Bendis, and Andrew D'Amato, who had cleared up his situation with the mob and was no longer shadowed by Mark Iuteri. Mucci was a good host. To keep the hotel on the threshold of bankruptcy, he allowed the promoters to stay for free. The food and liquor were also gratis.

D'Amato walked into the bar looking distraught. He explained that he owed $17,000 on his home in Connecticut and the bank was making noises about foreclosure. He was worried about his wife and three daughters.

Later that evening, Phil ran into Mucci. "Armand, is this true about Andy's mortgage?" he asked.

Mucci nodded, adding that he, too, was in a bind: When he'd paid off the balance of Phil's fee for Seven Oak paper back in February, he'd taken the $4,000 out of a client's trust account. Now the client was pressuring him about the money. Kitzer had an idea to help both of them: He would introduce D'Amato's Euro-Afro-Asiatic Trust to Fred Pro.

Phil had mentioned the Eurotrust back in New York, and Pro was intrigued. Once Pro took clients' money, they naturally expected him to produce. Since he had no intention of ever actually facilitating a loan, he instead began "bridging" his customers—

essentially, stalling. This involved "a lot of phony papers and fancy paperwork."

These tactics were central to Trident's success. Pro took pride in his lavish, multipart excuses, the language he would unleash in his baroquely worded missives—he called them "intellectual masturbation letter[s]." That year happened to be the twenty-fifth anniversary of Elizabeth II's accession to England's throne, and he used the queen's Silver Jubilee to great effect, explaining that he couldn't access funds in the United Kingdom because banks were shut down for the festivities. Pro might also attribute delays to drops in the dollar's value, or increases in gold prices, or a Mexican holiday, or Europeans' tendency to take holiday for all of August.

He also placated clients by arranging for other promoters to send bank telexes indicating that the promised financing was imminent. But the vehicles he tapped for such documents occasionally burned out. As a result, he said, "I always look for a fresh artificial lending source."

And that, naturally, often involved Kitzer. "I would call Phil," he said, "and Phil would supply a fresh one for me or use one of his own, because Phil always had a bagful."

Kitzer thought Pro might pay $30,000 to have the Eurotrust stall some particularly impatient customers. "I'll make a phone call and set up a deal in New York," he told Mucci. "If I set it up using EAAT, the trust, can you get Andy to do the deal?"

"Phil, if you set up any kind of a deal to get us $30,000 using that trust," Mucci replied, "I'll make Andy sign if I have to kill him to do it."

That wouldn't be the last time one promoter threatened to murder another one over a deal Phil conjured up.

Three days later, on Saturday, May 21, Kitzer, D'Amato, Bendis, and Mucci wove through the maze of overstuffed furniture clogging the offices of Trident Consortium and found seats. (Wedick and Brennan were still in Indiana.) Waiting for them were Pro and his associate, Silas Yoakum Guthrie III, an old-time promoter Pro had hired earlier that year. Guthrie, whom everyone called Sy, was appealing a wire-fraud conviction that had resulted in a two-year prison sentence. Guthrie had come to admire Pro months earlier after introducing him to a boxing promoter interested in staging a fight between Muhammad Ali and Michael Spinks. The promoter had already invested heavily in the project, but he needed money to extend an option he held with Ali. "Mr. Pro offered a series of rash promises, promises that I knew Mr. Pro could not fulfill," Guthrie said.

Pro took in the assemblage of talent that May morning and declared the event to be a summit meeting. Initially, things proceeded auspiciously. D'Amato delivered his Eurotrust presentation, flashing his copies of million-dollar CDs, which Pro found highly promising. The trust, Pro judged, "appeared very fashionable, and I thought it would be easy to use with my customers."

D'Amato also showed off a copy of a takeout commitment that looked better than Trident's—and was "almost as good as the quality of Phillip Kitzer's handiwork," Pro said.

Pro was particularly impressed with D'Amato's verbiage. The work featured "a certain diarrhea of words . . . he used in telexes that I thought would be very attractive. He had great expertise in writing beautiful letters."

Not to be outdone, Pro delivered a florid presentation on Trident, sprinkling his sentences with words like "colloquialism" and "multiplicity" and highlighting his own nearly unparalleled talents with "the mystic"—his term for the ability to con a person out of five- or six-figure quantities of money. Pro pulled out his passport—he "unfolded it like an accordion," Bendis later recalled. "He had been all over the world so many times . . . doing tremendous deals, making all kinds of money, and going on and on about that." Pro said he no longer even granted meetings unless potential clients arrived with a check in hand.

D'Amato and Pro sketched out a deal. For $30,000, D'Amato would help stall five Trident clients.

Pro sifted through sixty legal-sized file folders piled around him, one for each mark. He made two piles: one for deals he wasn't concerned about, the other for clients currently pressuring him. Occasionally he reached into one pile and thumbed through it, then moved a folder to the other pile.

The conversation became scattered and chaotic. D'Amato, Mucci, and Bendis began talking about various deals they were working on, and Pro occasionally interrupted to explain the details of one of his schemes, only to be interrupted by someone else. Phil suggested to him that no one cared about the details—they just wanted him to hand over the thirty grand.

Pro seemed wounded. "I do my homework on these deals," he said. That was why, unlike some others in the room, he hadn't been indicted yet, he said.

Phil shot back, "Well, Fred, with the bullshit that is going down in this office, you had better say 'yet,' because the indictments are coming down here."

He thought Pro was crazy to spend so much money on his living quarters; by planting himself in one spot, he was an easy target. Everyone knew where to find him.

"Hey, let's not talk about indictments," Guthrie chimed in. "I've had enough of those things to last me a lifetime."

Pro quieted the crowd long enough to make a presentation about the Iverson Cycle Corporation, which had recently entered Chapter 11. The manufacturer generated revenues of $80 million globally, and Pro believed that if he could take control, he could drain out about $20 million worth of assets. That would allow him to refund any clients who were bringing heat and still walk away with a gargantuan payday. He passed around a color brochure of the Iverson line, explaining that the company was a candidate to provide bicycles for the 1980 Olympics (although that seemed unlikely if Pro took the helm).

Busting out Iverson, Pro explained, was "our own in-house cherished proposition."

Pro wanted the Eurotrust to furnish paper to Iverson's largest creditor, Ambassador Factors Corporation, to persuade the bankruptcy court to make him debtor in possession. If this gambit was successful, he promised to pay D'Amato and the others another $250,000.

The room finally aligned behind the Iverson proposal, but Pro couldn't make up his mind about which of his other packages he wanted help with—partly because his list of outraged clients would look different by the time D'Amato's paperwork came through. Eventually D'Amato gave Pro a generic Eurotrust letter that he could use with any five.

Phil said, "Okay, Fred, now where is the money—the thirty thousand?"

"You can't expect me to have thirty thousand dollars on Saturday," Pro replied. "I'll have the money for you on Monday."

The promoters decided to stick around for two more days.

When they all returned to Trident on Monday morning, May 23, Pro still didn't have their payment but promised that it would arrive imminently. Mucci and D'Amato were incensed. Both had quick tempers, and D'Amato had been agitated about his imperiled mortgage all weekend. Pro described him as "a wild man."

Phil and the others walked to the Mayflower coffee shop. D'Amato revealed that he had another reason for being restless: He had Eurotrust clients waiting for him in London. They had even bought him an airline ticket, but he'd cashed in the ticket and spent the money. These clients were now calling daily. Exasperated, D'Amato said he wanted to kill the Trident deal.

"All right, Andy, if you want to forget the deal, just forget it," Phil said. "Let's quit right now."

"Fine," D'Amato said. He stood from the table and walked out. Mucci stood, but Phil stopped him: "Leave him go. He'll be back."

As predicted, D'Amato returned a few minutes later. He said he still wanted to do the Pro deal, but his London situation was giving him fits, which gave Phil another idea. Pro was keen to get the Iverson deal moving; the bankruptcy court hearing was in two weeks. Phil called Pro and asked him to provide two airline tickets to London, plus expenses, for D'Amato and Bendis. He said that everyone was sure he would come up with the $30,000 and liked the way he operated, and D'Amato wanted to get to London fast so he and Bendis could push the Eurotrust to make everything happen.

Pro agreed. Iverson was his kryptonite; he would do almost anything to latch onto the imperiled bike company. He walked to a travel agency on Forty-ninth Street and Fifth Avenue and bought two round-trip tickets on TWA, then gave Bendis $1,000 for expenses. He also handed Bendis a check for $25,000—strictly to flash, as an inducement for the Eurotrust to furnish the requested paper. Pro said the check would bounce if Bendis tried to cash it, but he would make it good if the trust came through.

But Pro's promises felt hollow. By the time D'Amato and Bendis flew out that night, he still hadn't handed over the $30,000. He assured them that it was coming the next afternoon, but when afternoon arrived, he said it would be the next morning—only to put them off again until the following afternoon. Mucci, who hadn't even brought a change of clothes from Cleveland, smoldered.

On Thursday, Pro guaranteed that he would pay them the next morning. At eleven a.m. on Friday, Mucci and Kitzer took seats at a table in the empty Essex House bar. Sy Guthrie arrived first and apologized about the delays, but said that Pro really had the money this time. Mucci, who'd known Guthrie for years, said he was relieved that Pro was finally paying—the money would help a lot, and they'd be able to do more business together in the future.

As they talked, Pro walked in and stood over the table. "You and your goddamn friends," he yelled at Guthrie. He threw a stack of bills down, and everyone watched as they drifted across the table and floor.

"What is the problem?" Guthrie said.

Pro said that D'Amato had tried, against his orders, to cash the check for $25,000 he'd sent to London—"and because of my good, good relationships with Barclays Bank, Barclays gave them the cash, twenty-five thousand without calling me. I went over to Barclays to get these cashier's checks and they told me to close our account. They didn't want us in the bank anymore."

"Fred, you didn't get the money?" Phil asked.

"No," Pro said.

Mucci curled his hands into fists and glowered.

Phil told Guthrie, "Get Armand out of here."

Guthrie led Mucci out into the morning sun, where he growled, "I'll kill him."

Phil and Pro stared at each other. Kitzer didn't know it yet, but the encounter had been staged. Pro still didn't have the $30,000, and as a way to deflect attention, he'd dreamed up this confrontation. It had come to him a few days earlier, after Barclays had sent him a certified letter informing him that it was closing Trident's account. Pro had called Guthrie over and laid out his idea. It was the only way he could think of to deal with a hostile Mucci, who earlier in the week had told Guthrie that Pro was "a windbag and full of shit."

Pro and Guthrie "rehearsed a little song and dance act," as Guthrie called it. Pro figured he would further divert Mucci's attention by doing "the most dramatic thing I could do, [which] was to give some of the magic ingredient."

He'd sent an assistant to withdraw $1,000 in tens and twenties, "so it looked like a big lump of money. Then I walked into the Essex House and I started my soft-shoe." He thought the money would "be like a tranquilizer pill and keep everything under control."

Pro started picking up the bills, but Phil stopped him. "You leave that money," Kitzer said. "Just get out of here."

Phil collected the $1,000 and paid everyone's bill at the Mayflower; then he and Mucci left town.

By the time Pro finally came up with the $30,000, this performance would cost him much more.

Myron Fuller was on a mission to take down Trident Consortium—and he was willing to try something new to do it. In 1968, Congress had passed the Omnibus Crime Control and Safe Streets Act, which established a system for law enforcement officers to apply for the use of a previously unavailable tool: a wiretap. Over the subsequent eight years, the FBI had generally avoided deploying Title III, the part of the law that regulates wiretaps, because of uncertainty over how it would hold up in court. (Tapping phones was also politically sensitive because of illegal bugging incidents during the Nixon years.) Agents instead tracked organized-crime activities using a "trap and trace" system, which allowed them to view the phone numbers of the parties involved but not to listen in on the call.

That sounded unsatisfying to Fuller—after all, Pro's gift was talking. He wanted the wiretap. To do it, he needed a full buy-in from the prosecutors who would eventually handle the case in court. Jake Laufer, an assistant U.S. attorney in Manhattan with whom Fuller had worked in the past, instantly expressed support for the idea—but advised him to go further up the food chain. Fuller flew to Washington, where at headquarters he met with Jim Boland, a unit chief, who told him to go for it. Boland also suggested that Fuller talk to Robert Blakey, an attorney at the Department of Justice who was known as the father of RICO. Passed in 1970, RICO—short for the Racketeer Influenced and Corrupt Organizations Act—created a way for the first time for the FBI to arrest people for taking part in organized crime. Blakey, too, gave Fuller his blessing.

As Fuller began the month-long process of applying for a wiretap, an investigative gift fell from the heavens in the form of Mel Weinberg.

Weinberg was a deeply connected Long Island–based advance-fee con man who operated under the company name London Investors. In March, the FBI had arrested him in Miami for trying to sell phony CDs, and he'd cut a deal to work as an informant. Weinberg had previously collaborated with Pro and Joe Trocchio, among many other people Fuller was interested in—and he knew lots of wiseguys. A few weeks after Brennan and Wedick had told Fuller about the Brookhaven mortgage business, Weinberg called offering the same information.

Fuller potentially had two promising avenues for pursuing Fred Pro.

It was nine a.m. on June 6 when the group of visitors arrived at the Trident Consortium offices. Bernard Baker, the farmer from Kansas, filed in with his Colorado representatives and broker Billy Hicks, all of them wearing cowboy hats and turquoise jewelry. They were three hours early, and their garb stopped everyone cold. "They had all my secretaries overwhelmed," Pro said, "because they are not familiar with that kind of people."

He called them "the rhinestone cowboys" after the Glen Campbell song, which had come out two years earlier.

Pro knew little of Baker or his application. He called Hicks into his office to make sure Baker had come with money, then spent five minutes flipping through Baker's development plan and appraisal, memorizing a couple of key facts. He then invited everyone in.

After some small talk, Pro said he needed Baker's Social Security number for a credit check, and that he would also have to commission an FBI background check. All of this, Pro later explained, was "a psychological method of getting the customer into an obsequious position so they'd think that we are sophisticated and had world-wide contacts."

When Baker asked for a list of references, Pro handed over a preprinted list of banks, including Seven Oak, and explained that the Eurotrust—which he called the Martini Trust, dropping in the famous name—was likely to provide funding.

Pro handed Baker his typical commitment letter: "Gentlemen: We are pleased to confirm our willingness to process our financing loan arrangement for the amount of five million five hundred thousand dollars ($5,500,000.00) for referenced property based upon the following terms and conditions." The loan would carry 9.75 percent interest—and if it didn't come through, Pro would return Baker's deposit.

The closing was scheduled for July 10.

Baker handed over the $110,000 money order and departed. Pro's first thought was to cash it as quickly as possible so he could send $30,000 to Cleveland. He still hoped to obtain Eurotrust paper for his Iverson Bicycle pipe dream. Pro ordered his chauffeur to rush an associate to a bank in Red Bank, New Jersey. (His track record with banks was so problematic, he now hired people to cash and deposit his checks.) Then he called Armand Mucci and told him that this time, he *really* had the money.

Unfortunately, word came back from New Jersey the next day that the bank wouldn't pay out the money order to a third party. Pro was frustrated; with the Iverson bankruptcy proceedings looming, he didn't want to wait the ten to fifteen days most banks would need to clear the payment.

Mucci, desperate for Pro's money, proposed another idea: Bob Bendis could cash the money order in two or three days at a Cleveland-area bank where he held a trust account.

Pro reluctantly agreed, dispatching his assistant, Larry Mangiameli, to safeguard the $110,000. Not that Mangiameli filled him with confidence. Everyone called him Dorian, or Dorian Gray, because he was an aspiring actor who was obsessed with the corruptible Oscar Wilde character. Mangiameli was a friend of Pro's former girlfriend's, and Fred had taken in the "frustrated twenty-four-year-old boy" in an altruistic gesture, hiring him as a $400-a-week gofer that spring. Pro had begun teaching him the CIA business and had recently tasked him with developing a Trident Consortium training program for bridging phone calls, so that Pro could hire a staff to placate frustrated clients. But Dorian was still a scatterbrained young man who mostly fetched coffee and cigarettes. Pro nicknamed him Dorian Laser Beam. "He talked about getting jet fighters and flying over to Saudi Arabia and having dogfights with some friends, and back and forth," Pro said. "A very unusual boy."

Dorian Laser Beam was the only person available. Pro prepared a corporate resolution appointing him the secretary of Trident; another document empowering Mangiameli to handle the check on Trident's behalf; and a third letter indicating how he wanted the $110,000 broken down. He wanted $30,000 paid to Mucci in three lump sums, $27,500 sent to Pro's broker, and the rest returned to him.

Pro instructed Dorian to babysit Bendis at the bank and to diplomatically inquire about the Eurotrust situation before handing over the $30,000. Mangiameli wrote a note to himself in which he toggled in and out of the third person: "Remember, Dorian is on a plane American 661-4242 to Cleveland with the check, ask yourself where is Andy what is he doing, what's happening with Iverson, Armand, Fred. Ask in a nice way for references to . . . bank commitments going out before handing over $30,000. Will call you when I land in Cleveland, also while in bank to keep you abreast."

Pro put him on a flight on June 8 that would touch down in Cleveland at 8:40 a.m.

Later that morning, Mucci knocked on Kitzer's door at the Shaker House. Phil was half-dressed, and he pulled on his shirt and shoes while Mucci waited. He also roused J.J. and Jack, who had arrived with him in Cleveland two days earlier and were staying in an adjoining room. "Get dressed," he said. "C'mon downstairs."

Phil and Mucci walked to the coffee shop, and Mucci produced the $110,000 money order. Mucci recounted meeting Mangiameli as the young man had exited his flight. "Before you go any further, do you have the check with you?" Mucci had asked.

"Yes, I do."

"Well, show it to me."

Now Mucci and Phil sat with Dorian at a round table. Phil ordered coffee, and Mucci told the hotel operator to hold his calls. Bendis entered and took a seat. "Dorian," Phil said, "where did you guys get this thing from?"

"Those cowboys brought this," Mangiameli said. "The farmers."

"On what?"

"The potato farm."

"Potato [farm], $110,000? This would grow all the potatoes in the world, Dorian," Phil said. Everyone laughed.

"A dumb cowboy brought it in," Dorian said. "It was a deal we never expected to work. They just walked in the door out of the blue."

"What did Fred give them?" Phil asked.

"Fred gave them one of his famous contracts. They accepted."

Dorian said that they should cash it quickly, before the rhinestone cowboys backed out. Mucci sent him off to check into the hotel so the promoters could speak confidentially. Jack and J.J. arrived; there wasn't enough room at the table, so they settled into chairs directly behind Phil. While loading a cigarette into a filter, Phil explained that Pro "had obtained the money order from a client—a victim—that it wasn't a stolen money order; it wasn't a counterfeit money order. We felt comfortable taking it on that basis."

Mucci announced that he wasn't sending any of the money back to New York. Bendis, agreeing, said that they were "very, very much down on [Pro] for what he had done in stalling us with the money."

Phil pointed out that Bendis couldn't just put the check into his trust account and withdraw it however he saw fit; Pro had sent written instructions. Phil came up with a solution: Bendis could type up a document giving himself the authority to disburse the money as he saw fit, on which they would forge Mangiameli's signature.

Bendis was useful because he'd maintained a veneer of legitimacy. He had a law degree—in contrast to the others, who only claimed to have graduated from fancy colleges. He'd even managed his kids' Little League teams. After law school, he had joined his father's real estate management company, which was involved in federally funded low-income housing. But the company went bankrupt, and Bendis opened his own practice, focusing on real estate law. In May 1976, he'd met Mucci and become entangled in the Shaker House deal. On numerous occasions they'd come tantalizingly close to acquiring the hotel, and in the meantime Bendis started referring his other clients elsewhere.

Before things went any further, Phil made his signature announcement about entering into a conspiracy. "Bob getting up, going back to his office, and typing this letter up . . . we'll have committed the first overt act," he said, using language that appears in an indictment.

Also, by taking the money, they were "jumping into Fred Pro's conspiracy out in New York."

Bendis argued that they couldn't be implicated in Pro's swindle. They were "receiving this check as innocent holders for value," he said. "How Fred Pro got that check in New York is his business."

"All right," Phil said. "If you're satisfied with that, let's go ahead and do it."

But as Bendis left, Phil caught up to him in the vestibule.

"Bob," he said. "Do you feel comfortable putting that check into your trust account? You are an attorney, [and] know what you are getting into here."

This was no accident, that Phil had cornered Bendis away from the others. He wanted to test Bendis, see if he could rattle him. Phil thought Bendis could be spooked into signing the $110,000 over for deposit in Seven Oak instead, so that Kitzer could have it for himself.

"I was trying to frighten him," Phil later explained, "to get the check away from him."

In other words, he was trying to swindle money from Bendis that Bendis and the others had just swindled away from Pro, who had originally scammed it from Baker.

But Bendis said he was willing to risk depositing the check, and Phil let it go.

Later that day, the promoters received word that Bendis had struck out: because the check was made out to a corporation, Cleveland Trust had refused to deposit it in his account. The promoters discussed what to try next. They debated flying to the bank that had issued the check, but they studied a map and found that Tribune, Kansas, was six hundred miles from anywhere.

Eventually, Mucci decided to call a manager at Central National Bank with whom he had a rapport. His account there was overdrawn by $2,200, but, he said, "If I promise to square that overdraft up out of the proceeds of this check, I think the deal will fly."

The next morning, they all huddled around the money order. Pro's corporate endorsement had been crossed out and covered by Bendis's signature and account number, and now Mucci signed his name next to Bendis's. Someone joked that it looked like a child's coloring book, all the different hues and outside-the-lines scrawl. Phil accompanied Mucci to Central National, where they explained their problem. The bank manager agreed to submit the money order for payment and let them know when the Kansas bank wired the funds.

Back at the Shaker House, Pro was calling hourly about his $80,000. The promoters estimated that he'd phoned fifty times during the past few days. Mucci finally called him back to report that they'd submitted the money order for payment—without saying he'd used his own account—and were waiting for it to clear.

Dorian was still hanging around the Shaker House. He'd flown back to New York once, but when he'd called Pro from the airport, his boss had ordered him to get on the next plane back to Cleveland and not come home without the $80,000. Meanwhile, Mucci ordered him to stay in his room. "I wanted him to sweat it out in a motel room like I did," Mucci said.

Soon enough, the situation would get far hotter for everyone involved.

17

Kick the Can

After everyone rattled around the Shaker House for a couple of days in a fidgety limbo, Phil spurred the promoters back to work on Saturday. They sat at a table in the coffee shop, picking over the details of various deals, until Phil and Mucci locked into a conversation and moved across the room so they could better concentrate.

During a lull, the other four—Jack, J.J., D'Amato, and Bendis—noticed the splintered faction. Bendis got up and walked over, then D'Amato. Soon the Junior G-Men joined them, reuniting the full group, until—fifteen minutes later—another pair of promoters cleaved off. In this way the meeting shifted, amoeba-like, throughout the day, conversations fizzling and ramping up. Schemes were proposed, batted down. Mucci handed Jack another of the stolen bonds from Pinal County, Arizona, that he'd shown the agents in February. Jack was free, he said, to try to fence it and split the take with him. Waitresses poured oily coffee and delivered plates of runny eggs and club sandwiches and pastries.

Near the day's end, J.J. looked around and said to Phil, "You know, we've sat at every one of these twenty tables and messed every one of them up."

No wonder the promoters seemed to age so quickly, he thought. They sat around eating diner food all day, smoked like Cleveland's steel mills, and drank coffee until they switched to cocktails, sometimes as early as eleven a.m. Phil liked crème de cacao with Scotch—a sweet drink he sometimes mixed with coffee. For dinner, the agents often ordered filet mignon and baked potatoes. Phil was uninterested in food, which he attributed to a bad stomach—he and Jack were always sharing cylinders of Tums—but he often asked for the most exotic entrée. The promoters' idea of a workout was walking from their room to the bar. Phil disdained exercise but maintained his weight of around 140 pounds. Jack, though, was naturally burly and starting to pack it on. Mucci was seriously overweight.

This lifestyle is going to kill us all, J.J. thought.

He made a decision: From that point on, his only meal would be dinner. He had started running back home, mapping out a two-mile route around the parking lot in his apartment complex. He'd brought his sneakers on this trip, and now he told everyone he was going for a run—partly as a stress reliever but also because it gave him a chance to meet with Bowen Johnson, who had recently started shadowing Jack and J.J. on their travels. The undercover agents always struggled to put together reports while they were with Kitzer because of Phil's hours and intrusiveness. Johnson would wait in his room for his colleagues to appear, often between ten p.m. and two a.m. They usually looked exhausted as they recounted the relevant happenings of the day for their case agent. When that was finished, they collectively agreed on what to do next. It was a small, highly functioning democracy. "It was really a good group to work with," Johnson said. "No one was out to be a hotshot, which was important because under those conditions you better be able to get along."

There were even moments of levity amid all the pressure. One late night in New York, Jack stumbled and stuttered, trying to dictate the details of a complicated scam. J.J., sitting on the other bed, grabbed the recorder out of his hand. "Jack, you don't know what you're talking about," he said.

J.J. spent the next ninety minutes trying to craft a lucid description of the fraud and noticed Jack lying on the other bed, his eyes closed. "You set me up!" J.J. yelled as Jack and Bowen started laughing. "You guys played stupid so that I would dictate!"

After the agents left, Johnson typically spent the next few hours alone, creating reports to send back to Indianapolis. If there were recordings, he drew up a list of key developments and leads for agents back home and around the country to move on even before the tapes arrived: *Let Kansas know about Bernard Baker, and inform New York that Pro just ripped off $110,000.* This material would first hit the desk of agent Steve McVey, who was coordinating OpFoPen full-time in Indianapolis. He would pass the tapes to the secretarial pool, which might spend the entire day creating transcripts. "We were generating enormous amounts of material on the road," Johnson said.

This left him equally sleep-deprived, but Johnson, a Texas native with a pronounced southern drawl, was a company man. His father was an army officer, and Johnson had been an Eagle Scout who'd felt drawn to law enforcement work in high school, when he began practicing firearms with a local police team. Once out of school, he obtained his pilot's license and ran charter flights; while teaching several FBI agents to fly, he learned about their work. "The FBI was magical, if you will, and I wanted to be a part of that," he said.

He never could have envisioned his life as a key part of OpFoPen. Even the logistics, in the days before mobile phones or beepers, were dicey. In hotels, Johnson arranged for a room on a different floor or wing from Brennan and Wedick's—or just stayed in another hotel—to minimize the chances of being seen with them. Generally, there was no way to make plans or coordinate. If Johnson needed to consult with the agents, he hoped to run into them away from Kitzer; he would ignore them if Phil was there. When they went to restaurants, he took a table across the room and studiously avoided glancing in their direction, while still staying vigilant to movement at their table. If J.J. was wearing the Nagra and needed a new cassette, he headed to the restroom. Johnson would wait a few minutes, then go pop in a fresh tape for Wedick, the two of them crowding into a bathroom stall. He carried a spare recorder, too, in case J.J.'s conked out.

Johnson settled at a table at a white-tablecloth Manhattan restaurant one night when Kitzer was particularly chatty. After working his way through a steak, then dessert, then coffee, only to glimpse Kitzer still chatting across the room, Johnson was stumped. Finally it hit him that the place had a humidor. He whiled away the rest of the dinner meeting puffing on a stogie, ignoring the unsubtle looks of displeasure from his waiter.

Operation Fountain Pen was like that: It could be unnerving, exciting, exhausting, and befuddling—all in a single day. "No one had done this stuff before," Johnson said, "and you're early enough in your career that more than anything it's a bit of a heady experience."

That day in suburban Cleveland, Wedick had made plans to meet Johnson during his jog. They'd picked Highland Park Cemetery, located down the street from the Shaker House, for a rendezvous. Wanting to work up a sweat, J.J. ran for a couple of miles before looping into the cemetery, looking back repeatedly to make sure no one was trailing him. Satisfied that he was alone, he started looking for Johnson, who was supposed to be pretending to be paying respects to a loved one. J.J. had told Johnson not to acknowledge him unless he approached and said it was okay. If he thought he was being followed, he would just run by.

But he didn't see Bowen anywhere. *What the hell is this?* J.J. thought. At more than six feet tall with a powerful farm-boy build and dark hair, Johnson was hard to miss. J.J. slowed to a walk, trying to figure out what to do—he had forty-five minutes, tops, before he would need to be back, and he'd already run for thirty or more. Just then, Johnson popped out from behind a tomb, startling him.

"Jesus, Bowen!" J.J. said. "You scared the shit out of me."

———

That evening, as Phil, Jack, J.J., and Mucci sat in the Shaker House restaurant, a mellowness pervaded the room. But the languorous mood ended when D'Amato stalked in and began pacing around, fixated on his delinquent mortgage. He fumed about Pro, and the money he'd promised, and about why Trident's schtick would never last: Pro always had to repay a certain number of advance fees when the heat got too high. "Rob Peter to pay Paul," D'Amato said. "Keep the cycle going. But it won't work, 'cause I tried the same thing.

"I was in the same business, and what happened? You always spend the deposit money as soon as it comes in, and people get angry. They start screaming, and the deal just doesn't work like that."

As he was talking, D'Amato repeatedly kicked an empty beer can against a wall.

"Andy, I'll explain to you what *your* schtick is," Phil said.

"What's that?"

"Someday," Phil said, "when this case gets before a jury and they're listening to the evidence, the only thing someone is going to be able to testify about . . . is that Andrew D'Amato was playing kick the can in the restaurant."

Everyone laughed.

The next day, Phil and the agents left. The money order likely wouldn't clear for another ten or twelve days. Before they split up at the airport, Phil offered J.J. and Jack another piece of advice: If they were ever questioned about the $110,000, they should say they were absent when the promoters discussed it and had no idea what was going on.

Dorian Mangiameli flew back to New York with a document for Pro instead of the $80,000. It was the letter D'Amato had brought home from London. It read:

Dear Mr. D'Amato,

We refer to the meeting we have had in London concerning a guarantee request by Iverson Inc. for an amount of up to U.S. Dollars $2.5 million in favor of Ambassador Factors Corporation.

As we have only received the information on this company in the last two days and because of the holidays in London due to the Jubilee, it will not be possible for us to make an offer for your client until next Thursday, 9 June 1977.

We wish to make clear that we are prepared to make such offer only on the basis of a Standby Loan commitment for 3 years for which we would establish reserves by depositing the necessary amount of money with prime international banks of our choice in London. Such deposit will constitute only the reserves of Eurotrust and would not be pledged or hypothecated in favour of Ambassador Factors Corporation. The proceeds of the deposit on the last maturity date after 3 years would be assigned to AFC.

We look forward to seeing you next week.

Yours faithfully, for and on behalf of Euro-Afro-Asiatic Trust,

G. R. Lanciault, Managing Director

Pro read the letter in shock. This was supposed to be the key that opened the vault to Iverson. Instead, the Eurotrust people were bridging him—using his own stall tactics!—and had even co-opted Queen Elizabeth's Silver Jubilee and his use of pedantic vocabulary words like "hypothecated."

"[W]hen Dorian gave me this," he said, ". . . I really figured I got stuck. I checked with Mr. Guthrie and he told me I could wipe my ass with it. It was the most ridiculous thing he ever seen in his life, and I got took."

He chafed for years afterward. "They really ripped me off," Pro said later. "I mean, don't get me wrong, I rip off other people, but I thought there was some standard of honor among con men."

Phil and the Junior G-Men returned to Cleveland a few days later, on June 18. Mucci had sent word that the bank in Tribune, Kansas, had wired the $110,000 to his account. Kitzer told him to have $5,000 ready when he arrived—a quarter of his cut.

The next day, Phil and the agents met Bendis with his wife and two kids at the Shaker House bar. Mucci was out of town at a funeral but had left Phil's money. Bendis gestured toward an adjoining ballroom, and he and his wife and Phil walked in, leaving Jack and J.J. behind. Bendis's two kids played a game by the revolving door. After a minute, the agents crept up to the window in the doorway and watched the threesome in the center of the ballroom.

Bendis asked his wife to hand Phil a brown Central National Bank envelope. "I'm glad to get rid of that," Bendis said. "That is a hot item to handle."

Phil removed several hundred-dollar bills and tucked them into his pocket.

Mrs. Bendis murmured, "Oh, so much money."

"Well, for all the grief and aggravation we gave you sending Bob away to London, here, get yourself a dress," Phil said. He handed her two hundred dollars.

The three of them rejoined Jack and J.J. "Gee, that was a good deal," Bendis said. "We should get one like that once a week. It came just in time. I was almost at the end of my rope."

J.J. smiled. "Yeah," he said. "You don't know how bad we needed it."

On Monday, Kitzer, Bendis, and Mucci climbed into Bendis's car to head for Mucci's bank. They stopped at a diner en route, and at a table inside, Mucci said, "Okay, Phil, how are we going to cut this up, the $110,000?"

"Are you bound and determined to take the whole $110,000?"

"Absolutely," Mucci said. "I'll not return one dime to Fred Pro."

"Armand, this is going to bring heat," Phil said. "You're not going to jerk that $80,000 away from Fred just that easy."

Mucci nodded. "I can handle any heat that Fred puts out."

"What about the FBI?"

"I don't care about the FBI."

Phil suggested that they leave $60,000 in the bank until they had a chance to see how Pro reacted.

"I think that's a good idea," Bendis said.

"Okay, I'll go along with that program," Mucci said. "But I don't care what happens. I won't return the money."

At the bank, Phil took the balance of his $20,000. Mucci cleared up his overdraft and picked up $17,000 for D'Amato's house, then withdrew some for himself and Bendis.

Four more days passed before Pro realized that the money order had been cashed. On June 24, Bernard Baker called to ask about his loan. Pro had started explaining that he was having trouble clearing the money order—Mucci had told him as much earlier that day—when Baker informed him that, in fact, it had been cashed in Cleveland, and the money was now sitting in an account at Central National in the name of Armand Mucci.

Fuming, Pro called Mucci and demanded that he send back the balance of $80,000. They began shouting at each other. Mucci told Pro, "You ripped off somebody, so how do you like it when we rip you off for a change?"

As Pro bellowed a reply, Mucci said, "Fuck you," and hung up.

Pro called back repeatedly, but Mucci wouldn't answer. Fred seethed. His coveted Iverson deal had fallen through, and now he'd lost the $110,000.

He picked up the receiver again. This time Pro dialed Joe Trocchio, his sometime mob muscle. He would not let this thievery stand.

Brennan and Wedick headed home to Indiana on June 20, but they had barely returned to their lives when Phil called again. He wanted them to accompany him to Haiti to work on starting up First National City Bank. They'd been expecting this: With Seven Oak on the verge of burning out, Phil was hungry to get the new vehicle running, but they needed a break. The travel was murderous: two weeks, then ten days, then nearly three weeks, during which Jack slipped off his wedding ring and had little contact with Becky, and J.J. abandoned a romantic interest in his apartment building.

Phil's neediness was easier for J.J. to handle. He now saw that he could build his future around this case, and he burrowed so deeply into the work that he scarcely noticed the absence of any personal life. After they returned home and caught a breath, he collared Jack to go to Indianapolis for meetings, and to finish reports and catch up on paperwork. They often returned home so late that Jack flopped on J.J.'s couch for the night.

Even still, they both struggled to fulfill their basic obligations—especially the routine paperwork. Jack found this aspect of the job particularly problematic. He had a tendency to start things and not finish them, and the scrap heap on his desk now resembled the aftermath of a rockslide.

At one point Jack submitted a reimbursement voucher for more than $7,000 that he'd charged on his personal American Express. Each expense was supposed to be assigned to an open case. "Jack would just say, 'Yeah yeah yeah, just put 'Miami, $4,000,'" J.J. recalled. Then he would send the invoice to the FBI's accounting office (run by the infamous Cox brothers, widely referred to as "the Cox-suckers," who were notorious for bouncing expense vouchers that had a single out-of-place number).

Inevitably, the form soon reappeared in Jack's box stamped with the word DISALLOWED. He regarded the paper as if it carried news of an office smallpox outbreak. Although J.J. also went months without submitting travel vouchers, he laughed at Jack's palpable allergy to the bureau's box-checking ways. The only letter of censure Jack ever received was for not submitting paperwork in a timely manner.

"Nobody's caring about your AmEx bill, okay, Jack?" J.J. said, laughing. "It's the harsh truth, get over it."

Sometimes the demands, the stress, and the pull of different worlds created friction. J.J. wanted to work long days, even when they had time away from Phil—they had prosecutors to meet with, strategies to discuss. There was always another task. At some level he knew the case was consuming him, but he didn't care. Work, he later acknowledged, was "almost like an addiction."

Jack, meanwhile, wanted to go home and relax and see Becky and his sons after spending so much time on the road. He was acutely aware that his boys went without seeing his face for long stretches. He also enjoyed meals on a conventional three-a-day schedule, while J.J., who now ate only dinner, chafed at his partner's food breaks.

One day, everything boiled over. The agents retreated to a conference room in a far corner of the office and began screaming at each other. Even from behind the closed door, the shouting was so loud that everyone sitting nearby stopped working and looked at one another in alarm. No one had seen Jack get angry before. Eventually someone went to find Frank Lowie, who tentatively knocked on the door: "Are you guys all right in there?"

Lowie opened it halfway. J.J. and Jack looked over, flushed and startled. They said yes, sure, they were fine. They just needed to blow some lava out of the cone.

18

The Hit Man

J.J. Wedick pulled his car into the parking lot at Patoka Lake, opened his door, and breathed in the humid night air. Even he needed a break now and then, and he'd been looking forward to the long Independence Day weekend for weeks. His friend and roommate Kim Jordan had rented a houseboat to take out onto the eighty-eight-hundred-acre lake in southern Indiana. It was around ten when J.J. arrived, and the two men decided to crash on the boat and pick up supplies in the morning while they awaited their other friends' arrival. J.J.'s only ambition for the weekend was to sip a beer and catch the Fourth of July fireworks from the deck. Jack was with his family, and Phil was home in Minnesota.

J.J. woke to a warm, muggy morning, eager to push out onto the water. While waiting for the others to show, he walked to the park's pay phone to call his answering service. There was a message from Dorian Mangiameli, at the end of which he said, "Oh, and stay out of Cleveland this weekend."

Hanging up the phone, J.J. pondered what *that* was about. He sighed and decided he'd better find out. When Dorian answered in New York, he was circumspect: There was some trouble in Cleveland, but he couldn't elaborate. J.J. peppered him with questions until Mangiameli blurted the news: Pro had put out a contract on Armand Mucci's life. He was going to have Mucci whacked.

After saying good-bye, J.J. groaned, leaned his forehead against the phone, and absorbed the bombshell. He was astonished. He'd known Pro would be furious about losing $80,000, but *this*?

Walking back to his car, J.J. thought through the dynamics of the situation. He needed to pass the news to the bureau. If Mucci turned up dead in the middle of the undercover operation, OpFo-Pen would be finished, and the FBI administrators and the media would go crazy. The spotlight would hit J.J. and Jack: *How did these agents allow this to happen?*

So J.J. had to send word to Indianapolis. But when he did, he wanted to be able to say that he was on top of the situation and had a solution. He figured he had twelve hours. He told Jordan he was sorry, then jumped into his car and drove the three hours to Indianapolis. After checking into the Hyatt Regency, he started working the phones. He called Mangiameli back to see what else he could learn, then made calls throughout the day, contacting every promoter he could think of to find out what people had heard.

No one was saying much, but J.J. extracted enough to confirm the rumor. He called Jack and Phil and suggested that Kitzer call Mucci and Pro and have them get together to resolve it. Then J.J. called all the promoters again, this time not as inquisitor but as confidant: "Hey, did you hear about what Fred's doing?"

The more people knew what was going on and, in turn, asked Pro whether it was true, the less likely Pro would be to go through with it. The next step was to have someone in the FBI office in Cleveland warn Mucci about the contract—J.J. figured that enough people knew at that point that they wouldn't suspect that he was the source.

The next day, J.J. drove his bureau-issued blue Thunderbird to the arrival gate at O'Hare International Airport to pick up Jack. Phil had come up with a last-minute plan to fly to New York so they could try to make sure Pro had reined in his murderous impulses. J.J. kept hearing that the hit was off, then that it was on again. Phil didn't want to be associated with any violence, and he wanted Pro to stay out of trouble for selfish reasons: Pro was going to buy Seven Oak.

They'd been discussing this for a few weeks. Fred had agreed to the asking price of $200,000, with a down payment of $20,000.

Phil wasn't due to arrive from Minnesota for a few hours, so the agents anticipated having some time to catch up privately. They drove to where Phil's connecting flight would arrive, and Jack hopped out to unload their bags. J.J. figured he'd stash the car in a remote lot while Jack bought the tickets.

J.J. had just dropped his suitcase on the sidewalk when Jack hissed, *"Jim!"*

He looked up, startled. Jack was facing the opposite direction, toward the airport exit. His eyes widened, and he whispered, *"Kitzer!"*

Phil had changed his plans. Again. They would soon learn that John Packman, who ran Seven Oak, had managed to clear up his visa issues and had prevailed on Phil to meet to straighten out the bank's books ahead of its sale. Phil had canceled the New York trip and instead flown to Chicago early to meet Packman and a British accountant they could trust. They would all work in an airport hotel for a couple of days.

J.J. slammed the trunk shut and hustled into the driver's seat, trying not to look hurried. He called out the window, "Okay, I'll return the car, Jack!"

As he started the engine, J.J. could hear Phil calling out, "Hey, J.J., wait!"

Without looking back, he stomped on the gas pedal. From a certain distance, it was obvious the Thunderbird was a law enforcement vehicle—the elaborate dashboard radio system alone gave it away. But he wasn't sure how close Phil had come. J.J. glimpsed him as a shrinking figure in his rearview mirror, waving, as he rounded a corner and disappeared out of sight. *Objects in mirror are closer than they appear.*

Jack would have to think fast on his end, too, to explain why J.J. had taken off.

J.J. parked and sat for a moment in a far corner of O'Hare's long-term lot, taking a couple of deep breaths. That was probably their closest call yet. After he'd settled down, he walked to the shelter where a shuttle would pick him up and deliver him back to the gate. When he found the others, he acted surprised. "Phil! I didn't know you were here!" he said, grinning. "You came early?"

"I was yelling for you!" Phil said. "We could've used that car."

Jack stepped in. He said he'd just told Phil that J.J. had returned their rental car because they still thought they were flying to New York. It was all a misunderstanding.

J.J. apologized. "I was just trying to get the car back," he said.

When the agents talked later, Jack would relate that Phil had come within fifteen yards of the Thunderbird. Another ten or so steps and he would've been close enough to see inside.

The Brits arrived, and they hunkered down for the rest of the day and into the next, the Fourth of July, in Phil's hotel room. The goal was to cook the Seven Oak books—figure out a way to bolster the bank's net worth so they could file the quarterly financial statement, which had been due in March. They needed to conjure some accounting black magic in order to convince Britain's Board of Trade not to close or liquidate Seven Oak for another month or two. Packman produced a ledger that showed all the Seven Oak letters of credit Phil had issued.

The agents perused it, and J.J., who held an accounting degree, was amazed at the jumbled state of the records. The ledger showed the bank with a $300,000 balance—but Phil and Packman had long ago spent whatever money depositors had entrusted to Seven

Oak. Meanwhile, the bank was, at least on paper, on the hook for millions of dollars in CDs and letters of credit. With all the fraud festering inside the bank, no one wanted to put his name on any government report.

When Packman left, Phil confided that he'd issued even more securities that he'd never told Packman about and that, as a result, weren't in Seven Oak's books. But soon the bank would be Pro's headache. As the new owner, he would have a fresh opportunity to stall on the quarterly report, and he would be able to issue paper during whatever respite the British government offered.

Somewhere in a different part of the hotel, Bowen Johnson sat on his bed, trying not to think about his wife, nine-year-old son, and six-year-old daughter. Back home in suburban Indianapolis, they had fired up the grill without him for a Fourth of July cookout. The separation from his family for weeks at a time was the toughest part of Johnson's role—that and traversing long tunnels of tedium. There was no sightseeing when Jack and J.J. were attending private meetings; Johnson had to be there if they called or knocked. All he could do was flip through the few channels the hotel made available, hoping for something diverting. He didn't complain, though. His father had espoused the ethos that the job came first. "That was what you signed up for," he said. "That was part of the game."

Johnson couldn't ask for backup, either. Requesting help from agents in another city—which was otherwise normal protocol—would require him to walk them through OpFoPen's complexities. "I couldn't just go into another division," he said, "because I could not transmit the vastness of all that material."

But the case's recent revelations—in particular, the emergence of organized-crime figures—had galvanized the FBI. The next day, the bureau appointed three additional agents to travel with Johnson to help with surveillance, cover, communications, equipment, evidence handling, and whatever else he needed. They would coordinate with local FBI offices wherever Jack and J.J. followed Phil. These agents would send out daily teletypes, distributing background information about Operation Fountain Pen and forwarding leads. This was, in its own way, a remarkable development. Under Hoover, agents had rarely traveled beyond their own area. Now an entire backup unit was bouncing around America along with two undercover agents.

Things were just as frenzied back in Indianapolis. Brennan and Wedick had by now identified more than two dozen suspects around the world. Normally the FBI office would store information about a case in a single file. But OpFoPen spanned many dozens of cases involving shifting sets of promoters, victims, and paper. "It became a monumental nightmare," Bowen Johnson said. "To wade into something as vast as this was and to get on top of it with the technology we had at that time. . . . It was an incredible amount of paper."

These complexities had prompted the Indianapolis division to develop an entirely new data-retrieval system; by late June, there were already more than twelve hundred references in the indexes. Computers would have helped. Brennan had minored in computer science, and he argued that the bureau would be better off digitizing the files. The agents had pitched the idea to Jim Deeghan in the spring. Deeghan, in turn, had asked headquarters—but had received no reply. On June 30, he'd pestered the higher-ups again as the demands of the case mushroomed, but he had yet to receive any answer. Instead, the FBI delivered more bodies. During the month of July, Washington would send the Indianapolis office eight special agents and five support staff on temporary duty.

There were downsides to gaining the attention of the bosses in D.C. By the Independence Day weekend, the FBI brass had handed oversight of the case to three different units. Calling headquarters, Frank Lowie had spoken to seven different supervisors. Each new unit and bureaucrat had to wade into a stream of information that was moving so fast they needed hours of briefings to fully grasp what had taken place before. Naturally, this caused delays in decision making. When Lowie complained, the bureau made a huge concession: He received permission to hurdle all midlevel management and go straight to Jim Adams, the assistant director in charge of the FBI's entire criminal division.

But even this didn't resolve all the quandaries Johnson faced. In some cases, Phil cooked up schemes that carried the potential to damage the economies of small nations, as in one case involving millions of dollars in counterfeit notes from Swaziland. In that instance, Johnson spent hours trying to reach someone in the State Department.

That summer, the FBI conducted its annual inspection of the Indianapolis office. This was strictly a bean-counting exercise—a holdover from the Hoover era meant to assess whether each bureau office was generating sufficient statistics for the dollars it was allotted. According to one published account, the "arrest quotas were used to dress up the FBI's image at budget-crunching time in Congress" and led to jokes that the agents were really working for the Federal Bureau of Accountancy. It was, in other words, exactly the kind of exercise that would have, in the old days, set off klaxon sirens about Operation Fountain Pen, with its slow build and relatively high cost, and not a single arrest yet to show for it. But Assistant Inspector Tom Baker was new to the job, and he had never been indoctrinated into the mandarin sensibilities of the previous administration. When he called Brennan and Wedick in for interviews, they described hiding in restaurant bathroom stalls with a malfunctioning Nagra, taking notes on matchbook covers, sneaking out at two a.m. to call in reports. Baker had never heard anything like it. What particularly astonished him was the lack of "backstopping"—that the agents were doing this with no training or false identities.

"Really it just shocked me," Baker said. "They were going by the seat of their pants. The pressure these guys were under, that impressed me very much."

His report recommended that the bureau leave the agents alone to do their thing.

On their way through O'Hare, headed toward their flight to New York on July 6, J.J. spotted a caricature artist and had an idea. He walked up and handed the guy a twenty. Phil and Jack strolled over, curious. Phil tried to get J.J. to move along but stopped when he saw the image.

The scene showed a boat on a cerulean-blue sea with the words "Seven Oak Finance" printed on it. The boat was sinking, and there were three figures on it ready to leap off.

Phil smiled and said, "Oh, yeah, this is perfect." He then commissioned his own illustration. The artist wrote the words "1st National City Bank of . . ." and then "Haiti" appeared as characters with clown noses and roller skates. Dollar signs and a palm tree were scattered around. Across the bottom were the words "Board of Directors" and the names "Phil," "J.J.," and "Jack."

Phil took the cartoon, held it aloft, and smiled widely before they set off to catch their flight.

The first order of business when they reached New York was to close the Seven Oak sale with Pro, who handed over $17,000 as a first payment, saying he would deliver the other three grand soon. He also gave Phil a check for $14,000 from another deal, which led to a moment that rattled the agents. Phil no longer had Seven Oak available to launder the check, so he asked Jack to deposit it in his account. Jack tried to equivocate and change the subject, but Phil stopped him. "Now, come on," he said. "I saw a deposit slip in your luggage."

Jack stared at him. Five months they'd been traveling together, and Phil was still looking through their stuff. He'd discovered a mail-in deposit envelope in a crevice of Jack's bag. Jack tried to be careful about what he carried around, but he couldn't undo his nature—and at times, Phil was so companionable they could almost forget. Then something like the deposit-slip incident would happen. "There was always that tension," Jack said.

Jack told Phil that he would think it over, and the agents conferred with Johnson. Phil hadn't told the agents where the money had come from, so the FBI okayed the deposit.

Phil and Pro discussed an array of other deals, including one in Fort Lauderdale being spearheaded by Vinnie DiNapoli, a capo, or made man, in the Genovese crime family. DiNapoli was the leader of the organization's 116th Street Bronx crew. (The DiNapolis were seriously mobbed up: His older brother, Joseph "Joey Dee" DiNapoli, was a soldier in the Lucchese crime family; his younger brother, Louis, was also a wiseguy.) DiNapoli's idea was to open a place called the Lauderdale Beach Hotel and spread the word that it was gay-friendly. Operatives would surreptitiously take pictures or video of guests in intimate encounters, and the mafiosi would then extort payments from travelers eager to keep their activities secret. DiNapoli called his pet project the "fruit hotel."

On the same day, Pro was also dealing with Bernard Baker, the Kansas farmer. Pro had met him in Idaho a couple of weeks earlier, during "a cross-country tour of appeasing a few customers." The trip's purpose was ostensibly for Pro to meet with an Idaho banker to discuss facilitating Baker's loan. After returning to New York, Pro wrote a letter reassuring Baker that he would return the $110,000 deposit if the loan fell through. "I wish to again reaffirm to you that the unfortunate situation that has occurred in Cleveland has no effect to our transaction," Pro wrote.

But the charade continued. Between meetings with Phil and the Junior G-Men, Pro informed Baker that the closing would be delayed until July 11; a few days later, he attributed another delay to Queen Elizabeth's Silver Jubilee.

Pro gave Phil and the agents the same runaround on the $183,000 balance of the Seven Oak sale. They walked over in the afternoon for the money, and Pro said it was coming in the morning—but then it still wasn't there the next day. And so on. They started calling it the Parade. To placate them, Pro sent Dorian Mangiameli to the Essex House bar with a small good-faith payment of $5,800.

Pro wouldn't talk about the arranged hit on Mucci. J.J. and Jack still heard wisps of news about it, dropped comments. But no one knew for sure what was up.

The lingering specter of a mob killing added to the agents' growing unease. When they were in New York, they felt their parallel worlds bunching up, clattering into each other. One day after work, the threesome headed to the East Side for drinks. After they sat down, J.J. looked across the bar and spotted Peter Vaira, the head of the Justice Department's organized-crime strike force in Philadelphia, sitting with three or four FBI agents. Kitzer was unloading his Pall Malls and lighter when J.J. leaned over to Jack and nodded in Vaira's direction. Jack glanced at Vaira, then back at J.J. The agents exchanged a look that said: *Let's get the hell out of here.*

"Hey, Phillip, we're leaving," J.J. said, tugging at his arm.

There was another major development looming: The July 8 installation of a wiretap and bug in Trident Consortium's offices. That day, Phil, Jack, and J.J. headed into the elevator in Pro's building. Unexpectedly, the car went down and the doors opened in the basement, where two phone-company employees were working on the box. Jack glanced up and recognized a third utility worker as Rich Reeves, actually a fellow FBI agent, waiting to board the elevator. Brennan looked down, hoping Reeves wouldn't blurt out "Hey, Jack!" Reeves stepped on, rode wordlessly to the first floor, and exited.

Phil and Jack headed home that afternoon, but J.J. stayed in New York in case Myron Fuller needed help on the inside bringing the wiretap online. Knowing the FBI would need to break into Pro's office that night to install the microphone, J.J. offered to take everyone—Mangiameli, Sy Guthrie, Pro, and their dates—to dinner at the Essex House, then to a Lower East Side nightspot. He waved everyone out the door of Trident, then quickly twisted the knob so the lock popped open before he closed the door. They were all crowding onto the elevator when Mangiameli said, "Oh shit, I forgot my wallet."

He walked back to the office, pulling out his key. "Huh," he said when he found it unlocked.

"Dorian, what's the matter?" J.J. asked, following him. "Let's go."

"Yeah yeah yeah," Dorian said. "I don't know how that door was unlocked."

J.J. again positioned himself to leave last, and repeated what he'd done the previous time. But then they heard the phone ring inside the office. Mangiameli again left the elevator to answer it, and J.J. pretended to be baffled when Dorian again turned the knob and opened it. "I locked it," J.J. said with a shrug.

This scenario played out a third time when Dorian darted off the elevator to double-check the door. "How the hell could this happen?" he said when he again found it open.

Shit, J.J. thought, *I gotta stop.*

If Fuller was going to bug the place, he was going to have to break in.

19

The Blackout

J.J. was back in Chicago when he saw the headlines out of Southern California. A sensational daytime armed robbery had taken place at Swiss Vaults Inc., a private safe-deposit firm and gold and silver exchange in Santa Ana. News accounts said that police had found Vincent Carrano, the business's rotund forty-six-year-old co-owner and president, taped to his chair in a back office.

Carrano told a harrowing tale. A man who identified himself as Mr. Pena had telephoned at ten-thirty that Saturday morning asking to deposit twenty bags of silver coins—about $70,000 worth. That afternoon, a dapper man carrying a black blazer over his arm and wearing a wide-brimmed straw hat appeared at the door. Carrano was showing Pena toward the vault when the visitor growled, "Keep moving and don't say anything." Pena brandished a .380 automatic pistol. He walked Carrano past display cases and ordered him to open the locked rear doors, then they headed to the office. "The gun looked nine feet long," Carrano told a reporter.

The vaults, secured by bank-safe doors, harbored more than a hundred customers' valuables—coin collections, mostly. Carrano heard other voices and the sounds of heavy things being dragged. Eventually an accomplice peered into the office and told Pena, "Take care of that fat son of a bitch before you leave."

"I was so scared," Carrano later recounted, "I wet myself."

Carrano's captor cut strips of surgical tape and bound his arms and legs to the chair. When Carrano was sure everyone was gone, he worked at the tape until he was able to free his right hand. Then he scooted the chair across the room to a silent-alarm button. After pressing it, he lost his balance and toppled, hitting his head on a credenza and knocking himself unconscious. Police arrived to find the vaults emptied of three to four tons of gold and silver ingots, bullion, and coins; Carrano's cream-colored Lincoln Continental was also missing. The total loss: $1.1 million.

The chances of recovering any precious metals seemed virtually nil, because they could be melted and recast. "Silver and gold, no problem," Carrano's business partner, Jack Fulton, said. "Melt it down. It has no memory." (Fortunately, Carrano's insurer covered theft for amounts up to $750,000.)

Almost immediately, however, Santa Ana detectives seemed more interested in Carrano than in Pena. Parts of his story struck them as curious. And it turned out that in 1970, he'd been indicted on twenty-seven counts of mail fraud and conspiracy in the manipulation of stock in a Massachusetts railway company. He'd pleaded guilty to three of them.

Just as Myron Fuller's team was installing the wiretap at Trident, his informant Mel Weinberg received a call from mob-connected Joe Trocchio with a question: Did Mel know any hit men in Cleveland? Trocchio explained that Pro was looking.

Weinberg, who had roots in Pittsburgh, replied that he would call a guy named Jim Pagett, who went by J.P. Then he called Fuller at the FBI.

Fuller, not knowing that Wedick was already on it, came up with an idea. A short time later, Trocchio's phone rang, and the caller identified himself as J.P. It was actually Weinberg, disguising his voice. He said he could do the job for $10,000—with half up front. Trocchio agreed to send the cash through Weinberg.

With the wiretap live, Fuller listened in as Pro coordinated the hit. Referring to "getting lumber and hammers for the construction job" on the "Cleveland project," Fred said he planned to ride his limo to Trocchio's Long Island house with a dossier on Armand Mucci, including a map of the Shaker House and handwritten notes about Mucci's car and his preferred restaurants.

Weinberg, serving as the go-between with the fictional hit man, visited Trocchio to collect the contract money. But Trocchio gave him only $2,500—half the advance fee. Weinberg waited a week, then told Trocchio that J.P. wouldn't do the hit until he received the other $2,500. Trocchio grew angry. "I'll send out a hit on *him*," he said.

Weinberg, now enjoying the role, called Pro playing the part of Pagett, the hit man. "Pro, you didn't keep your promise," he said.

Fred swore he'd given Trocchio $10,000, leaving Weinberg convinced that Trocchio had skimmed some of it. "That's the kind of people these are," said Weinberg, the longtime con man. "There's no honesty anymore."

Fuller was pleased. The hit seemed derailed, and in the meantime, he sent another request to the FBI office in Cleveland for an agent to warn Mucci.

After learning of the plot, Mucci phoned Pro and confronted him. Afraid that word of the hit had spread, Pro called Trocchio, who, in turn, reached Weinberg—everyone trying to figure out who had talked.

"Mel, we got a leak," Trocchio said. "The FBI told Mucci there's a contract on him. Can we trust J.P.?"

"Absolutely," Weinberg said. "J.P.'s a mob hitter. He'd never talk to the feds. Maybe there's a tap on Pro's phone, or yours."

Either way, Trocchio was spooked. "Tell J.P. he doesn't have to kill him, okay? We still want our money back, but it's okay if J.P. just breaks his legs a little."

But Weinberg said Pagett was angry about being stiffed. "I ain't gonna push him, either," Weinberg said. "I'm not gettin' anything out of this, and he'd whack me out in a minute if he gets mad at me."

———

Fuller was riveted to the phone calls coming through the wiretap on Pro's phone. The con man talked in surging geysers of words, dexterously handling calls no matter how peevish or suspicious his clients had become about their long-delayed loans. One day he was claiming the stock market had closed early in London. The next: "Oh, didn't you hear? They had a bad storm, and the cable through the Atlantic Ocean broke."

Near midnight on the third day the wiretap was live, J.J. sat alone in the Trident offices. Pro had turned in, and Mangiameli was going out but was comfortable enough with Wedick to let him hang around. J.J. initiated a conference call with Kitzer and Brennan.

Phil had been drinking and was in a jovial mood. He decided that since Pro owed him for Seven Oak and was shamelessly stalling, as usual, they would rack up the most expensive conference call in history on Fred's nickel. They called Captain Jack Elliott in Southern California and a mutual friend in London. Soon there were so many people on the line that it was tricky to keep up a conversation. But Elliott held everyone's attention with an account of Vince Carrano's antics. Carrano, a longtime promoter, had over the past year embezzled many of his customers' precious metals and valuables—only to face a dilemma when a Swiss Vaults client showed up demanding his loot. "I think the problem is solved," Elliott said, "because they've been robbed."

Phil immediately guessed insurance fraud, and Elliott concurred that the theft was likely staged. "Hell, that shit's been gone for six months," Elliott said.

"That son of a bitch was trying to get me to buy that place," Phil scoffed.

In January, Carrano had asked Phil whether he wanted whatever remained on deposit. Phil wasn't interested in inheriting Carrano's mess, but, true to form, he'd had another idea. In the past he'd worked with a Swiss con man named Marco Koenig. If Carrano had enough left on deposit to make it appealing, Koenig would purchase Swiss Vaults and pillage the remaining loot. A different promoter would be listed as the new owner—someone claiming to be a priest at the Vatican. That person would "simply return to the Vatican and drop out of sight," Phil said.

Carrano had seemed interested, but he'd never advanced the proposal—and then, obviously, he'd come up with his own solution. "Well, maybe I'll come down there and shake him down for a hundred thousand dollars," Phil said.

Everyone laughed, and then Phil asked if the robbery had been staged plausibly.

"I believe the robbery, but I don't believe [they had enough of] the tape it would take to bind him to a chair," Elliott said.

Laughter filled the phone line. Before hanging up, Phil told Elliott to continue the call for as long as he wanted.

Later that night, J.J. phoned Fuller's surveillance operation and asked if they'd recorded the conversation.

"What conversation?" the agent replied.

J.J. instantly knew what had happened. Under the rules of Title III, the FBI had to disconnect during conversations that didn't involve illegal activities. When the agents had heard Phil's boozy opening lines, they'd figured it was late-night nonsense and hung up. J.J. had read that the FBI had joined the Swiss Vaults investigation, and he knew agents out there would have found the recording useful.

"You gotta be kidding me," he said. He and Jack would have to try to find another way to help.

J.J. was sitting in the FBI's Kitzer war room in Indianapolis, waiting for Jack to arrive to plot out their next moves, when another agent poked his head in. Jack was in the parking lot and needed help carrying up evidence, he said. But when J.J. walked outside, he found Jack sitting in his Buick station wagon with Becky, their two boys tucked into the back, suitcases jammed into every crevice and strapped to the roof. J.J. stooped to peer in the window.

"You going on an eighteen-month vacation, Jack?" he said.

"Look, I'll just be gone a few days," he replied. In Alabama, with Becky's family.

J.J. felt a surge of irritation, but there wasn't much he could do. There were children in the car. Jack had probably planned this, to avoid a scene, J.J. thought.

He understood that Jack needed to spend time with his family, but he found it hard to relate to. He had a different life—and the case, for the moment, *was* his life.

"Okay," J.J. said, lifting his forearms off Jack's window. "You're gonna come back, right?"

If he doesn't come back, J.J. thought, *I'm gonna kill him.*

Jack assured him that he just needed a week, tops.

J.J. sighed. It was a delicate time. The First National Haiti situation loomed as a major quandary. Phil wanted them along for the trip to Port-au-Prince, but Lowie had called around about travel to the troubled Caribbean nation. The SAC in San Juan, Puerto Rico, had said the agents should definitely not work undercover there while Jean-Claude "Baby Doc" Duvalier was in charge. Too much instability.

The agents had already elevated excuse making to an art form with Phil. They staged fights, one of them stalking off to go file a report. J.J. would say he was headed for a drink with a woman he'd met earlier. Or Jack would claim he had to call his corrupt commodities broker, which was a useful fib. Phil would sometimes turn to J.J. and say, "Come on, let's go down to the bar—he's talking to his pork-belly guy." They invented tales of wilderness treks in Montana and camping excursions in Canada. It helped that Phil and the other promoters constantly spun outlandish tales. Jack, who'd grown up hunting and sailing in the South, plausibly described fictitious moose-hunting trips and sailboat races. "We would tell him," Jack said, "whatever we thought he would believe."

The irony was not lost on them that they'd built a vast undercover operation, then had to find ways to get away from their target.

The more outlandish the excuses Jack and J.J. invented, the more Phil and the others embraced them. Story was currency in its own right, and the chance to repeat a good one conferred some of the riches on the audience. So any tale was accepted at face value, and considered a challenge for the others to try to top.

Haiti was different. This was their signature project, and Phil wouldn't countenance any casual excuses. If Jack and J.J. were going to be the president and vice president, as Phil envisioned, they needed to help set up the operation, which would include bribing government officials.

J.J. flew with Phil to Miami, feeling anxious. If he didn't handle this right, he thought, Phil might drop them from the Haiti project. When they bought tickets to Port-au-Prince at the Royal Embassy Travel Service in the Sheraton Four Ambassadors, J.J. couldn't delay any longer.

He pulled Phil aside. Several years earlier, he explained, he and Jack had been sailing the Caribbean when customs officials stopped them near Haiti, boarded the boat, and found an undeclared gun. They also had lots of cash. Customs towed the boat to Port-au-Prince, and J.J. and Jack paid some bribes to be set free—but the charge was still hanging over their heads. (The story, though embellished, was based on an incident Jack had once described involving a friend in Honduras.)

Phil looked at him. "Were there any drugs involved?"

J.J. avoided answering this. He wanted to leave some details to Phil's imagination, let him fill in the gaps. J.J. had watched Phil do this with his marks, letting customers extrapolate details about Seven Oak from his tailored suits and gold-embossed paperwork.

"Why didn't you tell me this earlier?" Phil said angrily.

J.J. apologized profusely. He found, to his surprise, that part of him actually felt contrite. He said he'd known that Phil was going to be unhappy and he'd just put it off—but that he and Jack really wanted to be involved.

Phil brooded a bit. "I always thought you guys were a little bit crooked," he said finally.

Then he told his own story about being asked for his passport while riding a train through the Soviet Union. The blue book was littered with visas and entry stamps from around the planet, and the Soviets—perhaps thinking he was some sort of spy—pulled him off the train for thirty-six hours of questioning. When Phil returned home, he sent a letter cursing out Premier Khrushchev; after that, the USSR was among the few places he wouldn't go.

J.J. smirked. He and Jack had to write off a Caribbean island, he said, but Phil couldn't travel in half the Asian continent.

"It's only July," Phil replied. "Let's do a recount in December."

They both laughed, and J.J. knew he was forgiven.

J.J. again sensed trouble when he and Phil returned to New York a week later. Jack was still away, and Phil again expressed irritation that he was assuming all the grunt work to set up First National. He said he was no longer certain that he could count on the Junior G-Men. The effort had taken on a newfound urgency, too. While in Haiti, he'd received word that Scotland Yard had made another visit to Seven Oak, this time with a search warrant to obtain whatever evidence was available to show that the bank was fraudulent.

The agents knew that Phil's relationship with Paul Chovanec had ended abruptly over some undisclosed rift. For his part, J.J. had spent the week working the phones solo, sometimes talking to mob figures. The job was getting edgy.

Plus, the city hummed with an apocalyptic vibe. Less than a week earlier, on the night of July 13, 1977, a series of lightning strikes had plunged New York into a twenty-five-hour blackout. Arsonists set more than a thousand fires, and rioters pillaged more than sixteen hundred stores from Harlem to eastern Brooklyn. The *New York Post* reported that "even the looters were being mugged." The Son of Sam was still on the loose.

J.J. told Jack to get back to New York so they could reconnect with Phil. When Jack reported that the next day's flights were sold out, J.J. told him to charter one.

"If you ain't got a plane, *find* a plane," he bellowed.

Jack chartered a plane to Atlanta, then caught a commercial flight to New York. He and J.J. knew the Cox brothers would go crazy when they saw that receipt, but by then they'd already had countless expense-reimbursement issues. What was one more?

When they all reunited and returned to work on July 20, Phil seemed pleased to have everyone back together. But even the cons felt grimmer. Jack Scharf, the promoter who dealt in weapons, wanted Phil to provide phony bid bonds for a deal with North Korea. The group met another con man, this one with a contract to provide pesticides to school districts and highway departments. The scam was simple: He poured a few quarts of kerosene into fifty-five-gallon drums, then filled them the rest of the way with water.

One night, the threesome headed home from an East Side bar at two a.m. and couldn't find a cab. Phil suggested they cut through the park. J.J., the Bronx native, shook his head. "Guys, are you crazy? We're taking our lives in our hands."

They set off anyway, jumping at every rustle in the sticky Manhattan night, the honks of cars and the whoosh of traffic fading like old memories as they skittered through the dark. "Violence," J.J. said, "was on everybody's mind."

Some of the mayhem hit unsettlingly close to home. The government's case against Joe Trocchio and two accomplices for the theft of $2.5 million in stolen U.S. Treasury notes experienced significant setbacks: On July 20, a potential witness, John Quinn, a Long Island resident who dabbled in mob activities, was found shot to death, his body dumped in the woods in Staten Island. Four days later, the bullet-pocked body of Cherie Golden, his nineteen-year-old girlfriend, turned up in Brooklyn in the trunk of a 1974 Lincoln Continental registered to Trocchio's girlfriend.

Maybe it was the palpable sense of society fraying around them, but Phil and the agents looked out for one another more than ever. One night J.J. fell asleep on the couch of their suite. Knowing his tendency to get cold with the air conditioner belching out chilly gusts, Phil spread a blanket over him. He had even offered the Junior G-Men their choice of rooms. He nudged J.J. to use his extra leather jacket when they headed out. Other times, J.J. borrowed his shirts and ties.

Phil often had stomach problems, sometimes even a searing pain in his midsection that he thought was an ulcer. Jack and J.J. took turns running to pharmacies for Pepto-Bismol and Tums. They carried his bags and fetched his dry cleaning.

Despite all this, Phil, as always, naturally gravitated toward fun. On a flight out of LaGuardia, a mechanical problem stranded them on the tarmac for an hour. Phil requested a deck of cards and organized a bridge game with Jack and some other passengers, ordering drinks and sparking laughter with his stories. When they went out, Phil taught Jack how to deploy his gold-plated Dunhill lighter. The key was anticipating the exact moment to swoop in next to a woman who'd just pulled out a cigarette. Jack experimented with the move, absentmindedly pocketing the device. Eventually Phil surprised him by buying him an identical model, and the two of them discussed the lighters endlessly afterward. During their nights out, Jack would return from cigarette-lighting excursions like a conquering king, wearing a triumphant grin.

They were their own band of three, and their protective bubble allowed some space for them to see beyond the carnage of the city. Walking down Third Avenue, barhopping, Phil scanned the skyline as if seeing the soaring parapets for the first time. For most of them to be built, he said, someone had to take a gamble on loaning millions of dollars. The buildings represented, in some form, trust. A group of strangers—bankers, contractors, insurers—had to believe in each other, and in a system, in a high-stakes game. From Phil's perspective, it was miraculous that there were enough honest people to make it happen.

In late July, Trident Consortium employees were having phone issues and called for service. Listening in, Fuller heard a service technician tell Dorian Mangiameli that while inspecting the box in the basement, he'd discovered that the business's phones were tapped. Mangiameli, shocked, spread the word that everyone should be careful about what they said.

Myron Fuller wondered whether the utility worker had connections to LCN—short for La Cosa Nostra, or the Mafia—because the mob seemed to be working its way into every legitimate enterprise. But there was good news: Fred Pro didn't know that the FBI had also bugged his office. Fuller's team could still hear everything said inside the office, and at least Pro's half of his phone conversations.

Pro also seemed constitutionally incapable of keeping his mouth shut. He would warn people who called—*the goddamn phone is tapped, don't say anything*—but then launch into an explication of an ongoing scam. Fuller later understood why: Pro had long heard that his phones were tapped; in one instance, someone had told him that his ex-wife or girlfriend had bugged him. "I really . . . think a lot of people are paranoid about it and I really did not seriously believe my phones were tapped," Pro said.

Mangiameli, who told him about the bug, "had illusions of grandeur, too," Pro said, "and I didn't believe everything he told me."

Pro had a booming business to run, and it defied every cell in his body to go silent. Fuller noted that Pro wasn't just talking to victims. He also spoke regularly with people the FBI recognized as associates of the Genovese, Lucchese, and Gambino crime families: Joe Trocchio, Sonny Santini, and Vinnie DiNapoli, among others. Both Mel Weinberg and Sy Guthrie, Pro's partner at Trident, told

Fuller that many New York–based promoters were mixed up with the mob.

Guthrie was also now talking to the FBI. He had lost his appeal on a fraud conviction and turned himself in to the Metropolitan Correctional Center in New York on July 20 to begin a forty-two-month sentence. He offered to cooperate with Fuller to shave off some time, and admitted that while working with Pro, he'd also been on DiNapoli's payroll.

Everything Guthrie was saying, and that Fuller intercepted on the wiretap, aligned with what the FBI understood of the Mafia's business methods. Historically the mob had focused on illegal activities like gambling and extortion. But during the previous decade, the five families had started tapping legitimate public enterprises as income sources. They cooperated in running construction and private sanitation firms and trucking and garbage-hauling companies. To mask their involvement, they took only a piece of the business, leaving a valid front in place. The mob took control of labor, after which "vast sums of money are siphoned from union pension funds, businesses are extorted in return for labor peace and an absence of strikes, and bribes are solicited for sweetheart contracts," said one report on LCN activities.

It was a propitious time for such rackets. President Carter was formulating plans to rebuild the Bronx, which meant hundreds of millions of dollars in government contracts. The Lucchese family, for one, already had ten or fifteen different straw builders lined up to grab government money, Fuller learned.

Guthrie said the families sought three elements to operate their schemes: a bank, an insurance company, and government contracts. For the first two, they turned to experts like Kitzer and Pro. "Can you imagine Vinnie DiNapoli walking into a bank and asking for a loan wearing his pinstripe suit?" Guthrie told Fuller.

Fuller immediately understood the ramifications. If the promoters delivered banks and insurance firms, the mafiosi could provide protection and enforcement. That would be handy for Pro when people started banging on his door, demanding refunds.

"The wiretap delivered evidence on a grand scale, all over the city, and it connected to all five families," Fuller said. "We had a great picture of how organized crime was working with con men."

As the wiretap's court-mandated run neared its end, Fuller hatched grander plans. On July 25, Weinberg, at Fuller's request, called a meeting with Joe Trocchio regarding Brookhaven, the mortgage company the mob was trying to acquire. Fuller and his colleague John Hauss attended, posing as buyers working for a Lebanese sheikh who, they claimed, wanted to invest his oil fortune in stolen securities, phony CDs, and counterfeit money.

It was the first meeting of what would become one of the most sensational investigations in FBI history.

That same day, Phil departed on a second trip to Haiti, leaving Jack and J.J. in New York to babysit Pro for the balance of the Seven Oak money. Pro had started working with Andy D'Amato on the endlessly discussed takeover of the Fontainebleau Hotel. As they all lounged on Trident's easy chairs, the door opened and a Francis Ford Coppola movie walked in. Gabe Cicale introduced everyone to Ralph Cantone, Ron Sablosky, and John "Sonny" Santini.

Santini in particular made an impression. He was five-eight and stocky, with thinning hair and a blotchy red face. He moved aggressively into the agents' personal space, talking close and peering at them as if scrutinizing scientific specimens. J.J. recognized his accent as full-blooded Bronx. As if to make sure no one misunderstood who he was, Santini launched into a story that involved shaking down a mark for payment. "The motherfucker wasn't doing what I asked," he said, "so I get an icepick and stick it in his fuckin' ear."

His scams took on a far more menacing tone. He'd been a ringleader in an early 1970s scheme to artificially drive up the stock price of a shell corporation named Elinvest, then used deception and threats of violence to foist the worthless shares on investors.

Eventually he and his co-conspirators cashed out. He moved on to an advance-fee operation run out of a midtown restaurant, Perilous Pauline's. On one occasion, he and Pro extracted $2,500 from a concrete contractor. When the mark hesitated, Santini snarled, "We spent enough time with you. You better come up with the money or we'll break your head." Then he would tell victims that he couldn't deliver the promised loans because the courier carrying the paperwork had come down with appendicitis or had a heart attack.

Over time, Pro had become ensnared in Santini's tentacles, and he now kicked a percentage of everything to his "partner." Santini had installed a "girl" to answer phones at Trident to make sure Pro didn't stiff him on any payments.

Jack was holding a gun, and J.J. went at him.

They were back in J.J.'s apartment in Griffith, working on ways to manage the suddenly elevated level of risk in their operation. They had never worried about their safety with men like Phil and D'Amato, but now they were hanging out with guys who carried ice picks around.

To prepare for potential confrontations, they began practicing techniques for disarming a wiseguy. They knew from their training that when someone pulls a gun, the natural reaction is to back away. The agents drilled each other to do the opposite: They practiced instantaneously moving to within an arm's length of their assailant, grabbing his hand, and breaking a finger or wrist. Speed and surprise were essential. As long as they were able to get within an arm's length, the agents believed, the gunman couldn't react fast enough to counter an attack. It was action versus reaction. After practicing the moves hundreds of times, switching roles back and forth, Jack and J.J. believed in their decisive first strike. Still, to survive that kind of situation unarmed, they would need skill and luck. The agents would need to be close enough to reach the gunman within a second or two, then survive the subsequent struggle.

FBI officials were coming to the same realization about OpFo-Pen's elevated risks, thanks in part to Fuller's wiretap. In late July, the bureau approved the Indianapolis office's request to designate the case as a Bureau Special. This top-tier classification mandated that every supervisor around the country dispatch agents immediately to support the investigation and pursue any leads within his region. Each office had forty-eight hours to shuffle their caseloads to make this possible.

Soon after that, headquarters came up with another, even more meaningful designation for the undercover operation: Major Case Number One. This meant that the FBI was designating Fountain Pen as its top priority, signaling a further move into a new kind of policing. The bureau would finally provide the computer support that the besieged Indianapolis office had been requesting for months.

Phil returned to New York at one-thirty a.m. on July 27, reporting that First National Haiti was nearly ready. He'd obtained government approvals in Port-au-Prince, set up a telex machine and phone and hired someone to handle them, and reserved space in the offices of a friendly attorney. It was his version of an Old West town on a Hollywood set: There was nothing behind the facade, but it looked impressive from the outside. The next step would be to extract $100,000 from investors to meet the minimum capitalization requirement.

This left Phil feeling jaunty. That night, they went to dinner at the Essex House with D'Amato, Pro and his Trident pack, and a clutch of women. Such gatherings infused the promoters with a certain brio, and by the time dessert arrived D'Amato was jousting with Pro over who was the bigger operator and bragging about the Eurotrust's $10 billion in assets. Phil leaned over to J.J. and said, "Ten billion in assets? Let's see how many fucking assets he's got in his pocket."

He told J.J. and Jack to excuse themselves to make a call and to meet him in five minutes in the lobby. At the appointed time, Phil led them out onto Central Park South, where they watched through the window as the waiter approached with the check for more than $300. Phil laughed as D'Amato noticed their absence and gazed at the bill, his face suddenly pale.

They were sitting in Trident's offices around noon the next day when an unexpected visitor appeared: Bernard Baker. Until recently, the Kansas farmer had been unsure of what to make of Pro's machinations. "I couldn't say that I felt that he wasn't trying," he recalled, "but I had the feeling that sometimes he wasn't."

His patience was now gone. He'd flown in from Kansas to collect a $110,000 refund and threatened to go to the FBI if he didn't get it. His bank was pressuring him to start paying the money back.

Pro tap-danced for a while, enumerating the challenges involved with securing multimillion-dollar loans. But when he realized that Baker wasn't going away, he wrote a check on his Merchants Bank of New York account for $109,000 (subtracting a thousand-dollar processing fee).

Baker departed, and Gabe Cicale arrived with news: Sonny Santini wanted to see Phil the next morning.

Phil sat back. This would be a delicate meeting, he said. He was cautious in his interactions with the Outfit. During one deal that had gone sideways, someone had tried to push Pro out of a twenty-ninth-floor window of the Park Lane Hotel. "Sonny is a heavy guy," Phil said. "We got to be very careful in dealing with him."

When they all sat around a table at the Windjammer Bar at the Essex House the next morning, Santini objected to Jack and J.J.'s presence. Phil explained that his protégés would be the new bank's officers and needed to be there. Santini relented and got to the point: He wanted in on the Haiti vehicle. He was expecting an advance-fee windfall soon, and proposed putting in $100,000 in return for the right to sell the bank's paper.

Phil nodded and said he would be happy to have Santini as a partner—but FNCB would be a poor investment. The bank, as Sonny knew, would be a vehicle for fraudulent paper—which meant that eventually, inevitably, it would vaporize. "Any money in there is going to be lost," Phil said. "You need to know that, Sonny."

The agents had seen Phil execute these sorts of diversionary tactics many times. He might tell a client, "Okay, when we sign the appraisal and you give me $10,000, we'll have everything in place." Before the client could protest, Kitzer would steer the conversation away, and later he would come back and say, "Now, as you indicated before, this would be the time to give me the check for $10,000."

Phil's black lullabies were always remarkably effective. He would present them so seamlessly and change the subject so quickly, the mark had no hope of keeping up. By the end of the conversation, the victim would be convinced that the $10,000 payment was a bargain—even his idea to begin with.

In this instance, Phil had another suggestion for channeling Santini's talents. Pro had agreed to pay $200,000 for Seven Oak, but so far he'd handed over less than $25,000. If Santini wanted to collect the balance, Phil would happily split it with him. Santini liked that idea; collections were his specialty. Phil then pivoted to other deals. One involved a Southern California precious-metals refinery run by his friend Jack Elliott. Santini, who had run a gold-prospecting scam in Las Vegas, was intrigued.

Before the meeting broke up, Santini shared a story about a recent money-collection episode. Neither the debtor nor the money was present when he arrived, so Santini dangled the guy's child out of a window several dozen floors up until someone delivered the cash.

Kitzer had dealt with organized-crime figures before. (He'd

recently talked with legendary mob lawyer Morrie Shenker about issuing paper for a refinance of the Dunes Hotel in Las Vegas. Shenker was a close Jimmy Hoffa ally.) He was happy to make money with Santini—as long as he didn't come out of it with Sonny owning a piece of him. On the way to the airport, Phil said that a friend in the Outfit had warned him about Santini.

"Don't ever owe Sonny a nickel," the friend had said. "He'll kill you."

Sifting through his wallet one morning in New York, Jack discovered something that scared him more than anything else he'd experienced undercover. He'd kept a scrap of paper in there with the phone number for Becky's apartment.

That paper was now missing.

Jack pondered various scenarios: Maybe it had fallen out and was lost. But maybe Phil had found it, or one of the mob guys had gone through his wallet. Each possibility seemed worse than the last. He was angry with himself for keeping the paper, because by then he'd memorized the number.

Becky was busy with the boys when the phone rang. She'd just traveled back from their Florida vacation—driving solo after Jack had bailed out—and the baby was rattling around, now less than three months from his scheduled arrival.

She was tired, but for the moment her outlook was sunnier than it had been over the winter. She and Jack had slowly rebuilt their relationship—as much as that was possible right now. They clung to the idea that life would improve when OpFoPen was over. Jack had also realized that the case could be his ticket out of Gary. He and J.J. had been exposed to dangerous characters, which might mean a transfer for everyone's safety.

She was at first relieved to hear Jack's voice, but she immediately picked up on the worry in it.

"That paper with your number on it," he said. "It's gone."

"What do you mean? What happened to it?"

"I don't know. I can't find it."

She had no clue about the ramifications. They had maintained a code of silence about his work. A friend of a friend worked for the local paper, and she feared that if she knew anything, she might let an idle comment slip and a story would turn up on the front page.

Jack faced a dilemma. He didn't want to scare her, but he also had to be brutally clear about the stakes. "Some of the people I'm with are . . . pretty bad," he said. "Do not let the boys say 'Brennan residence' when they answer the phone. And when you answer the phone, just say hello. If someone you don't know asks for me, say, 'I don't know who that is. You have the wrong number.'"

Jack told her he loved her and that he had to go. He knew that Becky was smart and believed she would handle the situation well, and he couldn't afford to worry. That would mean being distracted, which was not a good idea with the promoters. That was when you slipped up.

Becky had, many times, idly wondered what he was doing. She still had no idea, but now she knew for certain that it was danger-ous. She felt frustrated about being shut out—unable to evaluate the risks, ponder the timeline, circle a date to try to get to, after which they'd finally be clear of it.

But this was her life now: Her husband was in danger. And as she placed the receiver back in its cradle, another realization washed over her like a surge of electricity: As of that moment, she and their children were in danger, too.

Fool's Gold

J.J. Wedick hustled into the lobby of the Registry Hotel in Irvine, California. He'd been in his room, fiddling with the Nagra that Bowen Johnson had handed off to him on the far side of the hotel after they'd landed at Orange County Airport the night before, and now he was late. For this trip, J.J. had decided to wear the recorder differently so that he could keep the remote control in the vest of his three-piece suit. This required running the wire for the remote up over his shoulder instead of around his torso. The setup allowed him to avoid cutting a hole in his pants pocket.

He felt mildly exasperated to be wearing the suit at all; it wasn't an easy look to pull off in Southern California in July. But he and Jack and Bowen Johnson had all agreed that it was important to record that day's conversations. The plan was to meet with Captain Jack Elliott to discuss Vincent Carrano and the Swiss Vaults heist.

The Registry was a ten-story, 293-room behemoth that had opened the year before. J.J. wandered through the lobby, looking for the atrium decorated in the French Provincial style where they planned to meet. When he paused to gain his bearings, Phil and Elliott approached from behind, and Elliott, a gregarious Scot, clapped him on the back.

A bolt of adrenaline shot through J.J.'s body. Elliott's hand had just missed the recorder but instead struck a wire, causing the remote control to pop from his vest and fall inside his suit. J.J. felt it dangling against his stomach. He caught his breath and shook hands with everyone, then assessed the situation as they took seats. He instantly knew he wouldn't be able to reach the remote without unbuttoning his shirt and fishing around. And without the remote, he couldn't start the Nagra.

Elliott alone was worth the tape. A stocky man in his forties who had relocated to Costa Mesa several years earlier, he had jet-black hair and spoke with a jaunty brogue. Jack and J.J. immediately grasped why he and Phil worked well together. Elliott was gifted at talking his way into various businesses, then sinking his hooks into them. He operated something called the Commercial Corporation of London, registered in Panama and run out of his home, which he claimed was just down the street from John Wayne's. He purportedly owned a small airline and a ski resort and golf club in Salt Lake City. He'd recently run into trouble in England for handling two fraudulent bills of exchange worth $2.4 million written on the Bank of Swaziland. But Elliott had a Kitzeresque confidence in his ability to skate free.

Carrano was topic number one. Elliott launched into a play-by-play account of the staged robbery. Over the past year, Carrano had looted the place for more than $600,000, carrying out hundred-ounce gold bars and bags of silver coins and replacing them with twenty-six thousand metal washers. In early July, a customer had come in demanding access to his silver. In Elliott's retelling, what happened next was screamingly funny: On a Saturday afternoon, Carrano and several associates disconnected and rewired the burglar alarm; then someone taped Carrano to a chair and tipped it over, leaving the 350-pound promoter lying on his side with his mouth taped shut. Phil and Jack doubled over in hysterics as Elliott told the story. Carrano wanted to sell off the vault items that were taken in the "robbery"—but the police were sniffing around.

Holy shit, I can't believe this, J.J. thought. It was like a replay of when Fuller's surveillance team prematurely turned off the wiretap. J.J. now faced a dilemma: Listen to the story without recording it—again—or leave and fish the remote control from his suit. A film of sweat materialized on his forehead.

Phil looked at him. "What's the matter with you, J.J.?"

"I gotta go to the men's room," he blurted. "My stomach's bothering me."

He lurched to his feet. Inside the restroom, he latched the stall door and fumbled with the buttons on his shirt, then lifted out the device and put it back in place. He forced himself to sit for a few minutes—it had to be a plausible bathroom break—before returning to the group.

J.J. attributed the mild case of dysentery to the Southern California food. "My stomach was bothering me so much I couldn't even listen to you guys," he said. "So, what happened?"

The late-day California sunlight caramelized on the floor of Phil's hotel room. They were between meetings, wrestling with jet lag, when the phone rang and Phil answered. He perched on the edge of a bed, and it was immediately apparent that something serious was going on. Jack wandered out to get some ice while J.J. lounged on the other bed, listening. He inferred that Phil's wife, Audrey, was on the line. Phil went silent for a long stretch, looking at the floor. His face drooped. Phil said, "I can't get you that now."

He apologized and said he would try to figure something out. When he hung up, he stared toward the window and said his six-year-old son, Jeffrey, needed an urgent medical procedure that would cost $2,000. Phil had the money, but he wasn't carrying much on that trip, and whatever he had stashed away was out of reach for the moment. The man who had purportedly owned so many banks couldn't write a check.

The three of them rarely discussed family or anything that happened off the road. It was as if the pieces of their lives apart from one another might slow them down in the hyper-speed parallel existence they shared. Jack and J.J. knew that Phil was out of touch with some of his family; he hadn't spoken with his brother, Joe, for years. But when it came to Audrey and Jeffrey, Phil apparently took his role as provider seriously.

J.J. glanced over and saw the pain in his eyes. For the first time since they'd met, Phil's carefully constructed alternate universe was splitting its seams, and J.J. could see straight through into the abyss.

A quiet settled over them, and J.J. listened to bumps and footsteps coming from whoever occupied the next room. They had developed a familiar banter around the agents' American Express cards, one of their repetitive inside jokes. Phil would playfully try to get one of them to hand over his plastic. J.J. would say, "I love you, Phil, but I ain't giving you my credit card."

It was funny, but it wasn't. He and Jack had by then witnessed dozens of betrayals, small and large, among the promoters. As Elliott later described Phil: "I found him to be very keen. But I also found him to be very ruthless."

J.J. knew he should just get up and step out of the room, leave Phil to figure it out. Instead, he said, "Do you wanna use my credit card?"

Phil looked up. "Would you give it to me?"

J.J. felt something beyond the reach of the cold rationality that had guided his thinking—something in his gut that short-circuited his brain's executive functioning. They had crossed a threshold to where $2,000 didn't seem so important. J.J. wouldn't have even tried to explain it to anyone except Jack. But he knew Phil would pay him back.

"Phillip, if you fuck me over with this card, I'll kill you," he said. "Okay?"

He held out the AmEx. Phil nodded and picked up the phone.

That night they were all hanging out at a nightspot in Newport Beach when J.J. started dancing with a young blond divorcée.

Eventually he wandered over to Jack and Phil and told them that his new friend wanted to go to the beach, and they should head to the hotel without him.

Around midnight, J.J. climbed behind the wheel of his date's Mercedes convertible. They were waiting at a traffic light on MacArthur Boulevard, his elbow resting on the window frame, when a cab pulled up next to them. J.J. looked over and saw Phil and Jack sitting in back. They waved at each other, and he drove off. It struck him that the evening had played out with remarkable similarity to the way it would have if he was around his normal friends.

The next morning, J.J. showed up for breakfast late, dressed in a sport coat, a blue silk Brooks Brothers tie, and jeans. Phil was tolerant of his tardiness because of J.J.'s eventful night, but he didn't approve of the casual attire.

"What are you wearing?" he asked, smirking. He sounded like J.J.'s father back in the Bronx. "You look like you're dressed for a parade."

"Oh, c'mon, Kitzer," J.J. shot back, playing the rebellious teenager. "Look around. This is California."

But at Phil's insistence, J.J. went back upstairs and changed, and they headed off to Elliott's business in Costa Mesa for a tour of the precious-metals refinery operation set up in a storage area behind his offices. Elliott had had about thirty fifty-five-gallon drums of compacted mining dirt shipped in from Reno; he'd obtained them from Carrano the previous year in a trade for bogus Swaziland bills of exchange.

Elliott claimed to be making doré bars—bars of gold that isn't yet fully refined—out of the dirt. He then prepared sham assay reports indicating they were mostly gold, and created certificates based on the reports. Or he bribed an assayer to create certificates claiming the bars contained certain quantities of gold (the reports failing to mention that the cost of separating the gold from the other ores would be roughly equal to its value). Elliott rented out the certificates for 2 percent of face value.

Con artists had long mined veins of bogus gold and precious metals. Elliott and Phil had both handled millions of dollars in phony silver certificates. In other cases, promoters would claim that certain land was loaded with precious metals and sell claims to it. It was an easy con: As long as the materials were underground, you could assign any value you wanted to them.

Elliott fired up the smelter. With the temperature in the room soaring after Elliott poured the dirt into molds, Phil and Elliott removed their suit jackets. Jack, distracted by the spectacle, also shed his coat, drawing a glare from his partner. J.J. couldn't peel off his jacket because of the concealed Nagra. Jack caught the dagger look: *Thanks for the help, pal.*

Phil looked over. "Hey, J.J., aren't you roasting?" he said.

Wedick shook his head. "You know me," he said with a shrug. "Always cold."

Elliott continued his refinery seminar. The bars he produced were solid lead—but his schtick was to claim he was using a process called "iron interlock." If you separate, or unlock, the molecules in the minerals, you can harvest the gold, Elliott said with a grin. He showed the agents a book that backed up the science. "It was a great smoke-and-mirrors story," Jack said.

When the bars were finished, Elliott stamped ingot numbers on them—customers could choose their own—and stored them in an adjacent vault. Jack, J.J., and Phil walked into the vault, and Elliott pointed out one of his inspired touches: He'd chosen lightbulbs that cast a gilded tint over the bars. Jack and J.J. looked at each other and rolled their eyes. It was all just a collection of unconvincing props and stage lighting, but Phil told the agents the paper was still worthwhile. A client could take the certificates to his banker and say, "Will you hold this for me and give me a receipt?" He would then possess a document from a credible bank saying he owned $1 million in gold—and could use that receipt at a second bank as collateral on a loan. Before they left, Phil sent a few bars to Santini and Cicale, who wanted in on the scheme.

———

The Pasadena smog had settled in for the day and the football game was already under way by the time Phil, Jack, and J.J., all clutching beers, settled into their seats in the Rose Bowl. After a week of meetings, with their business in Southern California finished, Phil had surprised them with tickets to a preseason NFL game that Saturday, August 6: the Los Angeles Rams against his beloved Minnesota Vikings. Phil wasn't a huge sports fan, but he avidly followed the Vikings and their star quarterback, Fran Tarkenton.

Small and slender for pro football, Tarkenton didn't look the part. But when his opponents swarmed him and a sack seemed imminent, Tarkenton would duck, dodge, and feint and run for a big gain. He had an uncanny knack for slipping free just when trouble was closing in.

The trip's slower pace had afforded the trio a rare chance to soak up some local culture. Near one hotel in Los Angeles, Jack walked past a woman he recognized as cruise director Julie McCoy from *The Love Boat*, the hit TV show that had launched the previous year. Jack swiveled and wandered to the edge of a shoot. At dinner in Beverly Hills, Phil ordered steak tartare, then spent the entire meal amusing himself by badgering his wary friends to take a bite.

Back at the hotel the next day, the phone jangled to life. Pro was calling about the doré bars Phil had sent; apparently Santini had taken them to be assayed and was incensed to learn that they were pure lead. He felt Phil had suckered him somehow.

Phil chuckled. "You know Sonny's mentality," he said. Santini wasn't as mentally nimble as the other promoters, and was perpetually suspicious that they were taking advantage of him. Phil hung up, and they made plans for the evening. The phone rang again. This time it was a terse-sounding Santini, asking Phil to come back to New York as soon as possible.

"We need to meet," he said.

Phil replaced the receiver in its cradle and pondered this development, then told Jack and J.J. that he suspected that Santini and Cicale had conned themselves into believing the doré bars actually contained gold. They were already on the verge of leaving California, and Phil figured they might as well take a red-eye so they could tamp the problem down quickly.

New York's summer-long meltdown had shown no signs of abating when their flight from Los Angeles touched down. The daytime temperatures hovered around ninety, with smothering humidity, and at night it dropped only to seventy-five. The three men hopped in a cab to Manhattan and checked into the Essex House, then met with Pro, who was acting jittery and distant, as if he had a secret he didn't dare tell.

Phil and the agents were foggy from the red-eye, but they'd slept just enough to slog through the day. They sat down for breakfast around ten-thirty at the hotel's restaurant. Jack was the only one enjoying the food; J.J. had only coffee, as usual, and Phil was picking at a plate halfheartedly when Gabe Cicale and Sonny Santini walked in and the room ionized. Santini looked twitchy, his face blotched with swaths of red and tightened into a scowl.

Cicale was harder to read, but his usual joviality was absent. "Okay, guys," he said, his voice chilly. "Let's take a ride."

"Where?" Phil said.

"We're going up to the Bronx," Cicale said.

Santini stood there looking peeved.

Cicale was focused on Phil, but he gestured to the Junior G-Men, too. "We'll wait for you out front," he said. Then they disappeared into a pair of black Lincolns parked illegally on Central Park South.

Phil, Jack, and J.J. looked at one another: *What the hell is this about?* Their meals sat half-eaten.

Phil stood. "Let me find out what's going on," he said.

They watched him leave; then J.J. turned to Jack. "I ain't going up to the Bronx with these guys, Jack," he said. "This does *not* feel good to me."

This seemed to be about more than just a few bars of lead. Jack agreed. They watched through the windows, envisioning Vinnie DiNapoli (a made man and Sonny's boss) sitting in the Bronx, waiting for them. There was no chance to get help. Bowen Johnson had a room on the fourth floor, but they had no way to alert him.

The agents stood and walked to where Phil was speaking with Cicale. He nodded and turned back toward the hotel alone, and the agents cornered him. "Phillip," J.J. said. They used his full name when they wanted his undivided attention. "We are *not* getting in that car. There's something rotten here."

Phil told them he'd already come up with another suggestion: They would go up to his hotel room and have a private conversation there—just him, Santini, Cicale, and Ralph Cantone, who had emerged from one of the waiting cars. "Whatever it is," Phil said, "they want to talk to me. You guys wait here."

The four of them, Phil and the mob guys, walked through the lobby and disappeared into an elevator. The agents watched as Phil pushed the button for the eleventh floor and nodded at them.

Jack and J.J. moved immediately, without discussion. They boarded the next elevator to the fourth floor and went straight to Johnson's room. Both were thinking the same thing: *Get the guns.* They banged on the door, and J.J. called, "Bowen!" But he was gone—probably on a coffee run, since he had also flown a red-eye. No one had expected that they would walk directly into this kind of trouble during their first hour back in New York.

Whatever. There was no time to find Johnson. Jack and J.J. darted back onto the elevator, and on the ride up to the eleventh floor, they riffed on potential strategies. *We could just listen. If it sounds okay, stay outside. One of us could go back for the guns. But what if it sounds bad?*

They had no idea what to expect, but J.J. was furious that they didn't have their guns the one time they really needed them. They exited the elevator, turned right at a T intersection, and came within a few yards of Phil's door. They could hear bellowing and creative variations of *motherfucker* and *son of a bitch*—obviously Santini.

It sounded bad. The agents were unarmed, and the three mafiosi in the room were almost certainly packing. Strictly speaking, this was not the way the FBI had trained them to execute their missions. The right move would have been to call for backup before entering—but they couldn't just stand out in the hall: Santini sounded like he was on the verge of throwing Phil out the window.

"If they shoot him and we're out here, that's fucking ridiculous," J.J. said.

Jack raised his fist and pounded on the door.

Sonny's Mentality

AUGUST 8, 1977

Everything went quiet. That was the first thing the agents noticed after Jack banged on the door—Santini stopped bellowing. When Jack and J.J. leaned closer, they heard only Phil's voice. It sounded even and measured, as if he were making one of his presentations.

Phil answered the door, looking flushed but calm. Jack and J.J. were breathing hard.

"Phil," J.J. said, peering around him. "What's going on?"

Phil held his hands up. "Everything's fine."

J.J. and Jack could see the three Outfit guys toward the back of the room. Santini, his neck crimson, stood against a wall.

"Can we come in?" J.J. said. They wanted to make sure no one was holding a gun—though it was unclear what they would do if someone was.

Phil said, "There was a misunderstanding."

He turned back to Santini and picked up where he'd left off: "So, Sonny, like I was saying. Am I wrong about this? You're the kind of guy, somebody screws you, your mind-set is that you're not going to let that happen. You're going to go grab the guy by the neck and hang him out a window. Or stick an ice pick in their ear."

Santini agreed.

"Well, then, Freddie's the guy you need to be concerned about," Phil continued. "That $200,000 for Seven Oak—he still hasn't paid most of that."

Santini nodded.

"And he knows you're the guy trying to collect it?"

Santini conceded that this was true.

"You *know* Freddie's making money over there," Phil said. "He's got so many deals going he can't keep up. You ask me? He's got that $200,000, and he's holding out on us." He sat on a bed. "And like I said," he continued, "you're not the kind of guy who lets someone screw you like that right under your nose. *That's* what I was saying yesterday. Was I wrong about that?"

Santini shook his head.

"So, Sonny," Phil said, "if anyone's got money here, it's Freddie. *He's* the piece of shit who's cutting you out."

Santini mulled this over a bit longer and stood and nodded at Cicale and Cantone. The Trident Consortium offices were next door. Before they left, Phil reminded them to be careful about the phones—the FBI had bugged them.

"Yeah, well, if the FBI arrests him, I'm gonna kill him," Santini said. "Fred can't keep his fuckin' mouth shut."

Santini, Cicale, and Cantone left, and Phil and the agents passed a few moments in stunned silence before Jack said, "What was *that*?"

They returned to the restaurant, where Phil recounted the episode. It turned out that when Pro had called them in Orange County, he'd been using the speakerphone—with Santini in the room, listening. When Phil had said, "You know Sonny's mentality," Santini went apoplectic. He thought Phil was saying he was "mental"—as in intellectually challenged.

Once they went upstairs and Phil pieced this together, he turned on his mouth. *Sonny, you misunderstand. What I was saying is that you've got the mentality to succeed in this business, because you know how to bring in the money. That's an attribute to be admired, and it has nothing to do with your intelligence. In fact, you have to be smart and resourceful to be so good at what you do.*

Phil had spun an insult into "Sonny is the brightest guy in the Bronx."

He laughed recounting the story—how Elliott's lead bars had caused Santini and Cicale to "catch gold fever." They had just ordered a round of drinks when Pro burst into the restaurant, breathing hard, his toupee askew.

"You motherfuckers!" he shouted. "You sent Sonny over to my office, and he's had me hanging out the window with an ice pick in my ear, saying I better come up with the rest of the $200,000 or I'm a fucking dead motherfucker. Whatever you told him, it's not true, but *you* better fix this."

They all turned to Phil, who was grinning as he swished the water in his glass around. "You started this, Fred," he said calmly. "You'll come up with the money. I know your mentality. You'll figure it out."

Back in the room that evening, Phil was drinking and thinking. In Orange County, Jack Elliott had said something that had stuck with him: Los Angeles–based FBI agent Phil Hanlon had interviewed Elliott about Vince Carrano's robbery, and Kitzer's name had come up. Hanlon had been asking about him.

Phil had spent the past couple of days considering phoning "the alphabet," as he called the FBI. (That was the term you used, he said, if you were "in the game.")

Jack and J.J. had heard this before. Phil had often preached taking a preemptive approach with the bureau. Be helpful: *Hey, I wanted to let you know about something I heard.* Build a friendly relationship, just like in any con. In the past, Phil had sent telexes to the FBI and the Department of Justice. Later, he would say: *If I was doing something wrong, why would I cooperate? I brought this up in the first place.*

Now, with Scotch surging through his veins, Phil announced to J.J. that he was going to call Hanlon.

"Oh, yeah, Phil, that's a *great* idea," J.J. said.

Phil ignored the sarcasm while he dug Hanlon's number from his briefcase.

"Hey," J.J. said, getting serious. "We don't want any agents showing up at our door. The lion is sleeping in the corner—why do we have to stir the bear?"

Phil wasn't in the mood to debate. He could be pigheaded when he drank. He stood and headed for the phone, but J.J. intercepted him.

"You are *not* calling the FBI, Phillip," J.J. said.

The agents had worried about this in the past. There could be crossed wires; someone in Los Angeles could get confused or mistakenly say something about OpFoPen. They couldn't risk that. J.J. was standing between Phil and the phone when Jack walked in and asked what was going on. They stood facing each other, and Kitzer looked irritated. "C'mon, get outta my way," he said, moving toward J.J.

Jack turned to where the phone sat on the hotel-room desk and picked it up. He curled the wire in his hands and, with one yank, ripped it from the wall.

"You want the phone, Phillip?" Jack said. "Here."

Phil stalked out, J.J. following to make sure he didn't call from a pay phone. He was irked, but by the time the three of them replayed the scene the next day, it would be uproariously funny. Still, the incident made the agents think about the investigation, and the eventual endgame for their now six-month-old odyssey. They'd recently heard rumblings from Johnson that the operation wouldn't last much longer. Couldn't. The menace lurking on the organized-crime side of OpFoPen was too alarming to ignore.

In private moments, Jack and J.J. sometimes talked about Phil, about how it would end. Oddly, Phil also talked about winding down, phasing out the promoter life. He talked about buying a restaurant in Hawaii and retiring there, to create a comfortable base of operations. He was a complicated guy, the agents now understood, and it was hard to hold all the different parts of him together in their minds at once, to reconcile them. They couldn't help imagining different outcomes. In some unquantifiable but real way, they cared, and worried, and hoped that his life, after all he had done, might in some way be redeemable.

Of course Phil was a criminal who needed to be stopped, needed to pay a steep price, though he didn't think of himself in those terms. Years later, when a lawyer asked him about "stealing" $60,000 from Jimmy Kealoha, Phil objected: "When you say stole, sir, you make it sound like a stick-up with a gun."

The lawyer contended this: "There isn't much difference."

"I gave letters of credit," Phil countered. "I gave [him] some papers. . . . They were worthless. He bought something worthless. Cheated would be a better word."

But the cheating inflicted enormous pain. When he fraudulently insured millions with the likes of American Allied, he suckered end-of-the-rope working folks who, after filing claims on their crumpled cars, ended up with two or three cents on the dollar. Even for people who survived the financial calamity he inflicted, Phil would remain a specter—the feeling of dread in the pit in the stomach of everyone who signed a contract after scanning the dreary, impenetrable fine print. He created a wilderness pocked with land mines you couldn't detect until one blew your leg off.

But it was also possible to look at him from a certain angle, to place him on the sliding scale of humanity and judge him differently. He didn't abscond with senior citizens' Social Security checks. He didn't prey on veterans, or cancer patients, or charities. He was no Santini or Iuteri, traumatizing people with physical violence. His victims were mostly faceless: bankers and CEOs and developers who should have known better, who got greedy or didn't do their homework, or both.

"You think about, he's not that bad a guy, maybe, but then he's facilitating all this," Jack said. "You have that internal battle."

They liked him, and they knew Phil reciprocated the sentiment. They also knew that he'd chosen them because he thought they were criminals, too, and he would possibly lay the blame on them if the FBI caught them selling First National Haiti paper. "That's what we were destined for—to be the people left holding the bag,"

Jack said. "Although it may not have happened that way, because of how our relationship changed with him."

These were the nuanced, contrary puzzles they struggled with as August plodded forward. Phil was a corrupt, sometimes morally bankrupt guy who could also be good—capable of empathy and loyalty and moments of grace. He was a Gordian knot of contradictions: a man of countless sexual escapades who ditched a family—but remained loyal, in ways, to his new wife and son. He was a criminal who deceived and swindled people, yet he paid the agents back if they covered one of his expenses. He was a companion who could be frank and open in the way people tended to be in a crucible of an unfamiliar city—when you're disoriented and isolated and you lean a little harder on your friends—or in the gray light of a plane in a midnight sky, when a shared secret or an inside joke mark you as distinct from everyone else. He was that, too. But he also lied to them.

His justification for the lies? "That was part of the business," Phil said. That was because bankers lied, too, as a matter of routine. How many dreams had they crushed with their random deadlines and capricious decisions, their indifference?

As Phil framed it, his fraudulent paper could be a force for good—a way for the small guy to beat the banks, to get a loan he was denied and could very well pay back if given the chance. There was a Robin Hood quality to Phil; he believed he could help the desperate dreamer. Of one of his $30,000 letters of credit, he said, "[I]f somebody had a need for it, if it worked for somebody, it would have had a value of $30,000 or more." In that scenario, as bizarre as it sounded, Phil and his phantom banks would serve as an engine of real economic growth.

He would tell people: "We have letters of credit. These certificates and letters will stand up to a check. They can be put in a financial statement, given to a bank under certain circumstances; but at no time is it our intent to do an outright fraud on a bank."

A defense lawyer would later question him: "[W]hether it's an outright or a slight fraud, a fraud is a fraud, isn't it?"

"Not quite," Phil said.

"No?"

"No . . . not in our estimation."

Life did not resemble the set of hard and indiscriminate rules that banks created. Life was nuance, gray areas. Phil knew that if you took a black light to most people's souls, you'd find cheating on a tax return or a spouse, the insurance check that came from imaginary hail damage to aluminum siding, the shoplifting episode, the walking into a movie without paying.

Sure, these were minor episodes, mostly victimless—but, the agents pondered, weren't they different only in scale? *Get in on a deal, buy something, put your money in, earn lots more back, beat the system, beat the IRS by investing offshore.*

This was what Jack and J.J. wrestled with. Maybe everyone was part con man. Maybe everybody was in the game, and Phil just knew better than anyone else how to play.

When the phone rang the next day, the news was not good for Bernard Baker. His banker was calling to say that the $109,000 refund the Kansas farmer had extracted from Fred Pro had bounced. The check had been written on a closed account.

Raging, Baker dialed Pro's number. Predictably, Fred was out of reach or in conference and would call back. When Baker finally reached him, Pro proposed a five-year payout plan. Baker rejected this latest ploy and insisted that Pro send the entire amount. But Pro continued to stall and bluster, later explaining that he never returned the money because Baker "didn't get nasty enough."

Baker had his own way of getting even, though: He called an FBI agent based in Kansas, then sent Pro a telex: "Return of escrow funds have not arrived First National Bank of Tribune, Kansas per our agreement. Authorities have impounded your 'account closed' check and are proceeding."

Baker relished the idea of Pro in handcuffs, but it was cold comfort. With no way to either pay back the $110,000 loan or go forward in acquiring the Idaho farm, Baker was trapped. His bank foreclosed on him and took his farm.

Bowen Johnson called in reinforcements the following morning, August 10, for that day's meetings. Everyone in the OpFoPen contingent had been rattled by Santini's eruption two days earlier.

Other unsettling things were happening. Myron Fuller had subpoenaed a promoter named Harvey Greenwald to appear before a newly formed federal grand jury. Greenwald's lawyer had negotiated for him to skip his appearance if he would agree to an interview. But as Greenwald headed to his meeting at the FBI offices, someone fired a shot at him, wounding him. Greenwald lived, but he never appeared for the interview.

After two witnesses in Joe Trocchio's trial turned up dead and Santini threatened to whack Fred Pro, the FBI leadership was no longer so blithe about letting the undercover agents attend meetings without protection. If Jack's and J.J.'s identities were revealed after all they'd heard and seen, the consequences could be dire. Santini had been unmistakable on Fuller's wiretap—all curses and death threats.

So when Gabe Cicale arrived to fetch Phil, J.J., and Jack from the Essex House that afternoon, Johnson had twenty-two agents scattered outside the hotel. It was by far the largest security blanket ever draped over Operation Fountain Pen. Everyone was armed. They were not just an impassive monitoring team; if something went wrong, these agents would have to take immediate action.

Oddly, though, Cicale never came back out. Neither did Phil or the undercover agents. Puzzled, Johnson went up to Jack and J.J.'s hotel room, listened for voices, then knocked. Nothing. He checked back in his room—after the Santini incident, Johnson had rejiggered the schedule so that someone would be available around the clock—but no one there had seen them.

Johnson felt a flush of anxiety tinged with exasperation. Maybe they'd just been fortunate before, always somehow bumping into one another to exchange information. Recently, not so much.

In one instance, Phil told Jack and J.J. they were heading to Denmark to work a scam—but then, in classic Kitzer fashion, he canceled the trip at the last minute. There was no way for Jack and J.J. to alert Johnson before he headed to JFK. Johnson went through customs and checked his luggage, including a suitcase with surveillance equipment and his gun, and boarded the plane, wondering why he hadn't spotted the undercover agents yet. He was fastidious about OpFoPen travel. At baggage claim, he always let the suitcase with his gear circle the carousel unclaimed until everyone else was gone—just to be safe. Johnson had no idea how deep Phil's—or the mob's—connections ran, and the idea of being the one who exposed the operation after all that work haunted him.

On the plane, Johnson walked the aisles, drawing the ire of fellow passengers and feeling tormented by the agents' absence. *Where were they?* If he guessed wrong about their whereabouts, they would be without his backup for a day at least. He agonized over what to do. When the flight attendants prepared to lock the doors, Johnson couldn't put off a decision any longer. He apologized, grabbed his carry-on, and darted to the exit. Only after he returned to Manhattan did he find that he'd guessed right—although his equipment flew to Denmark and had to be shipped back to Indianapolis.

But this situation was even more absurd. With a team of seasoned New York agents standing watch, Wedick and Brennan had vaporized. "If something happened to them, as far as I'm concerned it's my responsibility," he said. "It's a sick feeling."

Lacking a better idea, Johnson resorted to a door-to-door search: He walked the neighborhood around Columbus Circle, ducking into bars and restaurants they'd visited before. He feared that they'd been forced into a car for that ride up to the Bronx, and there was no way to help.

Becky Brennan jumped every time the phone rang. Ever since Jack had called with the news that he'd lost that scrap of paper, she'd wondered, *Will this be the one?* She always answered with a tentative hello.

The agony of not knowing more ate at her. Being seven months pregnant was uncomfortable, and she was still living in the apartment with two toddlers. When Jack stayed there, their queen-sized bed felt so small that to turn over she had to climb out of bed, stand, and clamber back in, in the new position.

With the high-energy boys and all the chores and bills, the last thing she needed was the free-floating anxiety the telephone now brought. The warmth of summer helped, but autumn was creeping in, followed by that full-throated midwestern winter. Jack was seven months gone now, and deeper in than ever, leaving Becky with no idea if it was ever going to end.

Cicale took a shortcut. After picking up Phil and the Junior G-Men and taking the elevator down to the lobby, he veered left in the lobby and pushed through a service entrance instead of heading out onto Central Park South. They walked through a vehicle bay that opened onto West Fifty-eighth Street. As they threaded through parked vehicles, Jack and J.J. shared a look that said, *So much for the surveillance.*

The group walked south for five blocks until they reached West Fifty-third; then Cicale led them into the Hilton. Upstairs, they walked into a room packed with organized-crime types: Santini; Ron Sablosky; a character named Vince Orlando, who was working on a scam involving a gold mine in Costa Rica; and Ralph Cantone and his father. There was someone else, whom Cicale introduced only as "a good Italian boy." The meeting began with a discussion of a scam involving a former pro football player who owned a failing cattle ranch but later veered into the subject of removing problem witnesses. Cantone's father chimed in helpfully that he owned a farm in Ohio that was convenient for stashing bodies.

Eventually Cicale stood up, saying he had something to take care of in New Jersey. From his demeanor, Jack and J.J. inferred that Gabe was going to shake someone down, or worse. It was hard to tell. All J.J. and Jack knew was that the usually gregarious Cicale seemed more menacing around Santini.

As the meeting broke up, Santini approached Jack, J.J., and Phil and spoke again about partnering on First National Haiti. "If someone's not paying," Santini said, smiling at the Junior G-Men, "we'll use this." He reached into his jacket and produced a handgun with a silencer.

Jack and J.J. nodded. There was no reason to believe that Santini suspected that they were FBI agents, but he always seemed to be making implied threats. It was unsettling.

On the way out, they asked Phil about the gun. "He's crazy," Kitzer said with a shrug. "What can I tell you?"

That night, Johnson took a break and walked past groups of New Yorkers hugging and cheering. The NYPD had arrested David Berkowitz, the Son of Sam, ending a reign of terror that had stretched across the summer.

There was a sense of things winding down. Jack and J.J. attended a few more meetings with Phil the next day, August 11, before all three of them headed back to their respective homes. They'd been together for twenty-three straight days. They hugged at the airport but made no plans. Typically, one of them would call the others and get everyone together. Phil would say he needed to go back to Ellendale to dry out, and Jack and J.J. never pried for more details; they didn't want him asking questions in return. That day the agents said they'd get back together soon. But they suspected that by the time they did, nothing would be the same.

Things happened fast. There was consensus throughout the FBI's chain of command that Operation Fountain Pen had gone far enough and the bureau was fortunate that everyone involved was—so far—unharmed. But that was it. The idea of sending Wedick and Brennan back to New York was now untenable. Too many people in too many FBI circles knew who they were, and at this point, with so many wiseguys involved, any slip could be fatal. The promoters knew their names and knew that they lived in western Indiana. Finding them wouldn't be hard.

The bureau had taken belated steps to provide additional measures of protection. Frank Lowie made sure that anyone who answered the phone at the office in Indianapolis denied knowing anyone named Jack Brennan or J.J. Wedick.

The nation writhed through a fever dream of a summer. In Oregon, a lunatic made national news by driving a pickup truck over two college girls sleeping in a tent and then assaulting them with an axe; they had been riding their bicycles across the country. The assailant was never caught. Five days after the agents parted ways with Phil, Elvis Presley turned up dead in Graceland.

On August 23, the bureau convened an OpFoPen conference in Indianapolis aimed at moving toward arrests and prosecution. Agents from around the country pursuing various cases—Fuller from New York, Hanlon from Los Angeles, and others from Memphis, Charlotte, Louisville, Miami, and Honolulu—joined an assortment of U.S. attorneys, prosecutors from organized-crime strike forces, and investigators from the fraud division of the Department of Justice. They identified thirty cases to move forward on, and a second tier of possible indictments to come later. They discussed whom to serve with search warrants, which suspects would be charged, and which might be flipped into government witnesses. Brennan and Wedick had unearthed so many potential cases involving so many characters, some prosecutors could have filled dockets for years.

The FBI issued a directive that "all leads set out in this matter be covered immediately." And because the OpFoPen cases were so complicated, and required so much prior knowledge, the bureau cleared agents to fly as needed around the United States to pursue them. But until arrests were made, agents were ordered not to make any reference to Wedick and Brennan. "Interviews conducted should protect the Indianapolis undercover operation," the memo said.

As the summer wound down, Assistant U.S. Attorney Glen Garland Reid Jr. of Memphis sent a memo to prosecutors in New York indicating that he was about to charge Fred Pro with interstate transportation of stolen property—the Presley airplane. Soon after that, Santa Ana police served a search warrant on Vince Carrano, who had been a suspect in the Swiss Vaults robbery virtually from the beginning.

The chief OpFoPen suspects would be searched next. Starting with Phil.

22

The Game Is Rigged

SEPTEMBER 20, 1977

FBI agent Donald Schlaefer pulled up just off Interstate 35 in Ellendale, Minnesota, and gazed at the farmhouse that matched the
address on his paperwork. It was an unlikely place for an international con artist to call home. Paint was curling off the clapboards,
and the chimney appeared close to surrendering in its struggle
against gravity. It was a pleasant Indian-summer Tuesday, temperatures rising into the mid-sixties, but someone had heaped straw
bales against the north side of the house to block the icy winds that
would soon start screaming down over the plains.

Phil Kitzer opened the front door and welcomed Schlaefer and
his team of fellow agents. Schlaefer, an agent in the Minneapolis office, showed him the warrant, explaining that they were to
search the house and take all relevant business records. Kitzer
waved everyone in.

Unlike on other, similar assignments Schlaefer had been part
of, the house was devoid of tension. Schlaefer asked Kitzer whether
he had any questions, and Phil said no, he understood they were
merely doing their jobs. As the agents pawed at his closets and desk
drawers, Phil chatted about the weather, about Minnesota, about
Fran Tarkenton and how this might be the year for the Vikings,
even though they'd lost their first game to the hated Dallas Cowboys. He watched the agents lift a Western Union telex machine
from the upstairs closet. They loaded up his address book, a key

from the Hôtel International in Geneva, a Disneyland Hotel phone message from John Calandrella.

Kitzer told Schlaefer that he'd intended to spend some time organizing his papers, and he was grateful that the FBI was doing it so that he would know where everything was if he needed to defend himself in court. He told them to be sure they had everything.

"It was," Schlaefer later said, "a very friendly atmosphere."

Jack and J.J. hadn't seen Phil in more than five weeks, having dipped into their bag of creative excuses for being absent while Phil pressed on with First National Haiti. Not long after the team of agents packed up and left, Phil's phone rang. It was Jack, calling with the news that the FBI had just hit him with a search warrant. J.J., too.

"I don't know what to do," Jack said, repeating lines he'd rehearsed with Wedick. He was sitting inside J.J.'s apartment, doing his best to sound scared.

Phil told him to relax. He'd been through this before and had always come away unscathed. Phil peppered him with questions: What did they say while they were there? Were they looking for anything in particular?

Before they hung up, Phil again told Jack not to worry and said he would call back. Jack had accomplished the agents' first goal: Deflect suspicion. The promoters would be on the lookout for a rat, and Jack and J.J. wanted Phil to think the FBI was targeting them. Jack hoped his anxiety, and the revelation that he had been searched, had tamped down any doubts.

But the agents had another goal, too: They wanted to know what Phil was thinking. If anyone planned to destroy evidence or flee, they hoped to find out in advance. A few minutes later, J.J. called Phil from the Indianapolis office. It was four-thirty p.m. The FBI had a "hello line"—a phone set up in a back office, where the surveillance equipment was stored, with an unlisted and untraceable number. The agents could safely take calls from Phil there.

J.J. and Jack had created an official, signed search warrant for J.J.'s apartment—1934 North Mansard Boulevard, in Griffith—that they could show the promoters. At Phil's request, J.J. read out loud the list of everything the FBI had asked for in the subpoena. J.J. was required to furnish any documents he possessed related to Executive Enterprises, Seven Oak, FNCB Haiti, and Trident Consortium.

The agents talked to Phil numerous times the next day, too. Jack said he was considering leaving the country, and Phil joked about the resurrection of the Parking Lot Fugitive. J.J. and Jack took turns calling, asking different questions—a technique the FBI calls "tickling the wire." They wanted a clear sense of what he was up to. If Phil destroyed evidence, he could be charged with obstruction of justice, which in some cases could result in stiffer penalties than the original charge.

Phil told them that the FBI had also executed search warrants on Jack Elliott's Costa Mesa office and Newport Beach home. Fred Pro called from New York to say that Myron Fuller and his crew had emptied Trident Consortium of small quantities of several types of drugs, $10,540 in cash, a telex machine, and a vast trove of records. "He had literally a room full of documents," Fuller said. The FBI also raided promoter Tom Bannon's business, Bannon International, on State Street in Boston, seizing voluminous quantities of records, including many generated by John Calandrella during various dealings with Phil.

Digesting these revelations, Phil explained the mechanics of a grand jury, how they could be called to testify. Jack called Pro and they explored the idea that Andy D'Amato might be a snitch.

On September 22, two days after the searches, Phil and Jack talked about getting a copy of the affidavit attached to the search warrants. Phil explained that the affidavits spell out the evidence the FBI agents have to present in order to convince a judge to green-light a search. If they could get a lawyer to the courthouse wherever the case originated, they might find out what the FBI was up to.

Jack obviously didn't say so, but the judge had sealed the warrants for that very reason: Phil and his attorney, Frank Oliver, knew the system intimately. That afternoon, Phil asked the agents to come to Chicago so they could all meet with Oliver the following day.

The government would undoubtedly have more questions, and the promoters needed to be sure everyone knew what to say.

Wedick and Brennan hustled to prepare for the meeting. At J.J.'s request, the FBI outfitted a rental car with a recording device. J.J. also wore a concealed Nagra to ensure that they would get an audio record of whatever took place. If Phil and Oliver discussed defense strategies, that could be useful later. Once the undercover agents revealed their identities, they'd never be party to such a conversation again.

Phil waited for them outside the arrival gate at O'Hare. The agents hadn't seen Phil for six weeks, and he smiled as he slid into the front passenger seat for the drive to the Hilton downtown. Jack and J.J. greeted him enthusiastically but quickly launched into a recitation of their anxieties. They didn't know who the feds were after, or who might be talking to the FBI. "What about that fucking Calandrella?" Jack asked, leaning forward from the back seat.

Phil held up a hand as the Junior G-Men buzzed about not wanting to go to jail. "Guys, listen," he said. "You don't understand how this works."

They stared at him while sitting at a traffic light.

"Look," he said. "The FBI is interested in other stuff. They don't give a goddamn about these kinds of cases. Think about it: Let's say Phil Hanlon goes after us. He's gotta convince his supervisor to open up a case, okay? What are the chances his boss is even gonna understand what it's about? And even if the supervisor agrees, this agent has to go down to the U.S. attorney's office and convince a prosecutor to act on it—like they don't have anything better to do? Now that guy's gotta convince the U.S. attorney that they'll be able to prosecute us. The chances of that are nil and none. They hate these kinds of cases, because they're too complicated for juries.

"But let's just say that all happens. They open a case up. That don't mean nothing. They now have to go around and find witnesses and collect evidence. You know what the chances are of them doing that and succeeding? Not very good. Our deals are spread all over the place. Huge headache. And we can explain everything they have, and come up with our own evidence that shows it was just a deal that went bad.

"Maybe this one time, they get enough evidence. Now they gotta convince a judge to start up a grand jury. Even if that happens, that grand jury has to understand the case enough to indict us. And if we get indicted, we're gonna have our day in court. And before the trial begins, we've got months to file motions and delay, and that's the best time to do new deals."

Jack and J.J. sat listening, astonished, while Phil explained that the single most opportune time to rip people off was when you were already under indictment. The FBI and the U.S. attorney's office has just invested months or even years building a case. The idea of piling on new charges as the process moves along—that was logistically impossible. An indictment was a free pass to commit more fraud, as Phil saw it.

And when the case came to trial? Phil anticipated from his escapade a decade earlier in Bismarck how that would go. Oliver would be outraged and swish his cape and confuse everyone with accounting figures, then distract them with peripheral drama. Phil laughed at the memory. *"Your Honor, I was trying to do this complicated deal right, but I guess we made some honest mistakes. It's high finance."*

"Maybe the judge makes a mistake and we get off on a mistrial or technicality. But say we get convicted. We post bond and go free while we appeal—and that's another good time to do more deals, make more money. That can go on for a year or more, and the prosecutor will say, 'This guy's already been convicted, why try to get him again?'

"We might lose the appeal. Big deal! Most judges don't get worked up about these kinds of cases and might let us off with probation. But worst case, we *might* get three years at the Danbury Hilton."

Phil said the minimum-security prisons were great places to meet politicians on the take, corrupt bankers, executives. With all that time to talk, they could cook up some incredible deals. Then, with good behavior, they'd be out in nine or ten months.

Think about it, Phil said. He spread his arm across the top of the seat, his hand landing within inches of where a wire ran over J.J.'s shoulder, connecting the Nagra to a microphone. "We've made a few million dollars over the last year, and we've had more fun than most people can imagine. And when we get out, we'll get to do it all over again."

He looked at his friends. "So, all right. Is it worth it? Are you having a good time?"

J.J. and Jack looked at each other and nodded. They were.

"Then all right," Phil said, grinning. "Let's get to that meeting."

They checked into a suite at the Hilton, Jack and J.J. in one room, Phil in another. J.J. excused himself to run errands and headed for Johnson's room, where he met a bureau engineer who had developed a new wearable recorder.

Wedick had griped all summer that the Nagra was too cumbersome—it felt like a brick on his back. Just before he left for Chicago, a technology specialist named Bruce Koenig had told J.J. that he'd recently developed a new device in which the tape wound around a single reel rather than two, allowing him to halve the recorder's dimensions. The six-figure prototype was the only unit in existence, but OpFoPen was now Major Case Number One, so Koenig had decided to hand-deliver it to Chicago.

With the device situated on his lower back under a blue three-piece suit, J.J. studied himself in a mirror. He was impressed. The thing was just about impossible to see, which was a huge relief.

After six weeks away from the promoters, he and Jack had no idea what to expect from that day's meeting. Under the circumstances, Phil and the others would be suspicious of everyone.

When they gathered in late afternoon in the Hilton's saloon, to their surprise, Paul Chovanec was there. Phil explained that he wanted to quiz his former associate on what he knew.

Oliver arrived with his law partner, Mitchell "Mickey" Kaplan. Phil and Oliver had been friends and business associates for almost thirty years, going back to when Phil was an assistant in his father's bail-bond business. In the autumn of 1975, Phil had rented space in Oliver's law offices to run Mercantile Bank, and he had cut the attorney in on a few deals.

At fifty-seven, Oliver was an eccentric and erudite man who kept a library of more than four hundred old and rare books in the areas of science, math, history, and philosophy. He had represented countless Chicago gangsters, along with war protesters, draft dodgers, and two men accused of plotting to poison Lake Michigan. (A few years later, Oliver would turn up in a *Chicago Tribune* story headlined "Missing Porn-Theater Owner Found Dead in Car Trunk"—as the lawyer and former business partner of the dead man.) He was known to clash with judges and torment hostile witnesses with sharp interrogatories. Another Chicago attorney described him as "one of the most feared cross-examiners that anyone has ever seen."

Oliver issued simple, cursory advice. He suggested that everyone keep their mouths shut—particularly with the FBI. You want to talk, he said, talk to me alone, so it's privileged conversation. Once they determined what the FBI was after, they would meet for a more detailed strategy session.

Happy hour arrived, and Oliver and Kaplan left the others to chat and order drinks. After a few rounds, Phil went into Friday-night mode and dragged the Junior G-Men into a wedding reception taking place in another part of the hotel. J.J. groaned and rolled his eyes at Jack.

Phil began working the crowd, asking women to dance. J.J. urged him to go easy; he and Jack were worried that Phil would start insulting people if they were confronted, and security would be summoned. But Phil was relatively subdued. A surveillance team hovered on the fringes, but J.J. slipped out after midnight and told them to go home. "We're into nonsense now," he said.

Jack and J.J. eventually hauled Phil upstairs to his room. J.J. lay on the suite's couch to mull over how to safeguard the expensive new recorder. It was two-thirty a.m., and Johnson was likely asleep. J.J. would feel bad about jarring him awake—but then again, he couldn't safely leave the device lying around.

Pondering all this but fatigued beyond the grasp of his anxieties, he fell asleep on the couch with the Nagra still lashed to his back.

They hung around for one final round of business meetings the next day. Phil had reached some sort of détente with Chovanec, who stayed to discuss an idea to defraud the Mexican government. Chovanec suggested a new scheme that involved renting labor-union funds to fraudulently obtain loans. The agents memorized as much as they could, aware that they were drawing water straight from the well possibly for the last time.

When everyone departed the next day, Jack and J.J. knew they might be embracing Phil for the last time. Soon there would be indictments, then arrests. They couldn't guess how he would react once they revealed their deceit. That moment loomed like a wall of swollen clouds before a heavy storm, but they shoved those thoughts aside to focus on the tasks ahead.

Becky Brennan was within days of her due date with their third son. For Jack, this brought a tumble of conflicting emotions and thoughts. He was thrilled, but his family's safety worried him more than ever. Once the promoters and their mob associates learned that they were FBI agents, Jack and J.J. would become targets.

The government took a few final steps to protect them. Prosecutors asked the courts to seal the indictments, like the search warrants, to shroud the agents' identities for a few more weeks. Lowie sent a teletype to headquarters asking that J.J. and Jack be relocated. "As a result of activities and conversations they witnessed while in this capacity, it is anticipated that numerous individuals will be indicted in approximately 12 divisions, ranging geographically from Honolulu to New York City," the memo stated.

> Beginning in mid Oct., 1977, and for one year or more, [Brennan and Wedick] will be in nearly a constant travel status, as their testimony will be required before grand juries and at time of trial in every division where prosecution is attempted.
>
> It is noted that [the agents'] testimony is crucial in proving intent on the part of subjects and that their identity as [special agents] will be exposed at the time of discovery motions, which is expected to occur in late Oct., 1977. It is also noted that subjects know [Brennan's and Wedick's] residence to be in the Lake County, Indiana area and that [the agents'] activities brought them into direct and indirect contact with several known LCN members, which included hit men.

Given Becky's status, Lowie asked that Jack be transferred to Mobile, Alabama, near her parents. Jack would never have requested Mobile himself, because the bureau so rarely awarded anyone the office they actually wanted, but he was hopeful. J.J. asked for a California assignment—he hated the cold, and he wanted to be as far away as possible from Sonny Santini and company.

On October 6, Jack rushed Becky to the hospital for what proved to be false labor—but Jack insisted that she stay in a room overnight. That was because of the drama that had surrounded the arrival of their previous son, Chris. He was coming so quickly that

Jack had raced a train to a crossing to get Becky to the hospital, and the baby was born before he returned from parking the car.

Their third son, Matthew, arrived on his due date, October 7, at a robust ten pounds, six ounces. Becky, in agony because of the size of the baby, conjured up some creative names for Jack during the delivery.

Over the next few weeks, Jack and J.J. kept tabs on Phil by phone.

The con man was plowing forward at full steam. Phil and Chovanec flew to Panama to try to defraud a Panamanian bank using the rented-money gambit. Phil was having a blast, and he tried repeatedly to talk J.J. into rounding up Jack and flying to Central America.

On October 7, a teletype clacked through to FBI offices in Indianapolis, Boston, Louisville, Miami, and New York. It stated that the Department of Justice would ask the court to seal a Louisville indictment connected to a case involving Seven Oak "so as to preclude any advance notification reaching subject Kitzer prior to finalization of surrender."

Even with Operation Fountain Pen shuttered, Phil was still creating logistical challenges. Jack and J.J. had no way to know how long he would linger in Panama, but the feds didn't want him fleecing a bank there while an indictment awaited back in the States. On October 13, J.J. called Phil at El Continental Hotel in Panama City and asked him to return home so they could get together. Phil sounded jaunty; he said he loved Panama and was negotiating with one of Manuel Noriega's deputies. J.J. heard bar chatter and laughter in the background. "We're having a great time," Phil said. "Get yourself down here."

Lacking any other options, the FBI arranged for the Panamanian police to arrest Phil for suspected fraud and expel him from the country. J.J. gave them Phil's room number at El Continental.

Later that day, it was done. The Panamanian authorities reported that they'd taken Phil into custody and would put him on a flight to Florida. At some level, this step left J.J. breathless. He could now clearly see the moment coming when they would have to confront Phil, tell him what they'd done. The dread he felt surprised him.

He and Jack each processed the countless hours they'd invested in the case, the angst, their squabbles, the lost sleep, the dollars spent and tens of thousands of miles flown. Most likely, considering everything they knew about Phil, the arrest would be the easy part. After listening to Phil's cynical deconstruction of the criminal justice system, they found it hard not to feel anxious about what lay ahead—about the hatch door he might open and slip through.

That was the only outcome that felt more crushing than telling Phil the truth—the idea that after giving so much to reel in their catch, they were destined to watch him wriggle out of the net.

They knew the classic story. Ahab gnashed his teeth and raised his fist to the heavens. The whale just swam on.

Part IV

THE RECKONING

"But he stays by the window, remembering that life. They had laughed. They had leaned on each other and laughed until the tears had come, while everything else—the cold and where he'd go in it—was outside, for a while anyway."

—Raymond Carver, "Everything Stuck to Him"

23

You Have to Believe It to See It

He looked composed and confident as he walked off a Braniff International flight from Panama City to Miami around five p.m. The afternoon was typical South Florida: sultry and warm. Phil Kitzer didn't know what to expect, exactly, beyond that he was swapping some unpleasantries in Panama for a legal snag back home. The Panamanians had told him that an indictment was awaiting him in the States, and Kitzer had boarded the flight ready to surrender. He'd been expecting this since the FBI had shown up several weeks earlier, so he was unruffled. He considered his firewall secure. He would call Frank Oliver, and they would go to battle.

As Phil walked into the customs area, a tall, balding man in his fifties stepped forward. Kitzer recognized Phil Hanlon immediately. Hanlon was an FBI elder statesman, a canny and seasoned Southern California–based agent whom the promoters respected. Kitzer had avoided Vince Carrano's mess in part because the Swiss Vaults were on Hanlon's turf.

Kitzer said, "Phil Hanlon? From Los Angeles? What are *you* doing here?"

Hanlon explained in his deep, stentorian voice that he was there to arrest Kitzer. He placed handcuffs around Phil's wrists and lightly guided him to a waiting car. They drove downtown and headed into the spacious office of the FBI's special agent in charge in Miami, where Hanlon uncuffed him. Kitzer was genial and cooperative but said nothing of substance.

But he was puzzled. He kept staring at Hanlon, as if baffled over why the agent had flown all the way across the country for this when any rank-and-file G-man would do. This was as Jack and J.J. wanted it. J.J. had the idea that Hanlon should be the arresting officer—considered a great honor in the bureau after a major investigation—because they knew his presence would telegraph that the FBI had built a huge case. They wanted Phil's full attention.

Hanlon explained that Kitzer faced charges in both the Elvis Presley airplane case and in a fraud conspiracy in Louisville headlined by John Kaye, the natural-gas entrepreneur who'd acquired a $100,000 certificate of deposit from Seven Oak and then foolishly tried to cash it. But there were more indictments coming. From all over the country.

Kitzer digested this and asked to call his attorney.

Then he said, "I want you to know that my friends Jack and J.J., they're not involved in any of this."

Later, when Hanlon told the agents what Phil had said, it was a gut punch. Why, at that moment, did he choose to try to protect them?

There was one possible selfish motivation: Phil believed that Jack and J.J. were inexperienced with the criminal justice system. He might have worried they'd veer from the script, or fall apart and confess. Or maybe he wanted them to stay out of prison so they could keep doing deals for him in the event he was convicted. There was the question, too, of whether they were who they claimed to be—Kitzer's doubts about their real identities sometimes seemed to gnaw at him like a recurring dream whose meaning could never quite be deciphered. But it was also possible that Phil simply cared about them—that he considered himself a father figure to two young men he believed were about to enter a world of trouble.

Hanlon told Phil to wait, then exited into the hallway where J.J. and Jack stood. He nodded.

A knot formed in the pit of J.J.'s stomach, and a twinge of nausea rolled through him. He felt short of breath, and his heart banged in his chest like that of a freshly caged animal as he opened the door to the room where Phil was waiting.

The arrest triggered an avalanche of activity around the country. Within minutes, the FBI in Louisville called a press conference to announce indictments involving "white-collar crime of a high magnitude." Teams of FBI agents mobilized in Miami, Boston, and New York.

The *Hammond Times* reported that both the FBI's director, Clarence Kelley, and U.S. Attorney General Griffin Bell had "been keeping a close watch over the investigation." Kelley's spokesman added that the probe "involves many, many people and financial institutions worldwide."

Agents arrested Fred Pro at the Trident Consortium offices, seizing his passport and almost $20,000 in cash. Pro walked with a limp, which his attorney described as "pre-phlebitis," and sported an unexplained bruise below his left eye. Myron Fuller needed five people to pore over all the documents he'd seized weeks earlier, which showed Pro had swindled between $3 million and $5 million over eight months by promising about $1 billion in loans. More indictments for Trident were on their way; the wiretap had "opened a new curtain" for the FBI in New York, Fuller said. Decades later, he added, "I could still be there working cases from that. It was incredible."

From the Presley case, the FBI arrested four co-conspirators in and around Miami and a fifth in Boston. Agents in Ohio collared John Kaye and Tom Bannon, already in prison for a prior conviction, in the Louisville case. In Boston, they took John Calandrella into custody. The FBI sent arrest warrants to Europe for John Packman, in London, and Jean-Claude and Pascal Cornaz, in Geneva. In its own ongoing probe, Scotland Yard had seized more than nineteen hundred telexes from Seven Oak Finance.

In the subsequent months, there would be more: Andy D'Amato, Armand Mucci, Bob Bendis, Mark Iuteri, Sonny Santini—in all, more than two dozen people. Beginning that day in October, the FBI systematically disassembled the Fraternity.

Phil's first expression was surprise. He turned and saw J.J. and Jack enter the room, and his eyes widened. "Guys," he said, jumping to his feet. "What are you doing here? I *told* them you weren't involved!"

He started to lecture them about not talking until Frank Oliver arrived.

J.J. held up his hand. They hadn't scripted anything, so he just took a breath and said, "Phil. It's not like that."

"I *told* them that you—"

"Phil, listen," J.J. said, louder, interrupting. "We're FBI agents."

Phil stared at him, his mouth frozen in place around his last word. Then: *"What?"*

"We're FBI agents, Phil." J.J. held up his badge. "We were agents all this time. We need to talk to you about all this."

Phil stared at them for long seconds. Then he turned away slowly, scoffed, shook his head. Looked back at them. "You're *FBI agents?"*

They nodded. J.J. was still holding his badge out, thrusting it into the space between them.

Phil crunched up his face. "Let me see that."

He took J.J.'s badge, then Jack's. He stared at the metal shields without actually looking at them. He had the glazed eyes of a man flailing to reconcile a stupefying new reality, struggling to balance as tectonic plates groaned and buckled beneath him. It was less about the present moment than about the previous nine months—every day of which now had to be reprocessed through the lens of this staggering revelation.

Phil handed the badges back, then asked to see them again. He stared at them some more. He returned the credentials and paced around, looking at the floor. Finally he lowered himself heavily into a seat and placed one hand over his midsection. Reflexively, Jack asked if he needed a Tums. Phil ignored him and stared at a photograph on the wall as if it were a thousand miles away. Then he stood again and blew out a breath.

"All right," he said. "Okay, you guys are FBI agents. Okay. I'm not talking to them"—he gestured toward the door, indicating Hanlon and the other FBI officers waiting outside—"but I'll talk to you guys."

They all sat. Phil leaned back, looking at them silently for a spell—long enough that the agents were tempted to jump in and fill the lull. Finally, he said, "So you guys are FBI agents." He shook his head and wore an incredulous grin. "When did you guys start this—was it Norman? Holy shit, he set me up?"

They started to explain, but Phil interrupted with questions: That time the FBI showed up in D'Amato's room in Hawaii—were you behind that? And Fred Pro's wiretap? Who else knew? Phil asked how they kept track of everything—all the deals and meetings and conversations. They explained about the Nagra and hiding a recorder in the curtain in Hawaii, and Bowen Johnson's spectral presence.

The agents could see the scenes playing behind Phil's eyes. He pulled at his face, stared at them. When Jack brought up the show tunes at the Graycliff in Nassau—reflecting on an authentic moment they'd shared—Phil smiled and said he hoped there were no tapes of them singing. They laughed again about Jack ripping the phone out of the wall. They talked about all the characters: Dorian and Pro doing lines of coke, and Calandrella trying to stiff them in Frankfurt, and, of course, Santini. "Oh yeah, Sonny," Phil said, shaking his head. "That piece of shit."

They spent almost two hours unspooling this movie reel before Phil's demeanor shifted back to the present. The agents didn't want to rush him, but they had a goal in mind: They wanted to convince him to become a government witness. With his hypnotic salesmanship, his skills as a raconteur, and his uncommonly strong recall for people and conversations, he would make a potent weapon in the effort to ship the members of the Fraternity to prison.

They knew what he was capable of, and they wanted him on their side.

The government would offer a plea deal, which they hoped he would take, Jack told Phil. True, he would have to plead guilty, and admit what he'd done, and accept some prison time—but then they could help him.

In making this pitch, the agents faced an impossible task: They had to convince Phil that they were now telling the truth and were on his side, after spending the past nine months deceiving him. J.J. wanted to pull Phil to him, get him to see that they could revive their old bond. He longed to convince Phil that he could still lean on the undeniably powerful connection that they'd forged, even in light of everything that had happened and would happen. Finally, finally, the agents could share the complete truth, if only Phil could be open to it and be truthful himself.

"Look at me, Phil," J.J. said. "We can get through this—you just have to trust me."

He tried to will Kitzer to see it. He felt in that moment that he could make a connection that would transcend the devastation Phil was feeling.

Jack concurred. "You need to do what you need to do," he said. "But we'll help you if you'll let us be your friends."

Phil agreed to think it over. The agents said he could reach them anytime—but once he had a lawyer, they couldn't talk to him until they had a deal. They also told him that none of what had happened between them that evening, or over the last nine months, would change one fact: If he fought the charges and staged another circus like the one in Bismarck, the government would go after him hard. And they would be first in line to testify against him.

Then they summoned Hanlon, who cuffed Phil again and told him they were headed to the Federal Correctional Institution of Dade County. The agents saw, for the first time, fear in Phil's eyes.

He seemed to shrink as an agent helped him clamber into a car. Another agent helped lower him onto the backseat. He didn't look back as the car pulled away, carrying him off toward an unknown world.

24

Hobson's Choice

OCTOBER 19, 1977

Phil wore an orange jumpsuit when he walked into the Miami courtroom to appear before U.S. magistrate Charlene H. Sorrentino, after spending the night in jail. The appearance was brief and procedural, intended to determine the first steps in his journey through the criminal justice system. The judge noted the charges filed in Louisville and Memphis: mail fraud, fraud by wire, interstate transportation of stolen property, and so on. The previous week, Charles M. Allen, chief judge of the U.S. District Court in Louisville, had set Kitzer's bond at $250,000 cash and ordered that he surrender his passport.

Phil needed a lawyer, and he was still trying to reach Frank Oliver, nearly fifteen hundred miles away. The fact that Jack and J.J. were agents would make it tougher, but Phil was still figuring he would take on the government. If he could team up with, say, Fred Pro and Andy D'Amato, they could stage a dazzling defense. He hoped Oliver would help coordinate his looming battle with that of his fellow promoters.

A few days passed in the Miami lockup with no response from anyone. At first, Phil likely wondered whether all of his friends and associates were in the same predicament: freshly arrested, sitting in jail. But then a darker thought must have occurred to him: Maybe everyone in the Fraternity now knew that Phil was the source of their troubles—Phil and his decision to travel with and vouch for a pair of undercover agents. Even Oliver could be implicated.

Phil managed to get a call through to Jack Elliott out in California, who by then was dealing with troubles of his own. Elliott later recalled that Phil sounded desperate: Phil "told me that he was broke and everybody deserted him and he had no money and would I send him some money?"

By then, Phil clearly knew he had a major problem. To the rest of the Fraternity, he was toxic.

That morning, Hanlon joined Wedick and Brennan for breakfast at the Royal Sonesta Beach Hotel. It was a warm, blue-sky South Florida morning. The three of them walked back through everything that had happened—Phil's reaction, how they'd felt as nervous as they'd been the day they first met him—and all that might happen next.

J.J. shook his head. "Holy shit," he said, "do you guys realize what just happened? I mean, like . . ."

They all sat there in silence for a few minutes while the weight of it passed over them. It was heady but bittersweet. This was an ending of sorts for Jack and J.J., too. Soon enough, they knew, they would go from traveling and working together nonstop to being three time zones apart.

On November 3, the U.S. Marshals Service moved Phil to the Jefferson County Jail in Louisville, where the government would prosecute its first OpFoPen case. Phil was still unable to talk to Oliver—who, it turned out, was defending someone in a murder trial. But Oliver had asked two Louisville attorneys, Robert Zeman and Richard Heideman, to stand in on his behalf.

Phil's first priority: Get out of jail.

On November 7, Zeman asked the court to reduce Phil's bail to $10,000. He pointed out that Phil had never been convicted of a felony and would return home to Ellendale and agree not to leave the continental United States with the case pending.

Assistant U.S. Attorney David Everett, arguing against the motion on November 9, called Wedick as a witness. J.J. testified that Phil had told them he kept a get-out-of-jail fund of $700,000—though other promoters had told him that they thought Phil had tucked away at least $2 million. It was impossible to know for certain because Phil kept no books or records. Kitzer had also told the undercover agents that he knew someone who could furnish phony birth certificates that could be used to obtain a passport. If he really had a cache of money, he clearly couldn't get to it from prison. But if he was allowed to walk free, Wedick testified, he might access the stash and vanish or use his freedom to operate more scams.

The bail remained intact.

One by one, every trapdoor Phil had expected to slip through was sealed off. A full-blooded extrovert who had routinely placed dozens of phone calls a day, Phil became increasingly anxious in his isolation. He grew suspicious that someone—possibly one of his lawyers—was leaking information about his case, potentially endangering his life.

On November 12, three and a half weeks after his arrest, Phil wrote a letter to U.S. District Judge Edward Johnstone, appealing for help preparing his defense for trial, which was scheduled to begin on December 5. He asked for phone access to round up the cash he needed to purchase writing materials and send mail. "I have made repeated requests to jail personal [*sic*] that I be given access to long distance telephone calls, which have not been denied, but as of this date the requests have never been granted," he wrote.

His captors wouldn't turn over the fifty dollars he'd had in his wallet when Hanlon arrested him in Miami. Phil added that he'd appealed to the U.S. Marshals office, to no avail. "The government already has the distinct advantage of time," he wrote. "They have taken one year to prepare their case against me, and I have been given less than one month to prepare a defence [*sic*], in custody, under conditions that border on being held incommunicado." For someone who had long lived in comfort and privilege, this was alien to him—but not a violation of his civil rights, Everett noted in a brief of his own on Phil's situation.

On November 15, attorney Heideman called Oliver. Neither he nor Zeman had been paid for defending Kitzer, and they saw no indication that any money was forthcoming. Zeman also called Audrey Kitzer, who said the family owned no property and that she had no funds. She said she'd filed for Aid to Families with Dependent Children. As far as the lawyers and the government were concerned, the Kitzers were—at least on paper—destitute.

Meanwhile, Phil faced harsh living conditions in the Jefferson County Jail—significantly worse than in Miami. The place was overcrowded, with several men jammed into each cell, and it reeked of urine. Phil's ulcers festered. Zeman visited him on November 21, almost five weeks after the arrest. Kitzer complained of a "severe, long-time stomach illness," according to Zeman, and said that he "had not been able to eat for some nine days." The attorney described his client, in a motion to the judge, as being "in an obvious deteriorated state of health."

Phil said he'd been denied medicine and care, and had become so ill that he'd been taken to Louisville General Hospital two days earlier for treatment and medication. But when he returned to jail, the corrections officers told him they'd lost his medicine and wouldn't be able to replace it until he returned to the hospital, a week later. Zeman wrote that Phil "was in need of immediate medical treatment," and that Zeman himself was writing to Johnstone because Phil was worried that his own letters to the judge might never be delivered.

Back in Indianapolis, J.J. and Jack knew little of Phil's precipitous decline. The agents had to keep their distance while he contemplated his next move—if he refused a plea deal, after all, they would be adversaries in court. And anyway, the agents were as frenzied as ever. They were part of teams putting together more OpFoPen indictments while also preparing to testify in Louisville.

They faced major life changes, too. The bureau had approved their transfers on October 27. Jack was astonished to learn that the FBI had agreed to ship him to Mobile, his hometown. Eager to deliver his newly expanded brood into the safety net of extended family, he packed up immediately, before some bureaucrat changed his mind about the transfer. His family relocated to the South before Thanksgiving. J.J.'s new orders were for Sacramento.

When a month passed with no word, Jack and J.J. began to wonder whether Phil had decided to fight the charges. If that was the case, the government stood ready to unleash its full payload of legal artillery: The agents had made recordings of forty-six phone calls and eighteen meetings with Phil and others, and the collective effort of the two undercover agents and their support team had yielded six fat three-ring binders of 302 reports. In all, they counted about a hundred major frauds in which Phil, along with around fifty co-conspirators, had been involved.

On November 28, Oliver mailed Phil a typewritten three-page letter. Finally receiving a missive from his old partner in crime might have momentarily heartened Phil—until he read Oliver's assessment of his situation. "Your problems come to me in the middle of a long trial," Oliver wrote. "While I have not done anything about them, other than to try to reach your 'friends,' I have thought about them for a good bit. My conclusion: I think you are being unrealistic."

Oliver had been worried for a while that Phil was "becoming less and less mindful of the consequences to you of what you were doing," he wrote. "When we talked in Chicago at our last meeting I had the feeling that you did not give a damn anymore, and that I was talking to a man who almost hoped to be prosecuted. In that connection, I am relieved that the people with you were agents. They impressed me as being a couple of really shabby little con men, and I was dismayed to see you with them."

The attorney wrote that he had a "strong feeling that the two pending indictments are the tip of an iceberg. . . . I suspect that if you survive these, there will be others popping up like spring flowers. How many can you survive? Three? Seven? Where does it all end?"

Oliver advised Phil not to extend himself in defense of the other promoters. "Some of those," he wrote,

> are desperados at best, riding with a gun in each hand, their reins in their teeth. In spite of your efforts to protect them they will be brought down. . . . What you have told me of Fred Pro, for example, would not endear him to me as a man for whom I would walk through fire. Some of them appear to be wanted on two or three continents. Consider whether or not you would be willing to do four or five years for each of them.
>
> As matters now stand it seems to me that you have to make a choice. You can defend yourself against the present charges. You can plead guilty and stand mute. You can make a deal.

On the first option, given Phil's lack of defense funds, he would have to rely on a public defender, which was not a promising prospect, Oliver noted. As for the second option? "Pleading guilty and standing mute is like a ninety-year-old man visiting a whorehouse," the lawyer wrote. "He gets nothing out of the excursion in the first place, but is there to be scooped up in the ensuing vice raid."

Oliver said he wasn't encouraging Phil to make a deal, but, he wrote, "I just can't see any other way for you to come out of it."

He concluded:

> Phil, I repeat that a time has come for you to get your thinking into an orientation of total, cold reality. . . . [N]o one is going

to come riding in with a verifiable CD that can be funded at the closest bank. Nothing magical will happen. The government will grind and grind. And when you think you have saved something of yourself, it will grind some more. If you are prepared to face that as your future for a few years, then face it. But for god's sake, face it without pretending that one day you will awake to learn that it is all over and was just a bad dream.

I am genuinely sorry for your troubles and wish that I might wave a wand and make them all disappear. If I had the resources to come to your assistance and to provide for you the best fight of your life, I would hope to have the good sense not to do so, for I think I might do more harm than good. But please be assured of my continuing regard for you, and my desire that you should now do what is in your own selfish best interest.

Oliver's letter had the intended effect. On Sunday, December 4, within a day or two of receiving it, Phil sent a telegram to Jack and J.J. saying that he wanted to meet with them and the prosecutor, David Everett, alone. No other attorneys. He had no one representing him at the moment anyway; Zeman and Heideman had resigned because of non-payment.

On December 11, Jack, J.J., and Everett visited Phil at the jail. The agents found the overcrowding and the stench horrifying. Some inmates walked around barely dressed. "It was disgusting," J.J. said. "There was no sense of decency anywhere in there."

Phil appeared diminished. His skin was ashen, and dark shadows encased his eyes; he looked like he'd slept little and eaten less since they'd last been with him. He seemed relieved to see them—they were familiar, friendly faces, even under the circumstances. He grimaced when talking about the jail. Every inmate received

Scope—a dental rinse composed of about 20 percent alcohol—in his toiletry kit. Some were so desperate for even a momentary high, they guzzled it.

Despite the bleak conditions, the old Phil was still very much alive and well. When they sat down to talk, he informed his visitors that if they wanted him to cooperate, they had to meet his conditions. He wanted to be released from jail by Christmas. He wanted all the indictments against him dropped, and no prison time. He wanted Everett to clear up his problems with the Internal Revenue Service. (Kitzer's troubles with the IRS—audits, assessments, penalties—dated back to the 1960s and the American Allied case. By one of his own estimates—almost certainly a conservative one, spelled out on a financial-disclosure form during his incarceration—he owed the government $1.5 million.)

Everett rejected each condition. Phil would face indictments in at least five jurisdictions, totaling more than a dozen felonies, the prosecutor said. There was no way Kitzer could escape a significant prison sentence.

Phil stood. He was done talking. The agents, who had watched him negotiate his way through countless deals over eight months, had expected such posturing. Phil being Phil.

J.J. flashed back to his work as a lifeguard at Coney Island's Bay 15. One packed Sunday afternoon, after spotting two swimmers floundering, he blew his whistle and sprinted into the water. The ocean was swollen and fitful, and as he swam the swells kept blocking his view of the flailing pair. By the time he reached one of them, he realized that he'd misjudged his approach. He'd been taught to always approach a rescue from behind, to keep the panicked swimmer from lunging for him and endangering both of them.

It was too late. J.J. rode a wave right into a wild-eyed man, who clawed at him. Fortunately, J.J. had also learned how to survive this worst-case scenario: He gulped in a breath and yanked the man down with him into the gray-green depths. Instead of a savior, he became an anchor. The gambit worked: The desperate swimmer pushed free and popped to the surface again, at which point J.J. grabbed him from behind and calmed him.

That was how it had to work with Phil, too. To save him, they first had to drag him under.

Everett and the agents returned the next day with a new proposal: If Phil pleaded guilty and testified, they would cap his sentence at ten years. Final offer. If he turned it down, they would try him in federal court in Louisville within a month. If he was convicted there, and in the multitude of cases to come, he could wind up in prison for much, if not all, of the rest of his life.

Phil knew the government was trying to make him as miserable as possible in order to strong-arm him into cooperating. The message was clear: Join us or suffer. He hated to lose, but he was a realist and had little leverage. Oliver was right: The government would pound away at him, year after year, case after case. If he had any decision to make, it was a Hobson's choice: He could take what was offered or nothing at all. The agents warned him: "There's no half measures here, Phil," Jack said. "You go halfway, you're done. You gotta go all the way. You gotta tell it just like it is in detail, and if you did it, say you did it."

Phil negotiated as hard as he could. Later, a defense lawyer attacking Phil's deal with the government would say, "You had conned a lot of folks, but you could only con them down to ten, is that right?"

"They conned me up to ten," he would reply. "I was trying to con them down to five."

By the next day, they had a deal. Jack and J.J. met him at the jail and shook his hand and asked, "Okay, who can you give us?"

They wanted the names of people he could testify against. Phil wrote out a two-page list: Andy D'Amato, Armand Mucci, Bob Bendis, Mark Iuteri—though he could never remember that last name. ("The guy who traveled around with Andy," he said.) Harold Silverkur, the promoter in Switzerland. The Cornazes. Fred Pro.

Phil signed the plea deal on January 4, 1978. He agreed to plead guilty to the three counts filed against him in Louisville and testify truthfully at all OpFoPen-related trials. He would provide "independently corroborative" information. In exchange, the government would not pursue further prosecution or seek more jail time. Phil could not, per the agreement, request a reduction of sentence, but Everett agreed to supply letters reflecting the nature and extent of his cooperation to appropriate parole boards, should his testimony merit such a step. And Everett would provide protection for Phil and his family. He also agreed to recommend that Phil be sentenced to a minimum-security prison camp—"a deviation from normal policy of the Federal Bureau of Prisons [that] is agreed to only on the basis of the uniqueness of this particular case and defendant."

Audrey Kitzer was baffled. When a reporter from the *Minneapolis Tribune* made the drive to Ellendale to ask about the drama surrounding her husband, she professed to know nothing of his fraudulent banks and laughed in disbelief at an article about his exploits. "Listen to these names," she said. "They sound like they're out of a bad novel. . . . I never heard of any of them."

She deflected questions about their marriage. "I just wish he wouldn't have given Ellendale as his hometown," she said. "If he would've said Chicago or Minneapolis, nobody would care less. But Ellendale—then everybody wonders why he was here."

The time after the arrest had been hellish, she said. Some folks told her that she'd "brought disgrace" on the town and should leave. But she had no plans to pull up stakes with their son, Jeffrey, almost finished with the first grade.

"I wish the whole thing would go away," she said.

Some folks claimed to have suspected Phil all along. "Everybody in town knew he must've been in some kinda funny deal because he took all these trips and he had all this big money," one resident confided. "You had to suspect something. But nobody thought he was into it that big—millions of dollars. I mean, geez, what's going on in a little dinky-assed town like this?"

As the Louisville trial of John Kaye and John Calandrella edged closer, the government secretly moved Phil to a lockup south of Louisville, in rural Hardin County. Though he didn't change his name, he was now in the federal witness protection program.

The new surroundings helped. Phil had a cell to himself, decent food, medicine. And just before he was due to take the witness stand, Jack and J.J. secured the sheriff's permission to remove him from jail. They needed to go over his testimony, and it wasn't safe for him to be seen having long conversations with FBI agents in his cell.

They checked into a Louisville hotel, where Phil took a shower, and they gave him some clothes and fed him. Then they hunkered into one room as they had done so many times the previous year, to talk business, only this time Phil faced a task unlike anything he'd tackled previously. From the questions defense attorneys had asked during cross-examinations in the trial earlier, it was clear that they were hoping to convince the jury that Phil duped Kaye and Calandrella into handling phony paper. (The government had been unable to extradite John Packman from England or Jean-Claude and Pascal Cornaz from Switzerland.) They tried to block Phil's appearance as a witness, claiming his many years as a con artist extraordinaire rendered him unreliable. Pondering this motion, Judge Allen was astonished to read transcripts of the recordings Jack and J.J. had made. In chambers, he characterized Phil as "a rip-off artist with the greatest dreams, and I shouldn't use the word 'great.' Most sordid dreams of any man I've ever read about."

Allen ruled that Phil could testify, but he told the lawyers that they had "a right to say that Mr. Kitzer is a massive con artist. . . . The gold mine deal, the Hawaii deal, my goodness. We could spend three or four months here if we talk about those."

Jack took the stand a day before Phil, on February 16. He described Phil as being "at the top level" of a con game involving banks that peddled phony paper, and he described how Phil operated, how he built in defense mechanisms. "We would travel," Jack said. "Kitzer did not believe that it was safe to stay in one location because . . . any law enforcement organization in particular who wanted to know where you were would always be able to locate you and keep easy track of you, what you were doing. So he was a believer in mobility."

Defense attorney Paul Redmond began his cross-examination by asking Jack whether "a great many of the things you have testified to here are things that Kitzer told you."

"That is correct."

"Now, Kitzer, I am asking you from your experience, is a congenital liar, is he not?"

"I would characterize him as a person who lies when it is convenient for him."

"A psychopathic liar?"

"I wouldn't be in a position to make that statement."

"A man who does not know the truth from falsity but, rather, uses it any way he wants for his own benefit?"

"He does make statements which are false when it serves his purpose."

"Habitually?"

"When it's convenient for him."

"He even makes them to associates of his, does he not?"

"That's correct."

"And over the period of time that you were with him, you saw

him habitually and continuously lie to people who were supposedly his associates, is that not true?"

"He frequently lied to everybody," Brennan conceded.

The next defense attorney, Kenny Grantz, questioned Jack
about Phil's drinking.

Kitzer "consumed a lot of alcohol and could handle it," Jack said.
"He could stay up until four in the morning and get up at eight the
next morning and attend a conference with individuals."

"Still drinking?"

"He would start drinking at nine-thirty or ten in the morning."

"I mean, we could say he was a constant drinker from morning
till night?"

"Well, frequently, yes."

The question for the government was whether, after all this,
Kitzer would be someone a jury of Kentuckians would believe.

J.J. and Jack tried to prepare Phil for what lay ahead—to expect
to be called a liar and a thief and a drunk, and worse. They hammered him on the importance of being honest about what he'd
done, regardless of how it sounded, and reminded him that the
government would add prison time if he committed perjury. "Phil,
no freaking monkey business," J.J. told him.

As the first trial spawned by Operation Fountain Pen, this one
carried an outsized significance. If a jury rejected Phil's testimony
and acquitted Kaye and Calandrella, prosecutors in the other trials
lined up over the next year or two might waver.

J.J. took a certain odd comfort from the resumption of their old
habits: going to fetch stomach meds, picking up Phil's dry cleaning, their verbal swordplay. It was a relief to no longer have to hide
in plain sight; now they only worried about Phil being discovered.
After reading transcripts of one of the FBI's recordings, one of
the defense attorneys had said he expected "they would have him
under deep cover."

The next morning, they all walked out of the hotel and into the frigid air, toward the next chapter of their lives. Phil's first appearance as a government witness came on February 17, 1978. Exactly one year and two days after they'd met for the first time at the Thunderbird.

The Phil Kitzer Road Show

FEBRUARY 17, 1978

Phil's suit looked two sizes too big when he walked to the witness stand in the federal courtroom in Louisville. Anyone who knew him would have instantly recognized the physical toll the past four months had taken. His already slender frame had shrunk noticeably, and he was pale and drawn. But an electricity rippled through the room as prosecutor David Everett approached to begin his questions. An intense curiosity about Phil had built over the previous three weeks.

"You have sworn to tell the truth," Everett began, "and there's been a lot of testimony about your lying. You have lied quite a bit in your life, haven't you?"

"I have lied in my life, yes," Phil replied.

"Quite a bit, haven't you?"

"Quite a bit."

"What is your occupation?"

"Insurance and banking."

"You're a promoter?"

"Yes."

"Is 'promoter' another word for 'con man'?"

"Yes."

Kitzer explained how he talked about scams in a way that sounded as if they were legitimate business deals. "You don't have to use the word 'scam,'" he said. "We never used the word 'scam' when we discussed something."

Although he'd fibbed often when executing these deals, he insisted he wouldn't do so in court: "To lie on the witness stand under oath is a foolish, foolish thing."

Talking in an even, unhurried fashion, Phil explained that during the first six months of 1977, he issued Seven Oak paper with a total face value of $25 million, despite never having more than a few dollars in the bank. He laid out the Kaye deal—how Tom Bannon sought him out, and how on a taxi ride into downtown Minneapolis, Phil spoke frankly. "I told him, if he chooses to do business with me, I said, just as sure as we're in the cab, you can expect the FBI to come visit you."

"Why would you want to tell him that?" Everett asked.

"Well, if I was going to do business with him, I knew the FBI would be there, and what would be the sense of starting a relationship with him, to do business for ten hours, twenty-four hours, thirty-six hours, spend money, telephone, telexes, maybe get $500 or $1,000 invested, receive a phone call from him [saying], 'Oh, wait a minute. The FBI was here, I don't want to talk to you any longer.' Might as well have it out right there if it worries him. If it bothers him, let's finish out the evening, have a few drinks, you go your way, I'll go my way."

When the time came for cross-examination, the defense attorneys pounced. Attorney Grantz asked, "During the time that you were negotiating . . . were you at that time participating in quite a bit of drinking of alcoholic beverages?"

"Yes sir, I drank," Phil replied.

"Constantly?"

"Yes sir."

"All right. And drinking like that, did that affect you in any way?"

"No sir."

"Could you give us an approximation of how much you would consume during this period? . . . [D]o you have a daily quota?"

"No, I have no daily quota."

Grantz was diving into the particulars of the Seven Oak deal with John Kaye, probing Phil for inconsistencies, when the judge recessed court for the long Presidents' Day weekend.

Phil and the agents holed up again for the three-day break. A snowstorm hit on the cusp of the weekend, pinning them down in their rooms. "The snow was up to my ass," J.J. recalled.

Everyone felt restless. Phil had done well so far, but Paul Redmond—the more aggressive of the two defense lawyers—had yet to take his turn. Late Saturday night, J.J., gazing out the window, watched car headlights lurch far below as drivers slid on black ice off an interstate exit ramp and, sometimes, into one another. The demolition derby was a vivid reminder of what he would soon leave behind when he relocated to California. He hoped it wasn't a metaphor for what was coming on Tuesday.

He needn't have worried. Phil seemed unperturbed when the defense, as expected, continued to target his character flaws. He answered everything in the narrow, straightforward way in which the agents and Everett had coached him.

Redmond labored to rattle him, at one point shouting so loudly that the judge ordered him to lower his voice. Redmond asked Phil how he could claim to be wary of the consequences of lying in court when he'd fibbed in many other potentially hazardous situations—citing Fred Pro's statements that Sonny Santini had threatened to kill him. "So what you're telling us is that you have a great danger of lying under oath because you might go to jail for a few years, but you have no . . . fear of the danger of lying to people like Santini?"

"No sir, that's not what I'm telling you," Phil replied. "I'm telling you if you lie under oath, I know that a judge will sentence you for perjury. What Fred Pro tells me doesn't make it so. He says Sonny Santini had an ice pick to my ear. That doesn't make it so."

The trial stretched on for two more weeks, during which Redmond claimed that Calandrella was "a good-hearted guy who got conned by a couple of real pros," referring to Phil and Tom Bannon. But on March 7, the jury spent just three hours deliberating before finding both defendants guilty on all four counts, including making false statements in an application for a bank loan and fraud by wire. The *Louisville Courier-Journal* attributed the conviction to Kitzer's "damaging testimony."

Three days later, Judge Allen handed down ten-year prison sentences for both men.

After the trial, on March 12, the Department of Justice finalized its deal with Phil. He received his ten-year prison sentence and was whisked off to a prison designed for witness protection in San Diego.

The facility brought another moderate uptick in Phil's living conditions, though his cellmate was Aladena "Jimmy the Weasel" Fratianno, a mobster who had admitted to strangling three men and shooting two others during his time in the Mafia. When J.J. visited to discuss their next trial, a guard let him onto an elevator and pressed an unmarked button so there was no way to know what floor they were going to. The meeting areas had no furniture; J.J. and Phil sat on the floor. When J.J. asked for a chair, a guard told him that he was lucky to be allowed in with his pencil and notebook.

Phil seemed mostly at peace with what the agents had done. As they talked about his testimony, he sometimes asked how Jack and J.J. had managed specific parts of their investigation while they were all living together. He was impressed that this other world had been operating all around him without him once catching a glimpse.

The next trial, in Hammond, Indiana, covered the letter of credit purchased by undercover agent Dean Naum, acting as Nick Carbone; it brought the first Kitzer case J.J. had built full circle.

Phil and Norman Howard testified against Paul Chovanec, who was found guilty on all seven counts and handed an eight-year prison sentence.

So began what the agents and federal prosecutors referred to as the Phil Kitzer Road Show. By the time he reached Memphis, two months later, Phil had become something of a media sensation. One magazine writer described him as being "without peer as a con artist." Newspaper stories labeled Phil the "world's greatest con man" and, in a headline, the "King of Scam." One reporter characterized him as a "genie" who could "perform magic tricks of all sorts." A federal prosecutor described Phil as a "master con artist" who ran "one of the most cleverly designed schemes that's ever been uncovered."

Phil lived up to the hype. Defense attorneys worked furiously to rattle him, but the tenth-grade high school dropout matched them move for move. One lawyer described sparring with Phil as "going up against Dr. J"—referring to NBA star Julius Erving—"on the basketball court." Another attorney drew a contempt-of-court warning from the judge after complaining that Phil was "too smooth a talker for me."

Kitzer never spoke to the media, but in December 1978 *Charlotte Observer* reporter Robert Hodierne interviewed his father, then eighty-two. When asked about the American Allied trial, the elder Kitzer "smiles and says it was his son who was the crook, not he. It was a case, the father says, of 'too much money, and it went to his head. He got to be a big shot with so much money around and it just messed him up.'"

The indictments and trials and convictions piled up. In June, prosecutors in Charlotte charged Frank Oliver, along with Pro and Chovanec, in the fraud case FBI agent Allen Ezell had opened several years earlier in North Carolina. They referred to the scam as "the Phillip Kitzer method of finance."

Phil succeeded by being forthcoming, but there was one area in which he continually equivocated: He never revealed how much money he and his co-conspirators had scammed over the years. Because of the vast reach of their fraudulent activities—the trail of bad paper circled the globe, at what a Department of Justice official called "the absolute highest levels of international banking and swindling"—and the fact that many victims never reported the losses, exact figures were elusive. In one report, officials suggested $60 million, with the caveat that the number was "probably very conservative."

But after Phil's arrest, Richard Hanning, an assistant U.S. attorney in Hammond, tried to capture the enormity of it. His nine-page memo detailed how OpFoPen had "led to discovery of fraudulent schemes involving 48 judicial districts in the United States and offenses in England, Switzerland, France, Germany, Italy, the Netherlands, Canada, Mexico, Paraguay, Peru, Japan, Hong Kong, Singapore, Thailand, Costa Rica, Iran, Iraq, Nigeria, Liechtenstein, Australia and several island countries in the Caribbean. The investigation has led to date to the recovery of $3.8 million in stolen monies and stolen and fraudulent checks and securities, savings to individuals and financial institutions in excess of $15 million and identification of losses worldwide in excess of $2 billion."

Phil fancied himself a Robin Hood type, taking from greedy bankers to give to starving entrepreneurs, and the public's enduring enmity for banks made him a somewhat sympathetic figure. But when banks fail, the government bails them out, and the costs run into the billions—those are taxpayer dollars. And for every person Phil purportedly tried to help, there was a Bernard Baker or Jimmy Kealoha—people whose lives were derailed or ruined by his schemes. When Phil and his cronies busted out companies, people lost jobs, pensions. The societal cost was staggering.

Jack noticed that many fraud victims seemed uniquely damaged. They lived with the knowledge that they'd chosen to participate in the crime. "What you learn in this kind of work," he said, "you go back and talk to the victims of a con, you find the belief that 'I did this to myself. My judgment was flawed. I can't make good decisions.'"

The cons did more than ravage people financially. "It's much more devastating in the long term to a victim who willfully gave the money than somebody who's a victim from being in the wrong place at the wrong time," Jack said. "It destroys confidence. It destroys marriages."

Myron Fuller was shocked when few of Pro's victims sought reparations or even reported that they'd been cheated. Even after the FBI informed one developer that he'd been scammed, the victim refused to believe it, saying he still expected the funding to come through. Many were too embarrassed to admit that they'd been taken.

As for the banks Phil had scammed, many would instantly fire a teller who skimmed $150 but would clam up about a million-dollar error. Their lawyers advised them to "keep their mouth shut and eat it," lest they look gullible and lose the public's trust, he said. They generally didn't cooperate with the FBI. It was easier to say *That didn't work out* than *We got fooled.* The entire exercise likely seemed futile: The money, after all, was long gone.

Little of the money Phil ripped off was ever recovered, and attempts to pin him down on whether he had anything left usually ended up in a conversational corn maze. One attorney tried to elicit information about the $700,000 he'd once claimed to have tucked away.

"And that is what you have put away?" the attorney asked.

"No sir," Kitzer replied.

"How much do you have put away?"

"Nothing."

"So you're telling us . . . your net worth is zero?"

"I don't have anything put away."

"Okay. Maybe we don't communicate."

"Well . . . sir, when you say net worth, I mean when you say what money do you have put away, there is a big difference," Phil said, brandishing his skills of deflection. "Now, net worth can be real estate. It can be stocks, bonds, but when you say cash, you're talking about cash in a safe deposit box. I don't have any cash in a safe deposit box. A person can have a receivable. They can have real estate. Then you're discussing net worth when you're talking about Internal Revenue."

And so on.

In June 1978, Phil filled out a form pertaining to his ability to pay for legal counsel. He reported his income before his arrest at $20,000 a month—$240,000 a year, which translated to just under $900,000 in 2017. In addition, he reported earning another $100,000 in the previous year from Seven Oak. The FBI agents believe these figures represent a fraction of what he made and spent, without paying taxes. He listed $3 million in debts, about half of which he owed to the IRS.

But he left a few clues as to the wealth he accumulated. Sitting in his hotel room in July, he had scribbled the figures $209,000 and $185,000 on a piece of paper. Jack, sitting nearby, knew from their conversation that the numbers represented what Phil had made selling Seven Oak paper over its final month operating the vehicle. Phil tossed the paper into the trash, and Jack fished it out and tucked it into his pocket—a relatively rare piece of physical evidence that he quickly mailed to Indianapolis.

Extrapolating, the agents figured that Phil had cleared at least $2 million in seven or eight months from Seven Oak alone.

Becoming a government witness didn't translate into the country club prison life Phil had once envisioned. He testified in four trials in 1978, hopscotching around the country, and each local jail he stayed in offered its own distinctive menu of discomforts. "The witness protection program was not well developed then," said Tom Baker, the former FBI inspector who ascended to a management role.

Today, the U.S. Marshals Service takes responsibility for inmates in the program. But in 1978, FBI agents were frequently left to manage the witnesses they'd cultivated, and Jack and J.J. couldn't always travel with Phil and watch out for him. Corrections officers in local lockups were capricious in their care, sometimes negligent. Some believed Phil was milking the system, getting benefits as a government witness that he didn't deserve, and found ways to punish him; they would withhold his ulcer medicine or pair him with volatile inmates. At times, Phil was beaten. "When we met him," J.J. said, "sometimes he would be in a bad way."

There were other insults, some stingingly personal. After Oliver was arrested, Phil's old friend and attorney began savaging Phil in court filings, claiming Kitzer was mentally ill. Clearly concerned about Phil's ability to testify against him, Oliver cited Phil's "apparent willingness to state whatever suits his convenience at the moment, regardless of its truth; . . . his boastful self-glorification in his testimony thus far on behalf of the United States; his utter lack of appreciation of the consequences to him of his offenses; his pretensions to importance . . . as one of the top 'con-men' in the world." The lawyer speculated that Phil was either a psychopath or a sociopath.

Predictably, Phil was a pariah to Fraternity members he testified against. "He was a government witness, so there are automatically people that don't like him," Jack said. "You never knew who he was in jail with. And jail is not a safe place." The agents worried that an organized-crime boss would find a way to catch Phil moving between trials—or hire someone in an underprotected jail cell to whack him.

Baker was a new field supervisor in the FBI's Mobile office when Jack arrived. They became friends, heading out on sailing and shrimping excursions on Mobile Bay, and Baker tried to help as Jack and J.J. managed Phil's situation.

Phil would show up for an appearance bruised and raw, and the agents would spend hours tending to him, getting him his medicine and whatever else he needed so he could settle down and concentrate. Describing this to Baker, Jack once started crying. "It was breaking Jack's heart—literally," Baker said. "He was torn up about the way Kitzer was being terribly mistreated."

Baker called headquarters to try to get help. "The FBI is a big bureaucracy," he said. "Sometimes the right hand doesn't know what the left hand is doing."

When they were sailing, Jack also described what he and his family had gone through during OpFoPen. Baker was aghast that he'd been left to sift through the psychological aftermath of the operation—the danger, the long separations from his family—on his own. The FBI had even unhelpfully tried to transfer Brennan to Washington, D.C., not long after he'd arrived in Mobile; Baker scuttled it, citing all that Brennan had gone through in the past couple of years.

Today, the bureau screens agents carefully before sending them into undercover roles. A person needs a strong personality, a steady internal compass, and the ability to think quickly and independently. When undercover investigations end, the FBI provides counseling to help agents process their experiences. "Now, so much attention is paid to people who do long-term undercover work," Baker said. "Theirs was one of the first ones. These guys did a hell of a thing."

In the late summer of 1978, the government moved Phil to Federal Prison Camp, Montgomery, on the grounds of Maxwell Air Force Base, in Alabama. Wedick no longer had ready access to Phil in California, so he wrote Kitzer a letter bringing him up to date, and trying to lift his spirits.

The letter finally found its way to Phil on November 15.

"J.J.," Kitzer wrote in reply,

> You son of a gun, you really wrote me a letter, just like you
> said!!! I thought you were bullshit when you told me that.

Today I received your letter of Sept. 20, that you sent to Memphis! Took long enough to catch up with me.

Your Swiss people should be pretty happy. Now where do we go from here? Why don't we get one big courtroom & try everyone at once? I can't tell you how bad I want to get this all over with. It seems like it'll never end. The thing that is hard is to be put in those rotten jails. I was in that city jail in Calif. for 14 days, with only 3 days for talking. It's enough to drive you crazy. Have not heard from Jack. He said he would be in touch with me after I got back here. When are you going to come down? Put a bottle of Scotch in your pocket, I'm ready for a drink. I never went 14 months without a drink in my life. If we were to re-write that plea agreement I would put in a few "extra" things now that I have the hindsight! OK Jim, thanks again for the letter, will see you at the next stop. Phil.

A few weeks later, Phil testified in federal court in Kansas City. More than 90 percent of the criminal cases that enter the U.S. justice system never go to trial; agreeing to a plea deal often makes more sense, for various reasons, than attempting to win over a jury. Not with the promoters. They all wanted to try their luck.

An armed marshal stood three feet away as Phil sat on the witness stand while two other marshals kept watch nearby. When it was over, Armand Mucci, Bob Bendis, and Andy D'Amato all received five-year sentences for their roles in defrauding Bernard Baker out of $110,000.

Before the trial in Charlotte, Phil spent time with FBI agent Allen Ezell, whose pursuit of the con man had triggered OpFoPen. The night before Phil's testimony, Ezell and Kitzer went shopping downtown at J. C. Penney's and Sears, to buy a sport coat, slacks, and a collared shirt for Phil to wear in court. "I had never been out shopping with a subject before," Ezell said with a laugh. "It was just such an unusual thing to do during a trial."

The agent found his longtime target to be "a fun guy to be around."

Like many people who encountered Phil, Ezell grew preoccupied afterward by thoughts of what might have been. "He was a sharp guy," Ezell said. "If he'd have taken every one of his talents and channeled it in the right direction, he'd probably be a millionaire."

Or a millionaire who didn't end up in jail.

By the spring of 1980, Phil had fully settled in at Maxwell. That same year, the FBI created a formal set of guidelines for undercover agents and their supervisors. There were fewer trials by then, and when Phil traveled, a U.S. marshal loaded him on a commercial flight alone, to be retrieved by Jack and J.J. at the other end.

When he disembarked in Honolulu, the agents were waiting. They watched as Phil descended the stairs surrounded by a pack of people chatting with him and patting him on the back. "Bye, Phil!" they called out. "Enjoy your visit! Have fun!"

Grinning and waving, Phil strolled over to Jack and J.J. He said he'd flown with a Roadrunners Travel Club, and they'd all had such a good time—talking and laughing about all the same places they'd visited—that they'd made him an honorary member. Phil was wearing the club's pin on his suit jacket. Someone asked which hotel he was staying at, and he shrugged and said, "I'm traveling on the government's nickel." He and the agents laughed and climbed into a car to head to the local jail.

The agents had requested that Phil be incarcerated on Molokai, a nearly uninhabited island southeast of Honolulu. Jack and J.J. figured it was an ideal place to focus on the task ahead, which was testifying against Mark Iuteri. The next day the agents checked him out of the tiny lockup and took him to a hotel on a far end of the island. They spent a couple of days preparing with Assistant U.S.

Attorney Dan Bent of the Justice Department's organized-crime task force.

One late afternoon, the agents took Phil for a walk along the cliffs over the Pacific Ocean. When they were on the road together, Kitzer had often dragged them to happy hour, with the gold lighter, the Scotch, the women. Instead there was just softening sunlight and the thundering surf. They sat, and Phil lit a cigarette and looked at the ocean as if he were seeing it for the first time. After a spell, he told them that sitting there on the crags, amid the beauty of it all, was almost enough to make him forget the stress and headaches awaiting in court. It was good to put all of that behind them for a few minutes, Phil said. For the three of them to be able to sit together and talk.

Bent was struck by the threesome's dynamic—the tangible bonds between the men. "I got the impression that Kitzer was a very sharp guy, and he understood that they got him," he said. "Kitzer respected them, too."

Bent also gained an appreciation for how the agents had pulled off the operation. "They were completely unpretentious guys," he said. "They don't try to be the smartest guys in the room. . . . They had a real talent for it. They were two of the best federal agents I ever worked with."

The trial featured what had by then become the familiar assaults on Kitzer's character and history. Now a seasoned witness, Phil spent two days laying out the details of the Kealoha scam, including Iuteri's fraudulent appraisal of the condo project. A newspaper described Kitzer as "dapper, tanned, and dark-haired" and reported that "he was turned out in a conservative blue suit and blue tie and looking capable of running a bank or a trust company again."

After the jury convicted Iuteri, Judge Sam King imposed a fifteen-year sentence. "If ever a case required a maximum sentence," he said, "this is the case."

The FBI opened more than 130 cases as a result of OpFoPen, and federal prosecutors eventually convicted some fifty people. After about three years of trials, the government had taken down all the primary targets, including Sonny Santini, who in May 1981 was sentenced to eight years in prison. Jean-Claude and Pascal Cornaz and John Packman were the only key figures never to stand trial, because of extradition issues and because the elder Cornaz—whom Swiss officials described as "one of the main members of the Geneva financial underworld"—had a massive heart attack. But by then, the Fraternity had been fully dismantled.

Maybe more significant, though, was the culture change OpFoPen helped bring about.

In the four years after the operation, spending on undercover work more than quadrupled, and the number of investigations increased by more than 800 percent, to a total of 463. A congressional committee that studied this spike in 1982 termed the increased use of covert operatives a "sudden and dramatic change in the mix of investigative techniques used by this nation's premier law enforcement agency."

Under the terms of a typical ten-year sentence, Kitzer would have been eligible for parole in early 1982. But in May 1980, while Phil was testifying in Hawaii, his attorney, John J. Cleary, submitted a motion to modify his sentence.

"Since his arrest, the defendant has cooperated with the Government and its agents in the detection and prosecution of other large-scale financial frauds throughout the United States," Cleary wrote. "The defendant has more than complied with the original understanding executed as part of the plea agreement in this case, and has, at great personal hardship because of the intermittent confinement in local and county jails as a result of his testifying in various federal courts throughout the United States, suffered deprivation not ordinarily encountered by a regular federal prisoner."

The government signed on in favor of the motion, and soon after returning from Hawaii, Phil was released from Maxwell into a community treatment center. Meanwhile, Jack and J.J. talked about what would come next for Kitzer. Jack had been driving to Maxwell every few weeks to see him, to make sure he was staying out of trouble and didn't feel isolated. They wanted to do the same after he got out—help him resettle somewhere nearby so they could keep an eye on him.

The question was where. Mobile wasn't a giant metropolis, but there were plenty of big-city temptations. "We talked about, we gotta find a place for him where he's not going to get into trouble," J.J. said.

Phil had done well, but he was a threat to backslide. He'd been a con man for much of his adult life. The agents drove back and forth along the Gulf Coast before settling on Gulf Shores, a town of about ten thousand people on the southern edge of Alabama, between Mobile and Pensacola.

There was another reason they wanted him nearby: They hoped to harness his unique talents. While serving his sentence, Phil had begun lecturing on financial fraud to FBI offices around the country, including at the academy in Quantico. Dan Bent, the prosecutor in Hawaii, watched Kitzer explain his former vocation to trainees. "These were straitlaced young men," he said. "They weren't street-smart. Being told by a world-class con artist how fraud works was invaluable. I'm sure most of the people in the room were just dumbfounded that anyone could do those things."

Just before his scheduled release, in October 1980, after slightly more than three years in custody, Phil lectured at the FBI office in Birmingham, Alabama. That night, the accrued physical and psychic toll of his existence—the cigarettes, the booze, the lies, the stress, the mortal danger, the accusations, the jail, the verbal jousting in more than a dozen courtrooms, the ghosts of all the victims and his abandoned family, and the spectacular way that his parallel lives had collided, supernova-style, and merged back into one—finally toppled him. After his talk, a festering ulcer burned through the wall of his stomach.

Phil felt sudden, raging pain as the acid and digestive juices in his belly spilled into his abdomen. An ambulance sped him to a Birmingham hospital, where doctors awaited in surgical garb.

26

One More Thing

LATE SUMMER 1985

Jack watched as an FBI technician drilled a tiny hole through the shared wall of a beachfront condo unit in Gulf Shores, Alabama. The bureau had rented the apartment—along with the one on the other side of the wall—for his undercover investigation. The technician threaded a pinhole camera into the opening and masked its lens on the opposite wall with a decorative crock. The camera fed into a monitor that would allow Jack to watch a forthcoming meeting via a bubble-shaped video feed. Jack also hid a Nagra recorder inside a large ashtray in the middle of the room.

Hurricane season was gurgling to life over the Gulf of Mexico. The air crackled with an approaching storm.

Jack left to find J.J., who would be playing the role of Jim Gordon, a California-based racehorse owner, gambling figure, and general shady schemer. The staging was strikingly similar to a setup J.J. had overseen at the Holiday Inn in Hammond, Indiana, almost exactly nine years earlier, back when he was just twenty-six and an undercover novice eager to carve some notches in his belt.

And once again, Phil was at the center of the action.

Kitzer had been in a good place. After he recovered from surgery late in 1980, he was released into Jack's oversight. The agent helped Phil and Audrey and their son, Jeffrey, settle into a condo near the beach in Gulf Shores. The doctors wouldn't let Phil work at first, to ensure a full recovery, so he borrowed money from members of his extended family to pay bills. He liked the Gulf Coast, its weather and white-sand beaches, and felt overjoyed to have his freedom back. The following May, doctors recommended a follow-up operation.

Away from the prison and the trials and the road, Phil's health gradually improved. That summer, Jack secured work for him: Phil provided expert testimony in fraud cases. Earning $50 a day plus travel expenses, Phil, ever the gifted talker, was a devastatingly effective witness. "He could go in and say, 'This is how it works,'" J.J. recounted, "and the jury goes, 'Yeah, that's what these guys [on trial] did. Now I get it.'"

"Jim and I both have done expert testimony too," Jack said, "but Kitzer was more effective because he could always say, 'I did it. I know how it's done because I did it for years.'"

There were more grueling stretches of cross-examination by defense lawyers intent on painting Phil as a long-game grifter who had conned the government, but he rarely got ruffled. "He liked sticking it to defense lawyers whenever they were trying to put words in his mouth," Jack said. "He liked the U.S. attorney's offices, he liked that he was respected. He was an expert in an area, a guy who could do stuff other people couldn't do."

All the while, there was a risk he could backslide. In one case where he provided expert testimony, he conceded, "I would be capable of doing it again today if I so chose." The agents watched him carefully and tried to talk over the devil whispering in his ear, aware that Fred Pro and Norman Howard, among others, had been unable to go straight. "Phillip, don't screw this up," J.J. would tell him. "You fell far. There's real value in what you have now."

Phil gave lectures about fraud to groups of FBI agents and trainees. He spoke in Chicago, Denver, Mobile, and Charlotte. He addressed the Department of Justice and the Internal Revenue Service. He talked with bankers who once would've been his targets. He collected $500 per lecture and refused the protective services of the U.S. Marshals Services, believing that the dangers of his old life were behind him.

The world clearly needed him. Taking Phil out of circulation no doubt saved businesses, bankers, and entrepreneurs from being scammed out of millions of dollars, but the tide of financial fraud that he and the Fraternity wrought has scarcely ebbed. In March 1981, four and a half years after the *Wall Street Journal* article sounded the alarm on Phil's Caribbean briefcase bank, the newspaper ran a lengthy story headlined "Paper Pirates: Con Men Are Raking in Millions by Setting Up Own Caribbean Banks." And of course, still on the horizon were the innumerable financial-sector scandals, from inside and outside banks, in the decades to come.

Eventually he started a business, working as a kind of concierge for people in other countries trying to fill out paperwork to obtain visas or import or export products. In certain ways, he remained essentially Phil. He bought a thirty-foot powerboat with twin diesel engines and took Audrey and Jeffrey out for high-speed rides. Then he called Jack one day and said his boat had sunk in about eight feet of water and he'd sold it to the marina owner for $3,000. Jack, who was both frugal and a lifelong boat fanatic, and was storing a sailboat with Phil, tried to convince Phil to back out of the deal: Each of the boat's twin diesel engines was worth thousands, and they could easily be recovered.

But Phil waved him off. He was done with it, no regrets. He wasn't one to hold on to things.

Just before Christmas the year after J.J. got married, a deliveryman showed up at the agents' houses. Becky Brennan described the bouquet that arrived as "the largest, most beautiful arrangement of flowers I have ever seen in my life. . . . It was like something you see in a hotel lobby." Bewildered, she opened the card. It was from Kitzer.

Jack and J.J. were happy to watch him build a new life out of the smoldering shrapnel of his old one. More than eight years after they'd first met, the three of them together had clawed through a dark forest where most people get separated and lost. That they emerged on the other side of that wilderness closer than ever hinted at the mysteries and boundless possibilities of human friendship.

Somehow, an unthinkable breach of trust had become an unbreakable bond.

Everyone in the condo waited as Robert Eggleston and William Myers knocked on the door of the adjoining unit. The two men had served time with Kitzer at Maxwell when they'd all had less than a year left on their sentences and were cutting grass and tackling other jobs to ease their transition back into the world. Phil's movements had still been restricted by the witness protection program, but he'd become friendly with these two, entertaining them with stories about his life as a promoter.

Myers and Eggleston had been largely unmoved by the rehabilitative powers of the federal corrections system. Myers, of Fort Hunter, New York, was in his late thirties and had a bushy red beard and a powerful build, from years of construction work and prison weight rooms. By contrast, Eggleston, a New York City resident who wore dark-rimmed glasses, was a couple of decades older and professorial. He claimed to possess an advanced degree in chemistry. He had been working as a self-employed electrician after getting out of prison—but he and Myers figured they could make far more money manufacturing drugs.

Eggleston calculated that they could pull down about $4 million cooking crystal meth if they created their own operation, which meant they would need to round up the necessary chemicals and find a relatively isolated location where the ghastly exhaust from the processing could dissipate unnoticed. As Eggleston and Myers discussed how to check off these boxes, they had a revelation: Phil Kitzer. They knew that after leaving prison, he'd moved to Alabama's Gulf Coast—a place sprinkled with remote outposts exposed to steady offshore winds that would help disperse the noxious fumes. The two men targeted Fort Morgan, located on a peninsula that poked out across the mouth of Mobile Bay. They also knew from their conversations at Maxwell that Phil was resourceful and well connected.

After receiving the call from his Maxwell buddies, Phil hung up and called Jack, and they formulated a plan.

Phil answered the door, and Myers and Eggleston entered. The condo unit was decorated as if it were Phil's home, sprinkled with furnishings and photographs. Next door, everyone tensed. Jack thought it likely that the two men would be armed, so he'd summoned a SWAT team, which was with him in the adjoining apartment. They all watched on the monitor as the two visitors made their way inside.

Phil introduced his good friend Jim Gordon, who, he said, had worked with him on deals before prison and who would be an excellent source for meth-cooking supplies. A photograph of Gordon standing with his prize horses and jockeys in Hollywood Park sat on Phil's bookcase. (J.J. had recently spearheaded a California-based operation in which he'd created the character and, in classic Wedick fashion, convinced the FBI to let him purchase two racehorses.)

Eggleston and Myers shook Jim's hand and sized him up. They asked typical background questions—where was he from, what else had he done, where had he served prison time—and didn't seem particularly satisfied with any of the answers. When they were done talking, the two would-be drug dealers nodded at each other, and Myers produced an RF detector—a small wand-type instrument capable of detecting radio waves emitted by, among other things, wireless surveillance devices. They told Jim they needed to scan him. Nothing personal, they just had to be cautious.

Phil and the agents had anticipated that Myers and Eggleston would be wary of Jim, which was why Phil had hidden a transmitter in the breast pocket of his blazer. The device provided audio to Brennan to complement the beamed-in images, which was especially important if the men wandered out of the camera's view.

The RF detector immediately picked up a weak signal, and Myers looked over at Eggleston. Certain household appliances—for instance, microwave ovens—emit signals. They asked Jim to go outside so they could scan him without interference.

They walked out the back door, which loomed over the beach, and encountered blasts of wind and rain. Waves crashed below. The three men turned and headed back inside. The RF detector continued to ping, and Myers and Eggleston paced around, frustrated. *Some*thing was triggering it.

J.J. saw where this was going: These men needed some harder assurances. "Look, if you guys are concerned or whatever, here," he said, opening his shirt. "I'll even take my pants off."

As J.J. stripped, Phil seized the moment. He turned and headed toward the front door, murmuring that the room felt stuffy. Jack, watching, intuited what Phil was doing. He bounded out onto the front stoop, then positioned himself against the wall next to Phil's door.

Phil cracked open his door and, with a flick of his left hand, pulled the transmitter from his pocket and placed it in Jack's outstretched right hand. The move was unrehearsed—something they'd never even discussed doing. But by now they knew each other's intonations and gestures. "Phillip was nothing but cool under pressure," Jack said. "He didn't get rattled, and if he could start talking, you'd be all right."

Jack had come to know these gifts well—which was why the U.S. government now employed Phil as a $36,000-a-year informant, working mostly with Jack and his colleagues in Mobile. Over the past four years, Phil had played versions of his old self, talking deals with the same verbal dexterity and salesmanship and exuberant bonhomie. He'd worked on more than a dozen cases with Jack and sometimes J.J., usually targeting con men and corrupt public figures.

Phil returned to where J.J. stood in his underwear. To help his visitors relax, he offered himself up for a scan, pulling off his jacket and shirt, but by then Myers had already noticed that the signal had faded. As J.J. and Phil dressed, they speculated on the source of the enigmatic signal: *It could've been the TV—we turned that off right before you got here. Or maybe the microwave.*

Back next door, Jack fidgeted. He could still see what was going on, but he could no longer hear anything. He was left to read body language—and only if everyone stayed in the living room.

J.J. figured that Phil had unloaded the transmitter. It was a smart move, but he also felt a jag of anxiety, knowing that Jack could no longer hear them. He didn't like cases with drug guys; they were jittery and prone to violence. And as they'd learned from dealing with the likes of Sonny Santini, violent people made undercover work trickier. Their volatility brought greater pressure to stay calm and avoid saying anything problematic, and as a result, it became harder to do both. He forced himself to focus and breathe easily.

Myers and Eggleston still seemed perturbed about the unexplained RF signal. Eggleston said he wasn't taking any chances and wouldn't go back to prison under any circumstances, even if that meant blowing up the lab if the DEA ever found it.

Trying to soften the mood, Phil riffed on some escapades with Fred Pro and Gabe Cicale. J.J. jumped in with his own recollections, he and Phil piling on details, enriching and reinforcing the stories. He knew that Eggleston and Myers had already revealed enough that they didn't want to believe they were talking to a federal agent. He and Phil just had to give them a little help.

"I bet Phillip told you some good stories about Freddie," J.J. said.

They nodded and Jim piled on, explaining how ol' Fred had tried unsuccessfully to manage the wiseguys in New York—especially Sonny Santini.

As the conversation took root, Phil wandered back toward the front door. Myers had stashed the RF detector. Seeing where Phil was going, Jack again leaped up and raced outside, and they executed their handoff in reverse: Phil reached toward where Jack was waiting, took the transmitter from him, and slipped it back into his pocket.

Phil closed the door and returned, saying something about the wind and the crazy weather. By then, Eggleston and Myers were settled enough to talk business. Jim would arrange to have the chemicals stolen from a pharmaceutical warehouse somewhere in the Northeast—he had contacts from the Bronx, where he'd grown up—and delivered to their beach-house lab in Alabama.

They all agreed to this plan, and over the coming weeks, Phil updated Myers and Eggleston on Jim's progress.

No one knew how long he could keep going. Phil was doing well, having altered his life and paid his debt to society, but he smoked and drank and had never lived in a way that promoted longevity. Becky had sat in the backseat of their car once when Phil was in the passenger seat, and she'd noticed his unhealthy pallor. But they knew better than to suggest that Phil change how he lived.

He and J.J. sat in the Mobile Municipal Airport in mid-December, waiting for Myers and Eggleston to land. The would-be drug dealers had altered their plans and had found a location for a lab back in the Northeast, and they were flying south to fetch the chemicals and cook a test batch. They all met in the airport terminal's minuscule dining area—a few tables wedged in along the margins. Eggleston unfurled a white tablecloth, explaining that they'd all gone without life's fineries in prison, and these were better days. He pulled out a sheet of paper containing typed notes: his recipe for cooking meth.

Phil told him everything was ready. Then he said, "But there's one more thing, fellas."

J.J. glanced at him, trying hard to look nonchalant. *One more thing?* What was this?

About the crew they'd hired to steal the chemicals up north, Phil said. The men had broken into a warehouse, just as planned—but something unexpected had happened. A night security guard had interrupted the job.

Phil gazed intently at his two former prison mates. J.J. remained expressionless, but his mind was churning. He had no idea what Phil was doing, or where this was going.

The guard had struggled with the burglars and been shot dead, Phil continued. And if that wasn't bad enough? The security guard was a *woman*. A single mom, two kids, working a nighttime job, going to school. The newspapers were all over the story. Had they heard about it?

Myers and Eggleston shook their heads.

So, Phil said. Things had gone bad. Myers and Eggleston needed to know this, because there was no sense getting too deep into this deal, investing all this time and effort and resources, only to have them back out. There would be some heat. Phil had been through situations like this, so he didn't mind, but he needed to hear that his co-conspirators knew *exactly* where things stood. Phil stared at them, his face cast iron.

Eggleston looked at his partner, who nodded. Then he said, "Well, I didn't tell that bitch to be there that night."

"You sure, guys?" Phil said. He held up his hands.

"No problem," Eggleston answered. He shrugged. "Let's go cook."

J.J. was speechless. He was wearing a Nagra recorder, and he knew that Phil fully grasped the nuances of the criminal justice system. If you were a defendant on trial, your best hope was to come across as sympathetic or confused about what you'd done. Phil was doing to Eggleston and Myers what Norman Howard had been unable to do to him nine years earlier: He had lured them into making clear statements that they intended to participate in a crime.

With one conversational flourish, Phil had eliminated any chance for Eggleston and Myers to claim innocence. The federal prosecutor would simply play the tape to the jury.

Decades later, Jack and J.J. would look back on that moment with a sense of awe. There was something almost supernatural about Phil's ability to peer into a person's head. As J.J. put it, "He could read people as good as anybody I've ever known."

"Okay!" Phil said, clapping his hands together. "Let's go."

Everyone stood. Within a few minutes they would walk out of the terminal into the mild Alabama day, and vans and police cars would barrel up and careen to a halt in front of them, and teams of agents and cops with guns drawn would hurl all four of them to the ground and snap handcuffs on them. A cabdriver would dive into his car yelling, "Holy shit, everybody's got guns!"

As they strolled toward the exit, J.J. looked around. Over his right shoulder he saw ticket agents conducting their business, clueless regarding what was about to happen, and glimpsed someone from their surveillance team casually following. Then he glanced to his left, at the man he'd taken down and lifted up and learned from and marveled at over the last nine years. The light through the airplane terminal's windows lit Phil's face. He sensed J.J. looking at him and shot his friend a sidelong glance.

Phil was careful to always stay in character. But before J.J. looked away, he saw a smile curl at the corners of Phil's mouth.

Epilogue

Around the time of Phil's arrest, Myron Fuller and an FBI colleague walked into a theatrical supply house in New York City. They were looking for a specific costume: the flowing robes of an Arab sheikh. OpFoPen was winding down, but Fuller's work with Mel Weinberg on a spin-off investigation was only just getting started. Over the past few weeks, they'd noticed that con men reflexively grew excited anytime anyone mentioned their fictional Lebanese sheikh, viewing him as the man controlling the spigot on a steady flow of oil revenues. Now they were ready to bring him to life.

Fuller honed his story. Kambir Abdul Rahman became a Lebanese builder who had married into the sheikhdom of the United Arab Emirates and had become enormously wealthy. They told the promoters that Rahman had hired Fuller—using the name Myron Wagner—to spend this wealth in the United States through a shell corporation, Abdul Enterprises Limited. Fuller dashed the promoters' plans to acquire Brookhaven, the mortgage company, but told them that Rahman wanted securities—including stolen or phony ones—as well as casinos in Las Vegas and Atlantic City and expensive pieces of stolen art.

Even Fuller couldn't have guessed where that first meeting with Wedick and Brennan in May 1977 would lead. As Abscam grew, Fuller and his colleagues recovered about $1.5 million in stolen securities, making eight arrests that led to six convictions. They also recovered millions of dollars in fraudulent CDs and gold certificates.

Then a contact introduced Fuller and company to Angelo Errichetti, the mayor of Camden, New Jersey, and the focus of Abdul Enterprises pivoted. Errichetti and others dangled offers to help the sheikh gain asylum in the United States, arranging for meetings with members of Congress who could sponsor private legislation to make it happen. For this service, Abdul offered to pay $50,000 up front and $50,000 later.

By the time Fuller, Weinberg, and the others shuttered the operation two years later, they had arrested seven members of Congress—including Senator Harrison Williams of New Jersey. Each of the seven was convicted, and the landmark case sent shockwaves across the nation, spawning an effort to further professionalize and institutionalize FBI undercover activities.

A straight line leads from two young undercover agents in Nowhere, Indiana, to that seminal investigation. "If not for those guys," Fuller said, "Abscam never happens."

Acknowledgments

Soon after this book came together, I met Jim Wedick (who no longer goes by the nickname J.J.), Jack Brennan, and Myron Fuller in Park City, Utah, for three days of storytelling, laughter, and show-and-tell sessions that featured yellowing newspaper clippings and copies of old court decisions. It was enormously galvanizing, and in the two and a half years that followed, they each collectively gave up many hours of their time answering endless questions, hunting through their basements for photos and other artifacts, piecing together timelines, and generally bending over backward and sideways to help me reach across almost four decades to construct this story. I'm endlessly grateful for their efforts. Much obliged, also, to Jack's wife, Becky, for trusting me with her story. Also thanks to her and Nancy Wedick for their forbearance, excellent meals, and the use of their spare bedrooms.

Many thanks to my agents Larry Weissman and Sascha Alper, a phenomenal duo for an author to have in his corner. They believed in this book from the first mention and provided invaluable help in lifting it off the ground.

Authors are lucky to have one talented editor; I was wildly fortunate to have two. Domenica Alioto and Claire Potter at Crown fueled my efforts with wisdom, enthusiasm, and good humor. They made the book vastly better, and made the effort fun throughout. Much gratitude.

Also at Crown, Phil Leung, the production manager, and

Craig Adams, the production editor, kept the wheels moving in the right direction on every aspect of this book from beginning to end. Copyeditor Bonnie Thompson's hawk eyes and language skills made me look better on these pages than I ever could manage on my own. A deep bow to Chris Brand for creating the book's ingenious and striking now-you-see-him-now-you-don't cover, and to interior designer Songhee Kim, who's responsible for the elegant yet appropriately jaunty layout. Sarah Grimm and Roxanne Hiatt, the book's publicist and marketer, respectively, knew exactly the right soapboxes to stand on, and did it with great humor and panache. And, of course, *Chasing Phil* might still be a waking daydream for me without the steadfast support from the start of publisher Molly Stern and deputy publisher Annsley Rosner. I'm indebted to this team and humbled by their efforts.

Thank you to National Archives facilities in Atlanta, Kansas City, Chicago, and San Francisco for being there. The court records stored in these places were vital to my ability to tell this story. Much appreciation to Charles Miller, Jerry Phares, Arlene Royer, Jeff Sample, John Sparling, and everyone else in the archives and federal court system who helped me track down files from old OpFoPen cases. Thanks to Jim Rice in the Orange County, California, superior court clerk's office for digging up files from a trial from more than thirty-five years ago.

Kim Horgan, Cathy Miller, and Elizabeth Hansen all provided extra sets of hands and eyes with trial documents and transcripts in the National Archives files when I was stretched too thin.

A big thank-you to John Wareham of the *Minneapolis Star-Tribune* for tracking down files of newspaper clippings on the Kitzers from the 1960s that had been shipped off-site. That was a huge find for me. Thanks to Vicky Weiss at the *Bismarck Tribune* for digging through the newspaper's story and photo archives for material from the American Allied trial in the 1960s. Thanks to Joe Slobodzian of the *Philadelphia Inquirer* for helping track down some key information from federal court.

A number of people helped me at various points, in New York

and Pennsylvania, with research and/or transcribing work: Julia Calderone, Lauren Ladoceour, Zoe Schaeffer, Maura Smith, Lara Sorokanich, Becky Straus, and Britt Tagg. All of it was critical in moving me closer to the finish line on a high-wire schedule. Thanks to Carla Lindenmuth and Terah Shelton for their library sleuthing skills, and to Sabine Niemeier for running down details about the Intercontinental Frankfurt from the 1970s.

I'm grateful to Helen Racan, Phil Kitzer's ex-wife, and their son Richard, for sharing their stories on what was a difficult chapter in their lives.

I benefited immensely from the sage feedback and buoying support of my readers: Lou Cinquino, Claire Dederer, Peter Flax, Jeremy Katz, and Sam Kennedy. Thank you all. And to my longtime friend and co-conspirator, John Murray: Thanks for your ideas and input and comic relief, and for the quiet space.

My wife, Ann, also read the book and provided hugely helpful commentary and suggestions, all while enduring (with our son, Vaughn) my obsessiveness and absences over nearly three years. You both have my gratitude and love.

Notes

A word about direct quotations: All dialogue is taken from a primary source—a party to the relevant conversation—or a court transcript. In fact, the latter proved to be critical to my reporting efforts with this book. Phillip Kitzer died in 2001 at the age of 68, but his testimony as a government witness and expert witness in more than a half dozen trials was transcribed and is now preserved in various National Archive branches. In researching this book I traveled to Chicago, Atlanta, Kansas City, San Francisco, and Orange County, California, where I gathered more than six thousand pages of court records and transcribed testimony. Kitzer's testimony in particular provides a powerful glimpse into his storytelling style; on the witness stand he furnished details and anecdotes only he could recount. He often told stories using detailed dialogue, to the point that defense lawyers questioned whether he had a photographic memory or was planning to write a book. (He answered no to both.) Direct quotations from others also come from transcripts, as noted below.

Prologue

The material in this section, as with much of the book, is built around interviews with James Wedick and Jack Brennan and their testimony in numerous federal trials that resulted from Operation Fountain Pen. Quotes from them are from these resources unless otherwise noted.

> 1 **five and a half inches:** A detailed description of the Nagra recorder can be found on the Cryptomuseum website: http://www.crypto museum.com/covert/rec/nagra/sn/.

2 **"Cocktail fantasies":** For photos and descriptions, see the blog *Dutch Girl Chronicle:* http://www.dutchgirlchronicle.com/?p=2135. Also see "A Final Farewell to Bloomington's Iconic Thunderbird Motel," *Minneapolis Star Tribune,* May 10, 2016.

Chapter 1: How to Steal a Bank

This chapter is drawn entirely from testimony given in *United States v. Paul E. Chovanec,* Docket No. HCR 77-93, which took place in federal court in Hammond, Indiana, in June 1978. The relevant testimony came from Phillip Kitzer and Kenneth Guilbert.

Chapter 2: The Informant

Most of the Jack Brennan biographical material came from interviews with Jack and his wife, Becky. I also drew Brennan family history from articles by Erwin P. Hair in *Grapevine,* the publication of the Society of Former Special Agents of the FBI. His story "Four Generations of Brennan Family Served as Special Agents of FBI" appeared in the March 1981 issue, followed by "Jack Brennan Represented Second Generation of Family in the FBI" in the April 1981 edition.

14 **Howard resigned in 1960:** "The Ultimate Con," Knight-Ridder Newspapers (*Ellensburg Daily Record*), August 7, 1981.

14 **systematically fleece them of cash:** See *Chicago Tribune* articles "Ex-Insurance Aide Indicted for Thefts from 2 Companies," October 20, 1971, and Neil Mehler, "Firm's Heads Told: Pay Policyholders," February 2, 1974.

14 **"history of fraud and flimflam":** Selwyn Raab, "FBI Is Duped by Own Ruse; U.S. Faces Suits," *New York Times,* May 18, 1979. For more on Howard's shenanigans after the episode described in this book, see "FBI's Link to Scam Suspect Fuels Debate on Informants," by Douglas Frantz and Maurice Possley, in the *Chicago Tribune,* September 23, 1984.

15 **"This is the perfect vehicle":** Norman Howard's testimony in *U.S. v. Chovanec.*

15 **writing illegal bail bonds:** Gary Galloway, "Gary Pair Charged with Writing False Bail Bonds," *Post-Tribune* (Gary, Indiana), March 14, 1975.

19 **Bobby and Susanna Duckworth:** From an interview with Allen Ezell; the indictment and court filings in *United States v. Paul E. Chovanec Jr., et al.,* Docket No. 78-0583, Charlotte, North Carolina; and Robert Hodierne's "A Con Man Gets Stung at His Own Game," *Charlotte Observer,* December 24, 1978.

20 **The agent approached Kitzer:** From Chovanec's statement, dated July 7, 1978, filed in *United States v. Frank Oliver,* Docket No. 78-59, Charlotte, North Carolina.

Chapter 3: You Owe Me Fifty Bucks

Wedick provided the noted memo from Orville Watts dated May 12, 1976, regarding his desire to work undercover. Wedick was also the subject of two lengthy *Los Angeles Times* stories: "The Agent Who Might Have Saved Hamid Hayat," by Mark Arax, May 28, 2006, and "The G-man, the Shrimp Scam, and Sacramento's Big Sting," by Mark Gladstone and Paul Jacobs, December 11, 1994. A tape of the October 21 meeting between Kitzer and Norman Howard was played for the jury in *U.S. v. Chovanec*, and was transcribed into the record.

Chapter 4: The Shell Game

The bulk of this material comes from transcripts of the Hammond trial, *U.S. v. Chovanec*. A tape of the Holiday Inn meeting with Kitzer, Chovanec, Howard, and undercover FBI agent Dean Naum was played for the jury and transcribed into the record, as was a tape of the subsequent phone call between Naum and Kitzer. The rest of the material comes from the testimony of Kitzer, Howard, Naum, Wedick, and Dan King and Steven Watts of St. Joseph Bank.

Chapter 5: The Thunderbird

This chapter was based on interviews with Wedick and Brennan. Kitzer also testified on multiple occasions about the circumstances under which he met the two agents.

Chapter 6: Hello, Cleveland

Much of the material in this chapter comes from testimony in *United States v. Andrew D'Amato, Armand Mucci, and Robert Bendis*, Docket No. 78-20070-01, which took place in federal court in Kansas City in December 1978. Kitzer, Mucci, Bendis, Pro, Brennan, and Wedick all took the witness stand.

59 **Kitzer had met them:** Kitzer's testimony details their shared history and the proposed Shaker House scam.

59 **a 160-room edifice:** See a description of the Shaker House at the Cleveland Memory Project, run by the Michael Schwartz Library at Cleveland State University: http://images.ulib.csuohio.edu/cdm /singleitem/collection/postcards/id/2034/rec/20.

59 **"a little warm":** Kitzer testimony in *U.S. v. D'Amato, Mucci, and Bendis*.

61 **"It's a pretty shocking":** Ibid.

62 **"hit the sheet":** Kitzer's expert testimony in *United States v. Peter Martell, aka Peter Raia*, Docket No. 81-129, a trial that took place in federal court in Philadelphia in July 1981. Martell was convicted of conspiracy to pledge stolen bonds for a loan, among other charges.

63 **a "dumb Dago" from:** Prosecution memo from Assistant U.S. Attorney Richard A. Hanning to U.S. Attorney David T. Ready, Northern District of Indiana, November 16, 1977.

Chapter 7: No Mickey Mouse

The Kealoha case was the subject of extensive testimony in the aforementioned Kansas City trial and in *United States v. Mark Iuteri,* Docket No. 80-1491, which took place in Honolulu in May 1980. Testimony on the latter trial came from Kitzer, Kealoha, Iuteri, Brennan, and Wedick, among others.

71 **his capstone project:** Walter Wright, "FBI Out-Cons Worldwide Con Man," *Honolulu Advertiser,* January 5, 1980.

71 **With the market sagging:** Walter Wright, "Con Man Tells Court Kealoha's Attorney, Builder 'In on Scam,'" *Honolulu Advertiser,* May 8, 1980.

72 **Fireside Thrift, which had:** Walter Wright, "'Phony Bank' Reportedly Used in Earlier Con Job on Kealoha," *Honolulu Advertiser,* January 7, 1980.

72 **Yee was connected:** Kitzer and Kealoha testimony in *U.S. v. Iuteri.*

72 **"What are you gonna do":** Walter Wright, "King of Scam Royally Conned Pigeons Until FBI Caged Him," *Honolulu Advertiser,* May 9, 1980.

72 **a takeout commitment:** An excellent overview can be found in the decision in the Iuteri case by the U.S. Court of Appeals for the Ninth Circuit dated March 9, 1981, Docket No. 80-1491.

72 **Liechtenstein-based trust:** The trust was discussed at length in the Hawaii trial (*U.S. v. Iuteri*). Also see Theodore A. Driscoll and Tom Condon, "State Financier, Under Probe, Key Figure in $30 Million Deal," *Hartford Courant,* December 12, 1976. For more on the Fontainebleau's purported sale, see "Famed Hotel Sold in Miami," an Associated Press story that ran in the *Naples Daily News* on November 9, 1976.

73 **would "stand up":** Kitzer testimony in *U.S. v. Iuteri.*

73 **"We do not question":** Final Report of the Select Committee to Study Undercover Activities of Components of the Department of Justice, December 15, 1982, p. 34. Available on the website of the National Criminal Justice Reference Service: https:www.ncjrs.gov/pdffiles1 /Digitization/124269NCJRS.pdf.

73 **"to secure a foothold":** Ibid., p. 35.

73 **Hoover nixed undercover work:** Tim Weiner, *Enemies: A History of the FBI* (New York: Random House, 2012), p. 212.

74 **"turning agents into investigators":** James Q. Wilson, *The Investigators: Managing FBI and Narcotics Agents* (New York: Basic Books, 1978), p. 171.

74 **"the dress code of the agents":** Ibid., p. 35.

74 **"shit cases with which":** Ibid., p. 97.

75 **organized crime, foreign counterintelligence, and white-collar crime:** From the FBI's online history; see "Aftermath of Watergate: 1970s." Available at https://www2.fbi.gov/libref/historic/history /watergate.htm.

75 **"quality over quantity" policy:** Final Report of the Select Committee to Study Undercover Activities, p. 39.

75 **"are far less valuable":** Ibid., p. 41.

75 **with 516 resident offices:** Wilson, *Investigators,* p. 91.

76 **"When the cash value":** Jonathan Kwitny, *The Fountain Pen Conspiracy* (New York: Alfred A. Knopf, 1973), p. 5.

77 **The superswindlers collectively:** Ibid., p. 4.

79 **"Wait," D'Amato said:** Kitzer testimony in *U.S. v. Iuteri* covers this entire passage.

80 **"you use that with the victim":** From Kitzer's expert testimony in *United States v. Sidney Gerhardt and Joseph Adornato,* in Mobile, Alabama, Docket No. 82-CR-8.

Chapter 8: The Junior G-Men

Beyond the FBI agents' recollections, I relied in this chapter on the Hawaii and Kansas City testimony (*U.S. v. Iuteri* and *U.S. v. D'Amato, Mucci, and Bendis*) and the thorough reporting of Walter Wright of the *Honolulu Advertiser.* His story of May 10, 1980, under the headline "Fleecing a 'Mark' in Hawaii No Beeg Ting," provided the material for the mock-trial scene.

Chapter 9: The Poodle Lounge

The *Hartford Courant* covered the exploits of Connecticut native Andrew D'Amato extensively and aggressively, as evidenced by the citations below.

94 **snowed in Miami Beach:** Bruce J. Schulman, *The Seventies: The Great Shift in American Culture, Society, and Politics* (New York: Free Press, 2001), p. 121.

95 **Associated Press even published:** "Famed Hotel Sold in Miami," Associated Press (*Naples Daily News*), November 9, 1976.

95 **Hartford Courant followed up:** Theodore A. Driscoll and Tom Condon, "State Financier, Under Probe, Key Figure in $30 Million Deal," *Hartford Courant,* December 12, 1976.

95 **"not involved anymore":** Theodore A. Driscoll and Tom Condon, "Hotelier Says Publicity Cost D'Amato Top Job," *Hartford Courant,* December 15, 1976.

97 **"The performance bond and such-type":** Kitzer provided this explanation as an expert witness in 1982, in *U.S. v. Gerhardt and Adornato.*

99 **scale and grandeur:** See Tom Austin's "Fontainebleau Hotel's Extreme Makeover" in *Travel + Leisure:* http://www.travelandleisure.com/articles/fontainebleau-hotels-extreme-makeover.

101 **"as father confessor":** Mark Gladstone and Paul Jacobs, "The G-man, the Shrimp Scam, and Sacramento's Big Sting," *Los Angeles Times*, December 11, 1994.

102 **order by Scotland Yard:** Affidavit regarding Packman given by Wedick and Brennan, signed September 1982.

Chapter 10: Mr. Mutt and Mr. Jeff

The narrative of Kitzer's early life was constructed from testimony, newspaper reports, and interviews with his ex-wife. Kitzer also testified extensively on his formative years and experiences. For example, see testimony in his aforementioned appearances as an expert witness.

106 **historic Graycliff Hotel:** To learn about its history, check out http://www.graycliff.com/graycliff-history/.

111 **people called him Junior:** Kitzer testimony in *United States v. John Kaye and John Calandrella*, Docket No. 78-5341, which took place in Louisville in 1978.

111 **He was only seven:** Finlay Lewis, "Insurance Firm Woes Related by Young Kitzer," *Minneapolis Tribune*, June 1, 1967.

111 **One afternoon, a friend:** Interview with Helen Racan.

112 **"I bought the book":** "Kitzer Jr. Relates Insurance Start," Associated Press (*Bismarck Tribune*), May 31, 1967.

112 **door-to-door salesman:** Kitzer's expert testimony in *U.S. v. Gerhardt and Adornato*.

112 **A bond agency he worked for:** "Two Bondsmen Sue Gutknecht; Demand $125,000," *Chicago Daily Tribune*, January 29, 1955.

113 **"I've been telling":** Thomas Powers, "Phone Threat to Bondsman Is Disclosed," *Chicago Daily Tribune*, April 12, 1959. Despite his disavowals, the elder Kitzer's firm again came under scrutiny. See also Sandy Smith's "Bail Bondsman Vows He Made No Kickbacks," *Chicago Daily Tribune*, December 2, 1961.

113 **demanded a $25,000 kickback:** Kitzer recounted this episode on at least two occasions: once as an expert witness in *U.S. v. Martell* and again in the federal trial in Louisville (*U.S. v. Kaye and Calandrella*).

Chapter 11: Rip Off Hawaii

Mark Iuteri testified in his own defense in his trial in Hawaii, arguing that he had just been acting as Andy D'Amato's unwitting assistant. As the *Ho-*

nolulu Advertiser wrote in a headline on May 14, 1980, with a tangible note of sarcasm: "Accused Con Man Iuteri Testifies That He Just 'Carried the Luggage.'" The jury didn't believe him. As for the Kitzer insurance adventures of the 1960s: The two Minneapolis newspapers, the *Star* and the *Tribune*, each wrote more than a hundred stories on the matter. I have listed only the ones that link directly to passages in this book.

118 **"Listen, Jimmy," he said:** Kitzer's Hawaii testimony in *U.S. v. Iuteri*.

118 **"phony claims of connections":** Theodore A. Driscoll and Tom Condon, "State Financier, Under Probe, Key Figure in $30 Million Deal," *Hartford Courant*, December 12, 1976.

123 **chatted up a woman:** Wedick provided most of the details of this (in interviews and in his testimony), and Kitzer confirmed it in his Hawaii testimony (*U.S. v. Iuteri*).

125 **"button man for the Outfit":** Walter Wright, "Iuteri Called a Killer for Mafia," *Honolulu Advertiser*, July 8, 1980.

127 **In 1962, they took over:** Paul Presbrey, "Kitzer Testifies for Self in Fraud Trial," *Minneapolis Star*, June 1, 1967. Also see Finlay Lewis, "Insurance Firm Woes Related by Young Kitzer," *Minneapolis Tribune*, June 1; and Presbrey's "Kitzer Tells of Firm's Rapid Rise at Expense of Other Companies" and "Kitzer Jr. Tells Tale of Sinking Into Debt" in the *Star* on June 2 and 3, respectively.

128 **"dad bust it!":** Lester Velie, "Riddle of the Vanishing Insurance Companies," *Reader's Digest*, September 1966. This extensive article covers Head's investigation.

129 **In July, a policyholder:** "Suit Charges Bell Insurers' Fund Misuse," *Chicago Tribune*, July 2, 1965.

130 **Federal prosecutors targeted:** Jim Parsons, "Magnusson Named with 16 Others in Fraud Indictment," *Minneapolis Tribune*, October 30, 1965.

130 **"A proper investigation of":** Gerry Nelson, "Atty. Gen. Mattson Says Magnusson Allowed Public to Be Damaged," Associated Press (*Winona Daily News*), November 3, 1965.

130 **The Kitzers were living:** Ibid.

130 **On November 10:** "Magnusson, Others Plead Not Guilty," *Minneapolis Star*, November 10, 1965.

130 **But the following January:** Louis Dombrowski, "State Sues Bell Casualty Chiefs; Charges Fraud," *Chicago Tribune*, January 5, 1966.

131 **Minnesota prosecutors charged Phil:** Finlay Lewis, "Goff, Kitzer Jr., Firm Indicted in Political Contribution Case," *Minneapolis Tribune*, October 28, 1966.

131 **"Phony charges and":** "Humphrey Asserts Republicans Vilify Rolvaag and Mondale," *New York Times,* October 24, 1966.

131 **In June 1966, they sued:** "Kitzer Files Suit Against Insurer Group," *Chicago Tribune,* June 2, 1966.

131 **filed a $3 million libel:** "Suit Charges Libel, Seeks Nine Millions [*sic*]," *Chicago Tribune,* December 20, 1966.

132 **"The marks in Hawaii":** This anecdote was recounted by several different witnesses in Hawaii, including Brennan and Wedick; see *U.S. v. Iuteri.*

133 **"No, you have the words":** Ibid.

134 **"Did you do your appraisal?":** Ibid. Multiple people testified to this interlude, most prominently Kitzer.

136 **John Kaye was one:** This was the subject of Kitzer's first trial, which Bill Osinski of the *Louisville Courier-Journal* covered extensively. See "FBI Agent Describes His World Travels with Con Artist," February 17, 1978.

137 **"Yes, we have done business":** Kitzer described the concept of a reader bank multiple times, including in detail in his testimony in *U.S. v. Gerhardt.*

137 **"What is your price?":** Kitzer's testimony in Louisville (*U.S. v. Kaye and Calandrella*).

138 **"Get lost," he said:** Described by multiple witnesses, including Kitzer and Brennan, in *U.S. v. Iuteri.*

Chapter 12: The Parking Lot Fugitive

This chapter is drawn from the testimony in Honolulu (*U.S. v. Iuteri*) of Kitzer, Brennan, Wedick, Iuteri, and Kealoha, plus subsequent interviews with the former FBI agents and Dan Bent, the government prosecutor who handled the case. Iuteri acknowledged during his testimony that he hid papers in his clothing while transporting them down to the pool.

Chapter 13: The Cold Plunge

Trying to embarrass Kitzer, the defense attorneys in Hawaii (*U.S. v. Iuteri*) brought up the incident involving the transvestite in Tokyo. Kitzer admitted to it but downplayed his intentions.

155 **They lived in an old run-down farmhouse:** Details of Kitzer's personal life come from Nick Coleman, "Ellendale Wondered About Phil Kitzer," *Minneapolis Tribune,* March 12, 1978.

156 **"an air of excitement":** Steve Andrist, "Sensational Trial Kept Bismarck Astir," *Bismarck Tribune,* May 16, 1979.

156 **"This case involves bribery":** Paul Presbrey, "Blackmail Charged in Insurance Trial," *Minneapolis Star,* March 21, 1967.

156 **"personal checking account":** "'Blackmailed,' Magnusson Said of Letter," Associated Press (*Daily Journal,* Fergus Falls, Minnesota), March 22, 1967.

156 **Several young women:** "Women Speak of Trips Paid for by Kitzer," Associated Press (*Winona Daily News*), April 18, 1967.

156 **Audrey Jensen said:** "Woman Writes of Jacket Kitzer Bought," UPI (*Winona Daily News*), April 26, 1967.

156 **"great concept of social":** Finlay Lewis, "Foley Calls Magnusson Minnesota's 'Trojan Horse,'" *Minneapolis Tribune,* June 20, 1967.

156 **"six North Dakota housewives":** Donald Janson, "Minnesota Insurance Trial Implicates Democratic Politicians," *New York Times,* March 26, 1967.

157 **lawyer for David Kroman:** Finlay Lewis, "Mistrial Declared in Kroman Trial; Mental Test Set," *Minneapolis Tribune,* March 28, 1967.

157 **were collateral damage:** The defense strategy is summarized well in Paul Presbrey's "Plot to Get Kitzer Attributed to Lord," *Minneapolis Star,* June 20, 1967.

157 **the "Caped Crusader":** Robert Hodierne, "A Con Man Gets Stung at His Own Game," *Charlotte Observer,* December 24, 1978.

157 **When Junior himself:** His testimony went on for more than a week; start with Paul Presbrey, "Kitzer Testifies for Self in Fraud Trial," *Minneapolis Star,* June 1, 1967.

157 **Kitzer said Lord once:** Paul Presbrey, "Kitzer Jr. Tells Tale of Sinking into Debt," *Minneapolis Star,* June 3, 1967.

158 **grew "very, very angry":** Drawn from multiple accounts. See Finlay Lewis, "Gift to DFL Is Explained by Kitzer Jr.," *Minneapolis Tribune,* June 3, 1967.

158 **"You won't let me":** Paul Presbrey, "Kitzer Jr. Charges Truth Not Wanted," *Minneapolis Star,* June 8, 1967; and Finlay Lewis, "Kitzer Jr. Claims State Insurance Division Defrauded Him," *Minneapolis Tribune,* June 8, 1967.

159 **"erupted into tears":** Finlay Lewis, "Joyous Tears Greet Verdict," *Minneapolis Tribune,* June 24, 1967. After the verdict, the question lingered about how much criminal activity Kitzer had actually engaged in. In Louisville he testified (*U.S. v. Kaye and Calandrella*) that those kickbacks to the Chicago bank were the only illegal activity he participated in at the time. But at other points he conceded that the federal government had botched its case against him.

159 **fined him $100:** Jim Shoop, "Kitzer Jr. Fined $100 for Making Illegal Donation," *Minneapolis Star,* July 18, 1967.

159 **lawsuits and millions:** Paul Presbrey, "Insurance Firm's Assets Listed," *Minneapolis Star,* March 13, 1969.

159 **wrecked a rental car:** "Kitzer Jr. Accused of Drunken Driving," *Minneapolis Tribune*, April 27, 1967.

159 **folks in the jury box:** Paul Presbrey, "Allied Jurors Believed 'Politics,' Acquitted 4," *Minneapolis Star*, June 24, 1967.

159 **In those pioneering days:** Joe Pistone with Richard Woodley, *Donnie Brasco: My Undercover Life in the Mafia* (New York: New American Library, 1987), p. 20.

Chapter 14: The Ha-Ha Certificate

Kitzer, Brennan, and Wedick testified extensively about the Frankfurt trip during the Louisville trial (*U.S. v. Kaye and Calandrella*).

162 **"Did you ever find":** Kitzer's testimony in Louisville (*U.S. v. Kaye and Calandrella*).

162 **City of Los Angeles:** For background, see two stories by William Farr in the *Los Angeles Times*: "Check Plot Suspect Seized," November 14, 1975; and "L.A. Check Fugitive's Border Incident Told," January 22, 1975. Wedick and Brennan furnished the $300,000 figure.

162 **A distinguished-looking:** Among other instances, Brennan testified to Cornaz's background in Louisville (*U.S. v. Kaye and Calandrella*).

163 **sleek five-hundred-room Intercontinental:** From a brochure of Intercontinental Frankfurt published during that era.

164 **"two-for-one deal":** Brennan describes this in his Louisville testimony (*U.S. v. Kaye and Calandrella*).

168 **"It killed us":** Bryan Burrough, *Days of Rage: America's Radical Underground, the FBI, and the Forgotten Age of Revolutionary Violence* (New York: Penguin Press, 2015), p. 377.

171 **"We can't just leave":** Kitzer's testimony in Hawaii (*U.S. v. Iuteri*).

175 **"I knew what happened":** Kitzer's expert testimony in *U.S. v. Gerhardt and Adornato*.

175 **consultant for the United Nations:** For background on this and other elements of Kitzer's career, see his expert testimony in both *U.S. v. Martell* and *U.S. v. Gerhardt and Adornato*.

177 **"I have the capability":** From Kitzer's expert testimony in *U.S. v. Gerhardt and Adornato*.

177 **"provide insulation from you":** Ibid.

178 **"Have you talked to D'Amato?":** From a recorded phone call transcribed into the record during Kitzer's testimony in Hawaii (*U.S. v. Iuteri*).

Chapter 15: Pilgrims in the Mayflower

Fred Pro was one of the most colorful witnesses in any of the trials related to Operation Fountain Pen. Much of this chapter is built around his testimony in Kansas City (*U.S. v. D'Amato, Mucci, and Bendis*) and in Memphis (*United States v. Frederick P. Pro et al.*, Docket No. 77-20201). The trial involving the scam of Elvis Presley's jet has garnered much attention over the years, for obvious reasons. For primary sources, see the trial transcript and materials in the FBI Vault (https://vault.fbi.gov), available by searching for "Elvis Presley."

183 **the Mayflower:** David W. Dunlap, "An Old and Comfortable Face Is Leaving the Park's Side," *New York Times,* November 4, 2004.

183 **"a good place to keep":** Ibid.

184 **Pro claimed to have graduated:** Much of Pro's background is from p. 22 of an FBI report dated January 18, 1977, and posted online in the Elvis Presley section of the FBI Vault. Pro also discussed it in his Memphis trial testimony (*U.S. v. Pro et al.*).

185 **called Parker West:** Tom Huser, "Firm to Add Classic '37 Cord to Their Line of Model A's," *Miami Herald,* June 11, 1973.

185 **"I had a severe emotional":** Pro's testimony in Kansas City (*U.S. v. D'Amato, Mucci, and Bendis*).

185 **Also, during a visit:** Interview with Myron Fuller.

185 **"basically my teacher":** Pro's testimony in *U.S. v. D'Amato, Mucci, and Bendis.*

186 **"Phil, we got it":** Kitzer's testimony in *U.S. v. Pro et al.*

186 **"I didn't put one nut":** Pro's testimony ibid. Also see "Dade Men Defrauded Elvis, Prosecutors Say," Associated Press (*Miami News*), August 22, 1978. The Elvis connection to the case has triggered enduring fascination and not a few conspiracy theories. These are chronicled in, among many other places, Stephanie McKinnon's "Dead or Maybe Alive, Elvis King of Rumors," in *USA Today,* August 15, 1991.

187 **room 1103A:** FBI report dated May 21, 1977, the Elvis Presley section of the FBI Vault.

187 **"You want me to answer":** Howard's testimony in Hammond (*U.S. v. Chovanec*).

188 **"playing this game of trying":** Joseph D. Pistone with Richard Woodley, *Donnie Brasco: My Undercover Life in the Mafia* (New York: New American Library, 1987), p. 48.

188 **the *omertà*:** For a riveting elaboration on this, see Selwyn Raab, *Five Families: The Rise, Decline, and Resurgence of America's Most Powerful Mafia Empires* (New York: St. Martin's Press, 2005), pp. 5–12.

189 **"You can't expect to collect":** Kitzer's testimony in Louisville (*U.S. v. Kaye and Calandrella*).

190 **There was also a kitchenette:** Descriptions of Pro's offices come from Kitzer's testimony in *U.S. v. D'Amato, Mucci, and Bendis.*

191 **"In the five-hour flight":** Kitzer's testimony in Kansas City (*U.S. v. D'Amato, Mucci, and Bendis*).

193 **The check would total $500:** Robert Hodierne, "A Con Man Gets Stung at His Own Game," *Charlotte Observer*, December 24, 1978.

195 **a Denver-based real estate:** From Bernard Baker's testimony in Kansas City (*U.S. v. D'Amato, Mucci, and Bendis*).

196 **"Nowhere, Indiana":** Tom Baker's phrase in a history he wrote about Operation Fountain Pen and Abscam and furnished to the author.

196 **Myron Fuller was still:** Interviews with Fuller.

197 **a "knuckle dragger":** Interviews with Fuller.

197 **Trocchio had been arrested:** Pete Bowles, "Four Indicted in Bid for Mob Take-over," *Newsday*, March 24, 1982.

Chapter 16: The Rhinestone Cowboys

This chapter was drawn almost entirely from testimony in federal court in Kansas City (*U.S. v. D'Amato, Mucci, and Bendis*) from Kitzer, Pro, Bendis, Mucci, Guthrie, and Cleveland Trust assistant manager David Sipari. The material involving Fuller's investigations came from interviews with Fuller.

Chapter 17: Kick the Can

This chapter largely relies on Kansas City testimony (*U.S. v. D'Amato, Mucci, and Bendis*), specifically from Kitzer, Wedick, Guthrie, and Pro.

215 **"It was really a good":** Interviews with Bowen Johnson.

216 **"The FBI was magical":** Jebb Johnston, "Training Center Boosting Law Enforcement," *Daily Corinthian*, March 25, 2011.

219 **"Dear Mr. D'Amato":** This letter was read into the record during Pro's testimony in Kansas City (*U.S. v. D'Amato, Mucci, and Bendis*).

223 **"almost like an addiction":** Mark Gladstone and Paul Jacobs, "The G-man, the Shrimp Scam, and Sacramento's Big Sting," *Los Angeles Times*, December 11, 1994.

Chapter 18: The Hit Man

Fred Pro denied in court putting out a hit on Armand Mucci, but the contract was common knowledge in Kitzer's circle and over Myron Fuller's wiretap. It also appeared, as noted below, in Robert W. Greene's book about

Mel Weinberg, which was, decades later, adapted into the movie *American Hustle.*

224 **Pro had put out a contract:** Robert W. Greene, *Sting Man: Inside Abscam* (New York: Elsevier-Dutton, 1981), p. 100.

227 **amazed at the jumbled:** Wedick's testimony in Louisville (*U.S. v. Kaye and Calandrella*).

227 **Phil and Packman had long ago spent:** Ibid.

230 **"arrest quotas were used":** Selwyn Raab, *Five Families: The Rise, Decline, and Resurgence of America's Most Powerful Mafia Empires* (New York: St. Martin's Press, 2005), p. 221.

230 **"Really it just shocked me":** Interview with Tom Baker.

231 **"Now, come on":** Interview with Brennan.

232 **"a cross-country tour":** Pro in Kansas City (*U.S. v. D'Amato, Mucci, and Bendis*).

Chapter 19: The Blackout

This chapter encompasses two of the big stories on either coast during the summer of 1977: the phony armed robbery in Los Angeles and the New York City blackout and subsequent riots.

235 **"Keep moving and don't":** From Statement of Facts in *State of California v. Vincent Carrano, Jack Fulton, et al.*, Docket No. C-39065, held in Superior Court in Santa Ana, California.

235 **"The gun looked nine feet":** Richard O'Reilly, "Clues in $1.1 Million Bullion Theft Sought," *Los Angeles Times*, July 11, 1977.

235 **"Take care of that fat":** There was some discrepancy as to which pejorative term the perpetrator claimed to have used to describe Carrano. I went with the one on page 36 of the Statement of Facts in *California v. Carrano et al.*

236 **"Silver and gold, no problem":** Mike Runzler, "Few Clues Left to Solve $1 Million Bullion Heist," *Orange County Register*, July 12, 1977.

236 **he'd been indicted on twenty-seven:** "FBI Can't Unlock Safe Holders' Lips," *News-Pilot* (San Pedro, California), July 21, 1977.

237 **"getting lumber and hammers":** Interview with Fuller.

237 **"I'll send out a hit":** Robert W. Greene, *Sting Man: Inside Abscam* (New York: Elsevier-Dutton, 1981), pp. 101–2.

238 **"Oh, didn't you hear?":** Interview with Fuller.

238 **"I think the problem":** Testimony of Jack Elliott (*California v. Carrano et al.*).

238 **"Hell, that shit's been gone":** Ibid.

238 **"That son of a bitch":** Ibid.

238 **In January, Carrano had asked Phil:** Summary of facts in decision of Court of Appeals of California, Fourth Appellate District, Division Three, in *California v. Carrano et al.*, April 30, 1984.

239 **Koenig would purchase Swiss:** Evan Maxwell, "This Fairy Tale Doesn't End 'Happily Ever After,'" *Los Angeles Times*, July 23, 1978.

239 **"Well, maybe I'll come down":** Elliott testimony in *California v. Carrano et al.*

240 **They invented tales of wilderness:** Brennan's testimony in Louisville (*U.S. v. Kaye and Calandrella*).

242 **Arsonists set more than a thousand:** Sewell Chan, "Remembering the '77 Blackout," *New York Times*, July 9, 2007.

243 **"even the looters were":** Leonard Greene, "Lights Out for Suffering City," *New York Post*, July 9, 2007. For more on the riots and New York's struggles in that era, also see Bryan Burrough, *Days of Rage: America's Radical Underground, the FBI, and the Forgotten Age of Revolutionary Violence* (New York: Penguin Press, 2015), p. 398.

243 **John Quinn, a Long Island resident:** This paragraph is drawn from an FBI case summary on Joseph Trocchio and others dated April 8, 1980, courtesy of Myron Fuller.

245 **"I really . . . think a lot":** Pro's testimony in Kansas City (*U.S. v. D'Amato, Mucci, and Bendis*). See also the coverage of the trial in the *Kansas City Times*, in particular Greg Edwards's "Witness Details Investment Swindle" on December 6, 1978, and "Fraud Trial Witness Says Defendant Out to Kill Him," December 7, 1978.

246 **Guthrie was also now talking:** From Guthrie's testimony in Kansas City (*U.S. v. D'Amato, Mucci, and Bendis*).

246 **Historically the mob:** This paragraph is largely drawn from James O. Finckenauer, "La Cosa Nostra in the United States," a United Nations Activities paper published on December 6, 2007: https://www.ncjrs .gov/pdffiles1/nij/218555.pdf. I also consulted Selwyn Raab's *Five Families: The Rise, Decline, and Resurgence of America's Most Powerful Mafia Empires* (New York: St. Martin's Press, 2005).

246 **"Can you imagine Vinnie":** Interview with Fuller.

247 **shell corporation named Elinvest:** From summary of U.S. Court of Appeals decision for the Second Circuit, in New York City, in *United States v. Eric Blitz, Peter Horvat, Richard Orpheus, and William Drew*, Docket No. 75-1237.

248 **"We spent enough time":** From *United States v. Sonny Santini and Richard Strum*, U.S. Court of Appeals decision, Southern District of New York, Docket Nos. 81-1249 and 81-1250.

248 **appendicitis or had a heart attack:** Ibid.

250 **"Ten billion in assets?":** Interview with Wedick.

250 **"I couldn't say that I felt":** Bernard Baker testimony in Kansas City (*U.S. v. D'Amato, Mucci, and Bendis*).

251 **"Okay, when we sign":** Brennan's testimony in Hawaii (*U.S. v. Iuteri*).

Chapter 20: Fool's Gold

254 **ten-story, 293-room behemoth:** Leslie Berkman, "O.C. Investors Buy Registry Hotel in Irvine, to Reopen as Radisson," *Los Angeles Times*, July 7, 1989.

255 **purportedly owned a small airline:** From Elliott's testimony in *California v. Carrano et al.*

255 **He'd recently run into trouble:** Joe Cordero, "OC Man Charged in London Forgery Case," *Orange County Register*, October 23, 1977.

255 **twenty-six thousand metal washers:** Joe Cordero, "Swiss Vaults Trio Faces Embezzling Complaints," *Orange County Register*, September 4, 1977.

255 **disconnected and rewired:** Evan Maxwell, "Swiss Vaults Operators Plead Not Guilty in Theft," *Los Angeles Times*, January 7, 1978.

257 **"I found him to be very keen":** From Elliott's testimony in *California v. Carrano et al.*

258 **prepared sham assay reports:** From *U.S. v. Santini and Strum*, U.S. Court of Appeals decision. There were a couple of variations on Elliott's gold-bar scam, as described by Wedick and Brennan and summarized in Bill Osinski's "Government Witness Ends Fraud-Trial Testimony," *Louisville Courier-Journal*, February 22, 1978.

Chapter 21: Sonny's Mentality

Some of Wedick's and Brennan's most vivid recollections involve Santini, because of the threat he represented. The first section of this chapter was crafted through interviews with both retired agents.

266 **phoning "the alphabet":** From Kitzer's expert testimony in *U.S. v. Gerhardt and Adornato*.

268 **"When you say stole":** This exchange took place during Kitzer's testimony in Hawaii (*U.S. v. Iuteri*).

269 **"That was part of the business":** From Kitzer's testimony in *U.S. v. Martell*.

269 **"[I]f somebody had a need":** Kitzer's testimony in Kansas City (*U.S. v. D'Amato, Mucci, and Bendis*).

269 **"We have letters of credit":** Kitzer's testimony in Louisville (*U.S. v. Kaye and Calandrella*).

269 **"[W]hether it's an outright":** Ibid.

270 **not good for Bernard Baker:** From Baker's testimony in Kansas City (*U.S. v. D'Amato, Mucci, and Bendis*).

274 **"a good Italian boy":** This and the rest of this passage are from interviews with Brennan and Wedick.

275 **a lunatic made national:** As described in Terri Jentz, *Strange Piece of Paradise* (New York: Farrar, Straus and Giroux, 2006).

276 **"all leads set out":** From a teletype issued by the FBI on August 4, 1977, available in the Elvis Presley section of the FBI's online Vault. The Reid memo referenced in the next paragraph is also stored in that location.

Chapter 22: The Game Is Rigged

Nick Coleman's story in the *Minneapolis Tribune,* mentioned below, provided some rare insight into Kitzer's home life. As much as Kitzer opened up to Brennan and Wedick, he rarely delved into life in Ellendale.

277 **Paint was curling:** Nick Coleman, "Ellendale Wondered About Phil Kitzer," *Minneapolis Tribune,* March 12, 1978.

278 **"a very friendly atmosphere":** Donald Schlaefer testified about the search in Louisville (*U.S. v. Kaye and Calandrella*).

279 **emptied Trident Consortium:** FBI report 87-16994, in the Elvis Presley section of the online FBI Vault.

280 **"What about that fucking Calandrella?":** From the transcript of the Louisville trial (*U.S. v. Kaye and Calandrella*).

280 **"Guys, listen," he said:** This conversation was recounted by Wedick and Brennan.

283 **Phil had rented space:** Oliver described his version of his history with Kitzer in an affidavit given on July 18, 1978, and filed in federal court in Charlotte, North Carolina, as part of *U.S. v. Chovanec et al.*

283 **Oliver would turn up:** Ray Gibson, "Missing Porn-Theater Owner Found Dead in Car Trunk," *Chicago Tribune,* July 27, 1985. In general, headline writers loved Oliver. Two others from the *Tribune:* "Key Witness in Bungled Mob Hit Attacked as 'Scum, Loser'" (November 7, 1984) and "Simple Trial Turns Diabolical, With Judge Labeled the Devil" (September 16, 1983).

283 **"one of the most feared":** Maurice Possley, "Frank W. Oliver: 1920–2006," *Chicago Tribune,* October 5, 2006.

285 **"As a result of activities":** Memo to FBI director dated October 3, 1977, courtesy of Wedick.

286 **"so as to preclude any":** FBI teletype 87-143601, available in the Elvis Presley section of the bureau's online Vault.

Chapter 23: You Have to Believe It to See It

291 **walked off a Braniff International:** FBI report 87-16994, FBI Vault.

291 **boarded the flight ready:** Affidavit from Kitzer's attorney, Robert Zeman, November 22, 1977, filed in Louisville (*U.S. v. Kaye and Calandrella*).

293 **"white-collar crime of a high":** Jim Adams, "Dozens Are Indicted in What FBI Calls Broad Scheme with Louisville Links," *Louisville Courier-Journal*, October 19, 1977.

293 **between $3 million and $5 million:** FBI memo on OpFoPen and Abscam dated July 17, 1980. Pro worked a plea deal in the aftermath, while D'Amato was among the defendants to plead guilty. See Tom Condon's "U.S. Won't Prosecute Case Against Onetime Promoter" in the February 21, 1979, edition of the *Hartford Courant*.

293 **"opened a new curtain":** Interview with Fuller.

294 **more than nineteen hundred telexes:** Robert Hodierne, "A Con Man Gets Stung at His Own Game," *Charlotte Observer*, December 24, 1978.

Chapter 24: Hobson's Choice

I pieced together Kitzer's plight in jail partly through his lawyer's court filings and through inferences made from Frank Oliver's three-page letter in November 1977, referenced below. Another key piece came from Jack Elliott's testimony in the Orange County trial of Vince Carrano and Jack Fulton. And, of course, Brennan and Wedick met him a few weeks after his arrest and saw his condition firsthand. Various legal motions and correspondence cited in this chapter—including the Oliver letter—are part of the case file in *U.S. v. Kaye and Calandrella*. To read about trial highlights, see Bill Osinski's stories in the *Louisville Courier-Journal*, including "FBI Agent Describes His World Travels with Con Artist," February 17; and "Con Man Testifies About Promoting Costly Fraud Schemes," February 18, 1978.

298 **set Kitzer's bond:** U.S District Judge Charles M. Allen's bail order for Kitzer is part of the case file in *U.S. v. Kaye and Calandrella*.

299 **"told me that he was broke":** Testimony of Jack Elliott (*California v. Carrano et al.*). Elliott testified that he sent Kitzer money a couple of times before losing contact with him. On October 23, 1977—a few days after Kitzer's arrest—Joe Cordero wrote a story in the *Orange County Register* about Elliott's own legal troubles in London ("OC Man Charged in London Forgery Case") in which Elliott is quoted as saying, "I've never seen Kitzer do a dishonest thing."

300 **Phil kept no books:** See Kitzer's testimony in *U.S. v. Kaye and Calandrella*.

300 **phony birth certificates:** "Illegal Donations Admitted," *Northwest Indiana Times*, November 10, 1977.

302 **forty-six phone calls:** From court filings in Louisville (*U.S. v. Kaye and Calandrella*).

304 **He had no one representing:** Kitzer's testimony in *U.S. v. Martell*.

306 **"They conned me":** Kitzer's testimony in *U.S. v. Gerhardt and Andornato*.

307 **"Listen to these names":** Nick Coleman, "Ellendale Wondered About Phil Kitzer," *Minneapolis Tribune*, March 12, 1978.

308 **"a rip-off artist":** From transcript of Louisville trial (*U.S. v. Kaye and Calandrella*).

310 **"they would have him under":** Paul Redmond's statements transcribed in Louisville (*U.S. v. Kaye and Calandrella*), during a pretrial chambers conversation.

Chapter 25: The Phil Kitzer Road Show

For a comprehensive summary of the Louisville case against John Kaye and John Calandrella, see the appellate decision of the United States Court of Appeal, Sixth Circuit, decided on August 31, 1979. The Docket Nos. are 78-5341 and 78-5342.

315 **"damaging testimony":** Bill Osinski, "Two Men Convicted for Involvement in Fraud Scheme," *Louisville Courier-Journal*, March 8, 1978.

315 **He received his ten-year:** "Two Sentenced for Attempt to Defraud," *Louisville Courier-Journal*, March 11, 1978.

316 **"without peer as a con":** Steve Hamilton, "How the FBI Cracked the $110,000 Con Game," *True Detective*, September 1979, p. 76.

316 **"world's greatest con man":** "The Ultimate Con," Knight-Ridder Newspapers (*Ellensburg Daily Record*), August 7, 1981.

316 **"King of Scam":** Walter Wright, "King of Scam Royally Conned Pigeons Until FBI Caged Him," *Honolulu Advertiser*, May 9, 1980.

316 **a "genie" who could:** Evan Maxwell, "Genie Flitted Around Swiss Vaults but His Bottle Was Corked," *Los Angeles Times*, July 17, 1978.

316 **"master con artist":** Assistant U.S. Attorney David Everett used the phrase in chambers during the Louisville trial (*U.S. v. Kaye and Calandrella*).

316 **"going up against Dr. J":** Greg Edwards, "Witness in Fraud Trial Sticks to Story," *Kansas City Times*, December 8, 1978.

316 **"too smooth a talker":** From Kitzer's testimony in *U.S. v. Gerhardt and Adornato*.

316 **"smiles and says it was":** Robert Hodierne, "A Con Man Gets Stung at His Own Game," *Charlotte Observer*, December 24, 1978.

316 **"the Phillip Kitzer method of finance":** Maxwell, "Genie Flitted."

317 **"the absolute highest levels of":** Evan Maxwell, "A Con Man Falls Prey to FBI's Sting," *Los Angeles Times*, March 13, 1978.

317 **"probably very conservative":** Evan Maxwell, "Fraud Suspect May Be Linked to Vault Theft," *Los Angeles Times*, October 21, 1977.

317 **"led to discovery":** Richard Hanning memo to David T. Ready, U.S. attorney, Northern District of Indiana, November 16, 1977.

318 **Even after the FBI informed:** Walter Wright, "How Undercover Pair Pulled Plug on Scam," *Honolulu Sunday Star-Bulletin & Advertiser*, January 6, 1980.

318 **"And that is what you have put away?":** This exchange took place during Kitzer's Louisville testimony (*U.S. v. Kaye and Calandrella*).

319 **In June 1978:** This document is part of the case file in the Hammond trial (*U.S. v. Chovanec*).

319 **"The witness protection":** Interview with Tom Baker.

320 **"apparent willingness to state":** From Oliver's affidavit dated July 18, 1978, filed in Charlotte, North Carolina, as part of *U.S. v. Oliver*. For more on Oliver's arrest, see John O'Brien, "Tax-Evading Chicago Lawyer Indicted in Bank-Fraud Scheme," *Chicago Tribune*, June 7, 1978.

321 **"You son of a gun":** Letter courtesy of Wedick.

322 **all received five-year sentences:** Theodore A. Driscoll, "D'Amato Receives Sentence in Fraud," *Hartford Courant*, February 21, 1979. Bendis's sentence was later reduced to one year because of family hardship.

322 **"I had never been out shopping":** Interview with Allen Ezell.

323 **That same year, the FBI:** Joseph D. Pistone with Richard Woodley, *Donnie Brasco: My Life in the Mafia* (New York: New American Library, 1987), p. 28.

324 **"I got the impression":** Interview with Dan Bent.

324 **"dapper, tanned, and dark-haired":** Walter Wright, "A Con Artist Explains the 'Condo Caper,'" *Honolulu Advertiser*, May 7, 1980.

324 **"If ever a case required":** Walter Wright, "Iuteri Gets 15-Year Prison Term in '77 Loan Swindle of Kealoha," *Honolulu Advertiser*, July 8, 1980. For more on Iuteri's past, see Walter Wright's "Iuteri Tied to Murder, Beatings" in the *Advertiser* on July 3, 1980, and "Iuteri Called a Killer for Mafia" on July 8, 1980.

325 **"one of the main members":** Letter from Elaine Hurni, examining magistrate, Geneva, to the FBI director, July 13, 1979. Provided by Wedick.

325 **"sudden and dramatic change":** Final report of the Select Committee to Study Undercover Activities of Components of the Department of Justice, December 15, 1982, p. 1.

326 **That night, the accrued:** Kitzer described his ordeal with his ulcer in *U.S. v. Gerhardt and Adornato*.

Chapter 26: One More Thing

Kitzer, by necessity, flew under the radar as an FBI operative. The *Barron's* story cited below is one of the few instances when he was publicly named in this capacity.

329 **"I would be capable":** From Kitzer's testimony in *U.S. v. Gerhardt and Adornato.*

330 **the newspaper ran:** Jim Drinkhall, "Paper Pirates," *Wall Street Journal,* March 23, 1981.

331 **$4 million cooking crystal:** "Suspects in Drug Lab Case Denied Bond," *Mobile Register,* December 20, 1985.

333 **$36,000-a-year informant:** Brennan and Wedick described Kitzer's work as informant, but this came from Barbara Conway, "Alabama Sting: World-Class Con Man Meets His Match in Mobile," *Barron's,* June 27, 1983.

335 **Mobile Municipal Airport:** "Two Sentenced in Drug Case," *Mobile Register,* August 2, 1986.

Epilogue

339 **a theatrical supply house:** Robert Hodierne and Mary Walton, "The Sting: From New York to Florida to New Jersey to Washington to Philadelphia," *Philadelphia Inquirer,* February 10, 1980.

340 **"If not for those guys":** Interview with Myron Fuller.

Index

ABOUT THE AUTHOR

DAVID HOWARD is the author of *Lost Rights*. He has written for the *New York Times, Outside, Men's Journal, Travel + Leisure,* and *Bicycling,* among other outlets. He lives in Pennsylvania with his wife and son.